HEALING THE CULTURE AND THE FAMILY

PRAISE FOR *HEALING THE CULTURE AND THE FAMILY*

Among John Paul the Great's defining achievements, by God's grace, were *Veritatis Splendor* and his *Theology of the Body*. In this richly insightful book, David Hajduk enables us to see why. Western civilization is in the midst of a war against human nature, natural teleology, body-soul unity, and marriage. Hajduk demonstrates that Pope John Paul recognized this and mounted a multi-layered campaign against the "New Manichaeism." This book shows the connections between modern body-soul dualism, the regnant mechanistic view of nature, the rejection of metaphysics, and moral utilitarianism. In challenging this dismal worldview, John Paul II charted the path for the Church in the modern world.

—**DR. MATTHEW LEVERING**, James N. and Mary D. Perry Jr. Chair of Theology, Mundelein Seminary

At times the victim of media simplification and campy propaganda, John Paul II's "theology of the body" has prompted skepticism on the part of those who have not taken the time to delve into it more carefully. A deeper look discloses not phenomenological subjectivism or a personalist subversion but a fresh rethinking of Aristotelian and Thomistic principles, deftly applied to the errors of modern philosophy that made possible the sexual revolution with its penumbra of exploitation, broken lives, and butchery. Dr. Hajduk skillfully locates Wojtyła's contribution within the history of thought and culture, reminding us that the world—and, sadly, the Catholic Church today, suffering from short-term and long-term memory loss—is far from having assimilated the wisdom of this Lublin ethicist.

—**DR. PETER A. KWASNIEWSKI**, author of *The Ecstasy of Love in the Thought of Thomas Aquinas*

An important study which traces the proximate (Cartesian) and more distant sources of what John Paul II calls "the new Manichaeism" in modern culture. Hajduk carefully examines the links which Wojtyla/John Paul II sees with these sources in light of current scholarship on Descartes and ancient Manichaeism, making for a nuanced appreciation of the great Polish pope's analysis. By framing this analysis as a diagnosis and Wojtyla/John Paul II's anthropology as a cure, the study adds to a growing body of literature which sees the vision of the *Theology of the Body* as a unique and prophetic response to the intellectual and moral challenges of our age. Highly recommended for both scholars and advanced students.

—**DR. JOHN GRABOWSKI**, Professor of Moral Theology/Ethics, The Catholic University of America

Almost 20 years after the death of John Paul II and 8 years after his canonization, the time for simply remembering and repeating his words has long passed. Now it is time to go further with John Paul II's intuitions and inspirations. This is exactly what David Hajduk does in his book. The inspiration drawn from John Paul II's theological anthropology enables Dr. Hajduk to provide an insightful diagnosis of the contemporary culture's illness that consists in neo-Manichaean attitudes toward the human body and sexuality. Dr. Hajduk rightly describes the four contemporary facets of the old Manichaean worldview: anthropological dualism, a mechanistic view of nature, the rejection of the philosophy of being, and relativism and utilitarianism in ethics. Only the careful description and analysis of these four currents of the contemporary reemergence of this ancient Christian heresy allows the reader to understand in depth the prevailing attitude today of manipulation with regard to the body. Everyone interested in understanding the post-modern challenges to the Catholic view of the human body, sexuality, the theology of marriage and bio-ethics should study this book.

—**DR. JAROSLAW KUPCZAK**, O.P., Chair of Theological Anthropology, The Pontifical University of John Paul II in Krakow

Healing the Culture and the Family

According to John Paul II

DAVID C. HAJDUK, PH.D.

Foreword by Deborah Savage, Ph.D.

AROUCA
PRESS

ISBN: 978-1-990685-16-3 (pbk)
ISBN: 978-1-990685-17-0 (hardcover)

Arouca Press
PO Box 55003
Bridgeport PO
Waterloo, ON N2J 3G0
Canada
www.aroucapress.com
Send inquiries to
info@aroucapress.com

Cover image:
"Nazareth" (1986), by Michael O'Brien
Used with kind permission of the artist

TABLE OF CONTENTS

ACKNOWLEDGEMENTS

SINCE THIS PRESENT BOOK IS A REFORMULA-
tion of my doctoral thesis, *The New Manichaeism: An Examination
of John Paul II's Label in Letter to Families, no. 19 and its Insights for
Understanding His Anthropology*, I wish to acknowledge those who
assisted me in the development of that study. I am grateful to
Dr. Petroc Willey, Dr. Andrew Beards, and Dr. Martin Stone
for acting as supervisors of my thesis in its initial stages. I am
especially appreciative of Dr. Stone's expertise in the area of early
modern philosophy, which helped to direct me in my investigation of the Cartesian tradition. My gratitude is extended to Rev.
Dr. Francesco Pesce and Dr. Deborah Savage who supervised the
thesis through its final stages. Their encouragement and support
for the project was of great consolation as I forged ahead to its
completion. In particular, my conversations with Dr. Savage served
both to inspire and to refine my ideas, and I am honored that she
has written the foreword to the book you have in your hands. Dr.
Harry Schnitker must be recognized for his guidance in my study
of the beliefs and practices of medieval heterodox communities
and Dr. Caroline Farey for her review of the sections on the
philosophy of St. Thomas Aquinas. I am indebted to the skillful
scrutiny of Dr. Mary Mills, whose suggestions proved invaluable.
At one point, I must admit, I thought I would never complete
my thesis successfully *because of* Dr. Mills. I now see that I could
never have completed my thesis successfully *without her*.

I am touched by the graciousness of Dr. Reinhard Hütter,
who generously offered his time to guide me as I sought to
reformulate the thesis, as well as by the kindness and assistance
of Dr. Matthew Levering in my search for a publisher. Dr. Peter
Kwasniewski deserves particular mention for his enthusiastic
advocacy of my work and for ultimately pointing me to Arouca
Press. I am deeply appreciative of Alex Barbas and Arouca Press
for believing in the importance and relevance of this book, and
for the professionalism and care they displayed in bringing it
to publication.

This book would not have come to fruition were it not for
the wonderful friends who encouraged me to pursue doctoral

studies at Maryvale Institute and who supported me as I sought to convert the thesis that resulted into a book for a wider audience. And, as always, I am sustained by the love of my wife Shannon and our children, thankful for the many sacrifices they made along the way.

FOREWORD

THERE CAN BE NO DOUBT THAT THE CATHOLIC vision of the human person and the *telos* of human life stands in stark contrast to the view that characterizes contemporary culture. Indeed, our era is marked almost daily by seemingly perpetual skirmishes, epiphenomena of the deep mortal conflict clearly underway, a battle between two irreconcilable worldviews: between Catholicism itself and a secular "humanism" that seems hell-bent on dismantling the person and destroying his natural habitat—the family. There is no need to repeat all the arguments in support of this claim. We have all witnessed the evidence for ourselves. While desperate parents prepare to take up arms to defend common sense policies on the use of pronouns, public restrooms, and women's sports—and confront the unspeakable horror of the surgical mutilation that threatens their children—an unseen enemy of the family continues to slink into every nook and cranny of our society and our institutions, ignoring, obliterating, or sliding around every obstacle. It seems impossible to gain any traction, to find a foothold from which to mount a full defense. We have the vague sense that we are losing ground, that somehow, we are missing the mark—for reasons we cannot quite name. In *Healing the Culture and the Family according to John Paul II*, Dr. David Hajduk administers the relief we are seeking. For the work pinpoints ground zero of the war on the family. He has provided us with a critical point of leverage in our hope to recover a culture of life.

The significance of *Healing the Culture and the Family* is two-fold. First and foremost, it shouldn't surprise us that the forces of darkness are arrayed against the family, that the family is the primary target of attack. What could be more obvious? After all, "the family is the first and vital cell of society." [1] Indeed, it is the very foundation of society. For "it is from the family that citizens come to birth, and it is within the family that they find the first school of the social virtues that are the animating principle of the existence and development of society itself." [2] If

---

1   Vatican II, *Decree on the Apostolate of the Laity* (1965), no. 11.
2   John Paul II, *On the Role of the Christian Family in the Modern World* (1981), no. 42.

we wish to take back our culture, the family is, without doubt, *the critical point of leverage.*

But second, we have Dr. Hajduk to thank for locating ground zero: a deadly idea that has seeped silently into the common sense of the culture, accelerated by those thinkers whose legacy has contributed to the dissolution of the West. Here Dr. Hajduk reveals clear evidence of the genius of Pope St. John Paul II by pointing to *the* central insight of the late Holy Father's *Letter to Families*: that our culture remains under the sway of the ancient heresy of Manichaeism, a view of the person in which the body and the spirit are thought to be in radical opposition to one another, reducing the body to mere matter, an object that is subject to the whims of passion and appetite, a mere appendage, affixed to the mind, to be manipulated and used as one sees fit. In identifying and unpacking that insight, Dr. Hajduk provides a reliable guide for our efforts to recover the culture of life and engage in the singular project that belongs to us all—the task of healing and preserving the family. He demonstrates with all the drama of a Shakespearean tragedy that *ideas have consequences.* For he illuminates the fact that, though the battle may have come more sharply into focus in recent history, it is a campaign that has been going on for centuries.

John Paul II's *Letter to Families,* arguably the most personal and heartfelt document of his pontificate, was promulgated in February 1994, evidently in response to the United Nations' declaration of that same year as the "International Year of the Family." That this is very much on the late Holy Father's mind is found in the opening lines of the document, where he declares that the "celebration of the Year of the Family gives me a welcome opportunity to knock at the door of your home, eager to greet you with deep affection and to spend time with you." It is the letter of a father to his children, full of love and good advice. He speaks, not in the abstract, but to the concrete realities of our own lives.

But we cannot truly understand his purposes without placing this *Letter* into the broader context of the time. For barely a month later, John Paul writes another letter, this time to the Secretary General of the UN's International Conference on Population and Development, to be held in Cairo in September 1994.[3] Let us

3   John Paul II, *Letter of His Holiness John Paul II to the Secretary General of the International Conference on Population and Development* (March 18, 1994).

pause briefly over the significance of this second letter. It has a somewhat different tone.

Here we see John Paul II exercising the fundamental charism of fatherhood—that of defender and protector. He is firm and unyielding as he seeks to protect his children from the forces that clearly stand ready to defeat and quite literally to destroy them. Here the Holy Father invokes the considerable moral authority of the Church in communicating his "thoughts on a topic which, we all agree, is of vital importance for the *well-being and progress of the human family*" (italics in original).[4] He pleads with the Secretary General to give "proper attention to certain *basic truths*," among them, the unconditional and inalienable dignity and worth of each and every person and the sacred meaning of human life, from birth to natural death.[5] And he appeals to the UN's own *Universal Declaration of Human Rights* which, he points out, itself affirms the family as "the natural and fundamental group unit of society." He implores the United Nations to respond to the challenge already implicit in its own declaration by "doing everything within its power to ensure that the family receives from 'society and the State'" that protection to which the same *Universal Declaration* says it is "entitled." He declares that "anything less would be a betrayal of the noblest ideals of the United Nations."[6] And he proclaims *unequivocally* the sacred nature of the family: "it is the place in which life ... can be properly welcomed and protected. In the face of the so-called culture of death, the family is the heart of the culture of life."[7]

Now, Pope St. John Paul II wrote another, earlier document on the family, his 1981 Apostolic Exhortation *Familiaris Consortio* (*On the Role of the Christian Family in the Modern World*), written at the request of the 1980 Synod of Bishops. It is an important contribution to the Magisterium and also worth reading. But it is, as one might expect, considerably longer—which is both a boon and, for some readers, a liability. In writing the *Letter to Families,* the Holy Father clearly has a different purpose, and a different audience in mind. Not unlike his equally intimate *Letter to Women,* written a year later on the eve of the United Nations' Fourth World Conference on Women in Beijing, the *Letter to Families* should be seen as a quite deliberate strategic thrust, intended to alert his listeners to what

4   Ibid., 1.   5   Ibid., 2.   6   Ibid., 4.   7   Ibid., 6.

is at stake in these public conversations. It is clearly an attempt to draw a battle line around their hearts and minds—to protect them and keep them safe. It is intended to arm us with a secret defensive weapon—a grasp of the hollow core at the center of the enemy's strategy.

A long time ago, the father of Positivism, Auguste Comte, declared that the only way to destroy something is to replace it. He, of course, is the author of what might be the enemy's primary strategy in this battle we are fighting. But a good military commander always tries to use the enemy's weapons against him. And Dr. Hajduk has provided us with a timely and impressive analysis of the specific threat we face. We need to leverage that knowledge now, exploit it, and *replace* the deadly error that is seeping silently throughout our culture. With what, you may ask? Well, the answer is readily at hand.

Dr. Hajduk offers us more than a mere diagnosis of the disease; he points to the antidote as well. In *Healing the Culture and the Family,* we are led to realize that Pope St. John Paul II has given it to us already in the *Theology of the Body.* His legacy continues, its meaning discerned anew, now illuminated by a new generation of scholars. It is our secret weapon—and we need only take hold of it in our own defense of the family. We need to teach our children the truth about the human person—that we are a union of body and soul, meant to live for all of eternity in full sight of the glory of God.

Deborah Savage, Ph.D.
Professor of Theology
Franciscan University of Steubenville
Steubenville, Ohio

GENERAL INTRODUCTION

A HERESY IS LIKE A SPIRITUAL DISEASE THAT infects the Body of Christ. One could also say that it infects all of Christian culture, and so would have a particular impact on the West. A number of significant churchmen have opined that Christendom is no more, and that we are living in a "post-Christian" age. Well, if Christendom is dead, what put it on the bier?

John Paul II once warned, "As the family goes, so goes the nation, and so goes the whole world in which we live."[1] The original spiritual disease, that first great earthly lie and sin, attacked the very relationship between man and woman, and thus struck at the heart of the family.[2] Satan knew that if the family fell—being the "fundamental cell of society"[3]—so would everything else. This is why defending the family and promoting its health has to be central to the work of the Church. In our "post-Christian" culture, it seems that the health of the family has rapidly deteriorated and that the family itself is on the bier. What are the root causes of its swift demise?

It is evident to many today that the culture and the family are in need of healing. Yet, before we can offer a cure, we need to know the disease. Every disease, even a spiritual one, requires a proper diagnosis. Otherwise, you will not know the precise remedy to prescribe, and you may make matters worse. Such stories abound. After carefully considering the symptoms manifesting themselves in modern culture, John Paul II offered his diagnosis. He proposed that the spiritual disease of our times is a "New Manichaeism"—a new expression of an ancient heresy, or, as the saying goes, an "old heresy in new clothes." He also prescribed a remedy.

Contemporary research on John Paul II's thought suggests that he developed his anthropology as a response to the errors of Cartesian Rationalism and as an "antidote" to "Manichaean" views and attitudes about the body and sex.[4] In fact, in his *Letter to Families*, no.

---

1   John Paul II, Homily in Perth (Australia), November 30, 1986.
2   Gen. 3
3   John Paul II, *Letter to Families* (1994), no. 13.
4   Scholars Michael Waldstein and Jaroslaw Kupczak support the thesis

I

19, one could say that these purposes converge. There, John Paul II discusses the New Manichaeism contracted by contemporary men and women, which has altered their understanding of themselves and ethics, and he associates it expressly with the Cartesian tradition.

If the late Pope's anthropology is a response to Descartes and an antidote to "Manichaean" views and attitudes, then an examination of what John Paul II meant by the label "New Manichaeism" would elucidate his diagnosis of the ills of the present age impacting the culture and the family, as well as the remedy he prescribed. Additionally, such an examination would provide a useful interpretive tool for approaching his anthropology, for it would demonstrate precisely how his anthropology was a response to Descartes and an antidote to Manichaeism. In so doing, it would offer a novel contribution to studies of John Paul II's thought. These aims constitute the purpose of this book.

A RESPONSE TO DESCARTES

Since John Paul II associates the New Manichaeism with certain elements of the philosophical tradition stemming from Descartes, the work of Michael Waldstein and Jaroslaw Kupczak is foundational to this present study, for they posit that John Paul II's anthropology is a response to the Cartesian tradition. Their commentary generally discusses those specific aspects of Descartes' philosophy that were of concern to the late Pope, as well as the main thrust of his response, focusing on his work *Man and Woman He Created Them: A Theology of the Body* (hereafter simply referred to as the *Theology of the Body*).[5] While Waldstein references the

---

that Pope John Paul II's anthropology was developed in response to the Cartesian tradition and method. Popular authors George Weigel and Christopher West suggest that the late Pope's work is an "antidote" or "rebuttal" to Manichaean attitudes and views about the body and sex. A discussion of the work of these authors follows.

5   Throughout this work, Michael Waldstein's translation of John Paul II's *Catecheses on Human Love in the Divine Plan* is used: *Man and Woman He Created Them: A Theology of the Body* (Boston: Pauline Books & Media, 2006). This translation has become somewhat normative in the English-speaking world, as has reference to the *Catecheses* as the *Theology of the Body*. These choices in no way deny the legitimate concerns some theologians have with the translation or the reduction of the theme of the audiences to a "theology of the body" (see, for example, the work of Gilfredo Marengo). Neither does it deny

section of John Paul II's *Letter to Families*, no. 19 that treats the New Manichaeism, he does not offer a critical evaluation of the term or its expressed relationship to the Cartesian tradition.

In his Introduction to the *Theology of the Body*, Waldstein states, "...the purpose of the theology of the body is to defend the body against its alienation from the person in Cartesian rationalism"[6] and to help overcome body-spirit dualism.[7] According to Waldstein, the practical, technical philosophy promoted by Descartes combined a "rigorous dualism," which splits reality into matter (extended things, *res extensa*) and mind (thinking things, *res cogitans*),[8] with the rejection of final causality, so that bodies in nature (including the human body) are like machines that can be manipulated for any purpose to which man determines they are suited.[9] Waldstein states that John Paul II saw a close relationship between this "predominant scientific picture of the world"[10] and utilitarianism, which he defined as "a civilization in which persons are used the same way things are used."[11] Waldstein understands "the scientific rationalism spearheaded by Descartes" to be "an attack on the body"[12] and sees John Paul II's response to such an attack as "a defense of the body in its natural intrinsic meaning,"[13] which rejects the thesis that the body can be reduced to mere matter.[14]

In his work, *Gift and Communion: John Paul II's Theology of the Body*, Jaroslaw Kupczak deliberately entitles his first chapter "Discourse

---

that the Italian text (*Insegnamenti*) of the *Catecheses* is the basic or "official" and "authoritative" version of the audiences. Due to its consistency in the translations of terms and its wide use in the United States, the Waldstein translation proved most useful for this present book. The citations from the audiences, therefore, follow the format of that translation: the audience number and section number within that audience are indicated, separated by a colon (e.g., 15:1 is audience 15, section 1).

6   Michael Waldstein, "Introduction," in Pope John Paul II, *Man and Woman He Created Them: A Theology of the Body* (Boston: Pauline Books & Media, 2006), 105.

7   Ibid., 44.   8   Ibid., 41–42.

9   Ibid., 40. Waldstein states that, for Descartes, man "is not bound by preexisting purposes in nature, but sets his own purposes."

10   Ibid., 42.   11   John Paul II, *Letter to Families*, no. 13.

12   Waldstein, "Introduction," 95. Italics in the original. In this book, italics and brackets that appear in quotes are part of the original unless otherwise indicated.

13   Ibid.   14   Ibid., 96.

on Method" in order to underscore that "the method of the theological anthropology of John Paul II is built in opposition to the Cartesian method which has become paradigmatic for modern humanities and social sciences."[15] Kupczak posits that "such a 'scientific' perception of the world necessarily led to dualism"[16] which, in dividing reality into two kinds of substances, "cleft man into two parts" and "led to a gross deformation of the *humanum*."[17] He states that, as a philosopher, John Paul emphasized that "'the Cartesian paradigm' thus understood decisively influenced the understanding of man in modern science and culture, especially in currents inspired by positivism and empiricism"[18] and that his theological anthropology "belongs to the tradition of critical reflection that tries to overcome this dualistic and reductionist way of approaching man."[19] He even goes so far as to call John Paul's epistemology in the *Theology of the Body* "anti-dualistic" and "anti-Cartesian."[20] Kupczak also clarifies that, for John Paul, these dualistic and reductionist errors in describing man have "far reaching consequences for ethical judgments regarding human behavior, ranging from sexuality to bioethics"[21] and that such errors lead to "the manipulation of the human body, or the practice of 'using' the human body."[22]

The fundamental opinion of these commentators is that John Paul II viewed the major ethical challenges facing contemporary society as being rooted in certain philosophical errors that have been passed down and become entrenched in western culture since Descartes and the dawn of modernity. They suggest that the Pope believed these errors to have led to a certain "split" or "estrangement" between the human person and nature, between man and the world, and to have fostered a dualistic and reductionist way of understanding the human person and a utilitarian view of the human body. They also see John Paul's anthropology, especially as expressed in the *Theology of the Body*, as his attempt to remedy the maladies of Cartesian Rationalism.

This current work seeks to corroborate and develop the insights of Waldstein and Kupczak. In it, I will offer a detailed analysis of

---

15   Jaroslaw Kupczak, *Gift and Communion: John Paul II's Theology of the Body* (Washington, D.C.: Catholic University of America Press, 2014), 1.
16   Ibid.   17   Ibid., 3–4.   18   Ibid., 5.   19   Ibid.
20   Ibid., 43.   21   Ibid., 13.   22   Ibid.

Letter to Families, no. 19 in order to identify the specific aspects of the Cartesian tradition with which John Paul II was concerned, and then I will explore these aspects in Descartes's philosophy with the assistance of contemporary Cartesian scholarship.[23] A closer examination of Descartes's own work will not only help to clarify the Pope's diagnosis of the heresy of our times and his prescribed remedy, but will elucidate the relationship between the errors of Cartesian Rationalism and Manichaeism, and thus the rationale behind John Paul II's choice to label the collection of symptoms he identifies as a "New Manichaeism." Subsequently, I will turn to John Paul II's anthropology as expressed in the *Theology of the Body* and demonstrate how it does indeed attempt to relieve these very symptoms and heal the culture and the family of this neo-Manichaean disease.

AN ANTIDOTE FOR MANICHAEISM

If one wishes to explore more deeply what John Paul II meant in diagnosing a New Manichaeism and how his anthropology represents a remedy for it, the work of George Weigel and Christopher West is also important to consider. Both suggest that John Paul's anthropology is an "antidote" or "rebuttal" to so-called "Manichaean" attitudes and views about the body and sexuality.

In his work *Witness to Hope: The Biography of Pope John Paul II*, George Weigel proposes that John Paul II's anthropology, specifically as found in the pre-papal work *Love and Responsibility* and the *Theology of the Body*, is a key response to Manichaean attitudes about the body and sexuality. Believing that a "Manichaean shadow" had been cast over Catholic sexual ethics in spite of the early Church's formal rejection of gnostic and Manichaean teachings on the intrinsic evil of the material world, the human body, and sex, Weigel considers Wojtyła's *Love and Responsibility* to be an "antidote to Manichaeanism and the outline of a personalistic, humanistic response to the claims of the contemporary

---

23 Such scholarship may indeed question the validity of Waldstein's and Kupczak's interpretation of Descartes's project, seeing labels like "dualism" and "mechanism" as either overly simplistic or as being more reflective of Cartesian tradition than of Descartes himself. For just one example, John Cottingham proposes that Descartes was more a "trialist" than a "dualist" and holds that the dualist label fails to explain the complexities found in his writings. See his *Descartes* (Oxford: Blackwell Publishing, 1986), 119-132.

sexual revolution."[24] Weigel seems to consider this outline to be brought to full development in the *Theology of the Body*, stating that it "may prove to be the decisive moment in exorcising the Manichaean demon and its deprecation of human sexuality from Catholic moral theology."[25] Weigel has good reason to view these two works as responses to Manichaeism, since they both explicitly reject Manichaean attitudes about the body, sex, and procreation and elucidate their incompatibility with Christian faith.[26] Yet, this is effectively where Weigel's considerations end. The cursory treatment of these themes is likely due to the nature of Weigel's work as a biography and the breadth of the material he endeavors to cover.

Christopher West shares Weigel's conviction that the *Theology of the Body* is a "rebuttal to Manichaeism."[27] In his *Theology of the Body Explained: A Commentary on John Paul II's Man and Woman He Created Them*, West likewise makes reference to the "Manichaean demon," which saw the source of evil in matter and condemned all things bodily in man, especially devaluing human sexuality.[28] West suggests that John Paul II sought to "uproot" this faulty way of viewing the body and sex that had "seeped into many Christians' minds and hearts."[29] Commenting on John Paul II's interpretation of Christ's words about "lust in the heart," West emphasizes that for John Paul "anyone who wants to see in Christ's words a Manichaean perspective would be committing an essential error,"[30] because, "far from devaluing the body and sex, Christianity assigns to the body and sex a value beyond compare."[31] However, West neither offers a thorough analysis of John Paul II's use of the Manichaean label nor any reference to sources treating Manichaean doctrine. This is likely due to the nature of West's commentary, which is explanatory for the sake of popular readership and not a theological or critical

---

24   George Weigel, *Witness to Hope: The Biography of Pope John Paul II* (New York, NY: HarperCollins Publishers, 2001), 142.

25   Ibid., 342.

26   See John Paul II, *Man and Woman He Created Them: A Theology of the Body*, 36:3, 41:4, 44:5–6, 45, 49:6, 55:3, 62:5, 78:6, 82:6, 83:3, 85:5, and Wojtyła, *Love and Responsibility*, 59, 188, 254.

27   Christopher West, *Theology of the Body Explained: A Commentary on John Paul II's Man and Woman He Created Them* (Boston: Pauline Books and Media, 2007), footnotes 15, 12.

28   Ibid., 230.   29   Ibid.   30   Ibid.   31   Ibid., 231.

analysis *per se*. What is significant, however, is that West's work points to a link between John Paul's anthropology and Manichaeism, even if his genre does not allow for an in-depth exploration of it.

A "NEW MANICHAEISM"

Weigel and West both boldly assert that John Paul II's anthropology is an "antidote" or "rebuttal" to Manichaean views of the body and sex, but do they offer any insight into the Pope's diagnosis of a New Manichaeism and its relationship to Cartesian Rationalism?

Weigel's references to Manichaeism pertain exclusively to certain negative views of the body and sexuality, generally attributed to Manichaean doctrine, which consider the body and sex to be fundamentally evil and corrupt. His work does not make mention of John Paul's reference to a New Manichaeism in *Letter to Families* or to any link between it, Descartes's philosophy, and John Paul's anthropology. Thus, while Weigel's work is helpful in identifying John Paul II's anthropology as a response to so-called "Manichaean" attitudes and views about the body and sexuality, it does not provide any commentary on the New Manichaeism specifically.

On the contrary, in his Prologue to his *Theology of the Body Explained: A Commentary on John Paul II's Man and Woman He Created Them*, Christopher West offers the most precise commentary to date on the New Manichaeism. West's work is quite informative and helpful to those seeking to understand John Paul's diagnosis, for it is the only direct discussion and elaboration of it in current commentaries on John Paul II's thought.

West discusses what he refers to as the "Cartesian 'crisis of the body,'" summarized by John Paul II in *Letter to Families*, no. 19,[32] which West considers "a precise diagnosis of what ails the modern world."[33] In West's commentary, he alludes to similar themes that were found in the work of Waldstein and Kupczak, namely, that "the Cartesian separation of body and spirit has led to a lost sense of human identity"[34] in which, due to a purely scientific perception of the world, the human body is seen not in accordance with the categories of its specific likeness to God, but only its likeness to other bodies in nature, like those of animals. Thus, according to West, "the ancient Manichaean devaluation of the body takes on a new face,"[35] in which the body is objectified as "raw material"

---

32 Ibid., 12.   33 Ibid., 13.   34 Ibid.   35 Ibid.

and becomes a source of manipulation.[36] West concludes that John Paul II's *Theology of the Body* is the cure for this dualistic ailment, this Cartesian "crisis of the body," for in it John Paul ponders "the profound understanding of masculinity and femininity found in divine revelation"[37] and seeks to recover the "full truth" about the personal dignity of man and woman, a dignity that demands that he or she may never be used or manipulated. For West, the *Theology of the Body* is also an attempt to recover a sense of primordial wonder at the beauty of the human body[38] and to rediscover human sexuality as a treasure proper to the person.[39]

West states that, in the New Manichaeism, "the ancient Manichaean devaluation of the body takes on a new face," one in which the body becomes an object of manipulation. This "new face," one may assume, is in contrast to the "old face" that viewed the body as intrinsically evil and corrupt. Yet, this is where West's analysis ends.

In this book, I seek to develop the bold assertion, made by both George Weigel and Christopher West, that John Paul II's anthropology provides an "antidote" or "rebuttal" to "Manichaean" attitudes and views about the body and sexuality. I also intend to paint a fuller portrait of this "new face" of the Manichaean devaluation of the body referred to as a "New Manichaeism" by John Paul II. This requires a critical analysis of precisely how this New Manichaeism relates to the errors of Cartesian Rationalism and the beliefs and practices of the Manichees, and how these correspond to John Paul II's anthropological project. Thus, not only, as previously stated, is recourse to contemporary scholarship on Cartesian philosophy needed, but also to contemporary Manichaean scholarship so as to clarify the Manichaean view of the natural world in general, and of the human body and human sexuality in particular. Additionally, an analysis of John Paul's anthropology in light of this New Manichaeism will offer insights into his anthropological project and show how it offers a remedy for the spiritual disease of a New Manichaeism infecting the human family.[40]

---

36 Thus, "we fail to see that every 'it,' every human body we dominate and exploit is, in fact, a 'he' or 'she,' a human subject, a person." Ibid.

37 John Paul II, *Letter to Families*, no. 20.   38 Ibid.

39 Ibid.   40 John Paul II, *Letter to Families*, no. 19.

OVERVIEW OF THIS PRESENT WORK

The initial chapter undertakes a close textual analysis of *Letter to Families*, no. 19 to establish the structure of the New Manichaeism as it pertains to John Paul's critique of Cartesian Rationalism in that section, drawing out the specific problematic features of Cartesian Rationalism that John Paul associates with it. A more precise understanding of these features is provided through recourse to other writings of John Paul in which he treats similar themes.

In light of this analysis, and with the aim of offering a greater degree of clarification of John Paul II's concerns regarding the ills of Cartesian Rationalism, Chapter 2 of this work explores those features of Cartesian Rationalism identified in *Letter to Families*, no. 19 in Descartes's own thought and writings, utilizing primary sources and contemporary scholarship on Cartesian philosophy. This exploration elucidates John Paul's diagnosis and shows to what degree these ideas can be considered "Cartesian."

With these specific aspects of Cartesian Rationalism established and clarified, an investigation of their relationship to ancient Manichaeism becomes necessary. This is the subject matter of Chapter 3. Through an examination of contemporary scholarship on Manichaeism, judiciously limiting its scope to those beliefs and practices of the Manichees that correspond to the problematic features of Cartesian Rationalism and their consequences for contemporary culture, the analogy between Manichaeism and Cartesian Rationalism is disclosed and John Paul's diagnosis clarified. Since the Manichaean label has its own implications in Christian tradition, no examination of John Paul's diagnosis of a New Manichaean in the *Letter to Families* would be complete without considering how it relates to the previous diagnoses of Manichaeism in Christian history. Thus, Chapter 4 compares John Paul's use of the Manichaean label in the letter with its typical use by Christian apologists to describe particular heterodox beliefs and communities. Such a comparison further clarifies the analogy the Pope is drawing between aspects of Cartesian Rationalism and Manichaeism, and provides a rationale as to why John Paul chose to diagnose a New Manichaeism over other possible diagnoses (e.g., Dualism or Gnosticism).

In Chapter 5, the study proceeds to show how John Paul II's anthropology can be understood as a remedy for the errors of

Cartesian Rationalism and an "antidote" to "Manichaean" views and attitudes about the body and sex (and, thus, as his prescribed remedy for the New Manichaeism). It analyzes John Paul's anthropology in light of those features of Cartesian Rationalism he associates with the New Manichaeism, and then demonstrates how his anthropology, superlatively expressed in the *Theology of the Body*, is offered as a cure.

WHY IT MATTERS

It is evident that a sharpened focus of John Paul II's concerns will lead to a fuller appreciation of how he attempted to respond to these concerns through his own anthropological project. In the time since I originally wrote the thesis upon which this book is based, we have seen an increasing assault on the Christian understanding of the human person, marriage, sexuality, and the family. We have been witness to the spread of a neo-Manichaean way of thinking, in which body and spirit are put into radical opposition, and human sexuality is an area of manipulation and use. As one commentator on the *Theology of the Body*, Damon Owens, puts it, we live in a "this is my body"/"this is not my body" world. Christopher West has suggested that we have seen Descartes's "cogito" attain its end: "I think, therefore I am what I think I am." A quick glance tells the tale: we see the rise of gender ideology and transgenderism, the destruction of what it means to be a man or woman, the attack on human life at its very beginning and its end, a redefinition of marriage that now creeps towards legal recognition of polyamory, the pervasiveness of pornography and sex trafficking—and the list goes on. The question that should burn within us is, "How did we get here?" It is a long and complicated answer. John Paul II offered his diagnosis and remedy. We would do well to take heed. For the life and health of Western Civilization, the family, and perhaps even of the Church Herself, as in centuries past, depends on rooting out the spiritual disease of heresy and applying the balm of Truth.

CHAPTER 1:
The Structure of the New Manichaeism

INTRODUCTION

It is interesting to note what John Paul II *is not* claiming by diagnosing a New Manichaeism as the spiritual disease infecting humanity. He is not claiming that this New Manichaeism is a resurgence of the third century religious sect commonly associated with Mani from Babylonia or even of some alleged medieval derivative. Instead, he draws a relationship between the New Manichaeism and certain features of Cartesian Rationalism that have deteriorated contemporary men and women's understanding of the themselves, the world, the body, and sex. In order properly to understand the Pope's diagnosis, a close reading of *Letter to Families*, no. 19 is necessary. This will clarify the particular features of Cartesian Rationalism that John Paul sees as "neo-Manichaean," and draw out how he connects certain contemporary ways of thinking and acting with them. There is also a need to compare John Paul's use of the Manichaean label in the *Letter to Families* and his other uses of the label to elucidate why John Paul considers this spiritual disease affecting the culture and the family in fact to be a New Manichaeism. This chapter will not only consider the pertinent sections of the *Letter to Families*, but will also consult other writings in which John Paul treats similar themes.

THE NEW MANICHAEISM IN CONTEXT

In *Letter to Families*, no. 19, John Paul writes:

> Within a similar anthropological perspective, the human family is facing the challenge of a *new Manichaeism*, in which body and spirit are put in radical opposition; the body does not receive life from the spirit, and the spirit does not give life to the body. Man thus *ceases to live as a person and a subject*. Regardless of all intentions and declarations to the contrary, he becomes merely an *object*. This

neo-Manichaean culture has led, for example, to human sexuality being regarded more as an area *for manipulation and exploitation* than as the basis for that *primordial wonder* which led Adam on the morning of creation to exclaim before Eve: "This at last is bone of my bones and flesh of my flesh" (*Gen* 2:23). This same wonder is echoed in the words of the *Song of Solomon*: "You have ravished my heart, my sister, my bride, you have ravished my heart with a glance of your eyes" (*Song* 4:9).[1]

The phrase "within a similar anthropological perspective" immediately conjures up questions in one's mind. With what does the New Manichaeism share a similar anthropological perspective? And what precisely is that anthropological perspective? Before this chapter shows how the answer to these questions is found in Cartesian Rationalism, it will prove helpful to situate John Paul's words about the New Manichaeism within the overall aims of the letter.

The *Letter to Families* was written in celebration of the Church's "Year of the Family," which was declared for the 1994 liturgical year to correspond to the United Nations' declaration of 1994 as the International Year of the Family.[2] The main purpose of the letter

---

1   John Paul here refers to the "spirit" more broadly and not to "soul" specifically, though the latter is included under the former term. It is not unprecedented for John Paul to refer to "spirit" in this broad sense (Cf. John Paul II, *Man and Woman He Created Them: A Theology of the Body*, 67:1, John Paul II, *The Role of the Christian Family in the Modern World* [1981], no. 11). Additionally, *The Catechism of the Catholic Church* (1994), no. 367, states, "Sometimes the soul is distinguished from the spirit: St. Paul for instance prays that God may sanctify his people 'wholly,' with 'spirit and soul and body' kept sound and blameless at the Lord's coming (1 Thess. 5:23). The Church teaches that this distinction does not introduce a duality into the soul (Cf. Council of Constantinople IV [870]: DS 657). 'Spirit' signifies that from creation man is ordered to a supernatural end and that his soul can gratuitously be raised beyond all it deserves to communion with God (Cf. Vatican Council I, *Dogmatic Constitution on the Catholic Faith* [1870]: DS 3005;Vatican Council II, *Pastoral Constitution on the Church in the Modern World* [1965], n. 22 § 5; Pope Pius XII, *Concerning Some False Opinions Threatening to Undermine the Foundations of Catholic Doctrine* [1950]: DS 3891)."

2   The *Letter to Families* is a papal letter, that is, a publication issued directly by the Pope or by an official delegated by him to a particular person or group of persons regarding some matter or event of importance. These can

is to reflect upon how the Church can promote the dignity of marriage and family in light of the current situation of the family in the world.[3] Thus, a goal of the letter is to draw attention to particular challenges facing the family and its stability in society. One such challenge, according to the Pope, is that contemporary culture is marked by a great "crisis of truth," which he sees as a "crisis of concepts," wherein words like love, freedom, sincere gift, person, and "rights of the person" no longer carry their essential meaning.[4] This "crisis of truth" gives rise to the acceptance of (and even normalizing or glamorizing of) situations and behaviors which contradict truth and love and disregard the dignity of persons. John Paul's reference to a New Manichaeism experienced by the human family in paragraph 19 can be understood as part of his reflections on this "crisis of truth"/"crisis of concepts," wherein the essential meaning of "person" and "love" have been obfuscated.

Paragraph 19 itself appears in Chapter II of the letter in the section entitled "The Great Mystery." In this section, John Paul explains how St. Paul's reference in his Letter to the Ephesians to the "great mystery," i.e., Christ's love for the Church, illumines the "great mystery" of spousal love and the truth about marriage and the family. He demonstrates how the love of the Divine Bridegroom, Jesus Christ, who "fully discloses man to himself,"[5] proclaims the dignity of the human person, reveals love as the affirmation of the person embodied in the gift of self, and summons spouses to a communion of persons formed, animated, and sustained by this love/gift of self. According to the Pope, an erroneous view of the human person and of love, one uninformed by Christ and his grace, will lead to distortions of the person, of conjugal love, of the family, and of civilizations, and will create a climate "dangerous" to the family.[6] By mentioning the New Manichaeism within this section, John Paul is identifying it as one such erroneous view.

---

range from matters pertaining to faith and morals to acknowledgements of special anniversaries.

3   John Paul II, *Letter to Families*, no. 3.

4   Ibid., no. 13. Since Pope John Paul II wrote these words, we have indeed witnessed the deconstruction and reconstruction of words and concepts on full display in our culture.

5   Vatican II, *Pastoral Constitution on the Church in the Modern World* (1965), no. 22.

6   John Paul II, *Letter to Families*, no. 19.

THE NEW MANICHAEISM AND ITS RELATIONSHIP
TO CARTESIAN RATIONALISM, ANTHROPOLOGICAL
DUALISM, AND A MECHANISTIC VIEW OF NATURE

Within this sub-section, however, a more specific context for the label "New Manichaeism" can be identified, one which begins with John Paul II's assertion that "Saint Paul's magnificent synthesis concerning the 'great mystery' appears as the compendium or *summa*, in some sense, *of the teaching about God and man* which was brought to fulfillment by Christ."[7] What immediately follows is John Paul's critique of the Descartes's philosophy, specifically of Modern Rationalism, which he considers to be a philosophical tradition that has moved Western thought away from this "great mystery." These are particularly essential passages to consider if one is to grasp the meaning of John Paul's label "New Manichaeism" and its relationship to Cartesian Rationalism, for the reference to the New Manichaeism is actually nestled within the Pope's critique of Modern Rationalism.

In John Paul's assessment, Modern Rationalism "provides a radically different way of looking at creation and the meaning of human existence"[8] than does the "great mystery." The Pope states:

> Unfortunately, Western thought, with the development of *modern rationalism*, has been gradually moving away from this teaching [about God and man brought to fulfillment by Christ]. The philosopher who formulated the principle of "*Cogito, ergo sum*," "I think, therefore I am," also gave the modern concept of man its distinctive dualistic character. It is typical of rationalism to make a radical contrast in man between spirit and body, between body and spirit.[9]

According to John Paul, Modern Rationalism—which originates from "the philosopher who formulated the principle of '*Cogito, ergo sum*'" (i.e., Descartes)—endorses a form of anthropological dualism which makes a "radical contrast in man between spirit and body" by positing that man is comprised of two separate and distinct substances, mind (the "thinking thing") and matter (understood as pure extension). Such a dualist view rejects the hylomorphic view, associated with Thomas Aquinas and derived from the works of

---

7   Ibid.   8   Ibid.   9   Ibid, my brackets.

Aristotle,[10] that man is a single composite substance comprised of form (soul) and matter (body), i.e., that man's essence "embraces both form and matter,"[11] since it is through form that matter, as the principle of individuation, becomes an "actual being" existing as a "particular thing." For Cartesian Rationalism, the person is identified with his or her mind, as "a thing that thinks."[12] The human body is pure extension or "mere matter." After a brief, yet vigorous, defense of hylomorphism in which he affirms that "man is a person in the unity of his body and his spirit," and declares that "the richest source for knowledge of the body is the Word made flesh," since "Christ reveals man to himself,"[13] John Paul laments that "the modern age has made great progress in understanding both the material world and human psychology, but with regard to his deepest, metaphysical dimension contemporary man remains to a great extent a *being unknown* to himself..."[14]

To provide a fuller sense of John Paul's critique of Cartesian Rationalism's anthropological dualism, one can briefly turn to an article "Thomistic Personalism," which he wrote prior to his election to the papacy. In it he states that Descartes's "splitting of the human being into an extended substance (the body) and a thinking substance (the soul), which are related to one another in a parallel way and do not form an undivided whole, one substantial *compositum humanum*...lacks a sufficient basis for including the body, the organism, within the structural whole of the person's

---

10   Other medieval philosophers likewise held this view, which was one of the fruits of the renaissance of Aristotelian philosophy during this period. Aquinas synthesized Aristotle's philosophy with Christian doctrine and thus developed Aristotle's thought, bringing it to a particular level of perfection.

11   Thomas Aquinas, *On Being and Essence*, II, 1, trans. Armand Maurer (Toronto: Pontifical Institute of Mediaeval Studies, 1968), 35.

12   "I am, then, in the strict sense only a thing that thinks; that is, I am a mind, or intelligence, or intellect, or reason" (Descartes, *Meditations on First Philosophy: With Selections from the Objections and Replies*, trans. John Cottingham [Cambridge: Cambridge University Press, 1996], II, 18).

13   John Paul II even goes so far as to state that "in a certain sense this statement of the Second Vatican Council is the reply, so long awaited, which the Church has given to modern rationalism." In this brief defense, he affirms that "man is a person in the unity of his body and his spirit. The body can never be reduced to mere matter: it is a *spiritualized body*, just as man's spirit is so closely united to the body that he can be described as *an embodied spirit*."

14   John Paul II, *Letter to Families*, no. 19.

life and activity..."[15] It lacks this, in his opinion, because it does not regard the Aristotelian-Thomistic hylomorphic notion of the soul being the form of the body.

After discussing the anthropological dualism he associates with Cartesian Rationalism, the Pope immediately highlights in the *Letter to Families* a broader, one could say "cosmic," form of dualism likewise associated with this philosophical tradition. According to Descartes, the world is essentially divided into two types of substances: mind (*res cogitans*) and matter (*res extensa*). John Paul states:

> The separation of spirit and body in man has led to a growing tendency to consider the human body, not in accordance with the categories of its specific likeness to God, but rather on the basis of its similarity to all the other bodies present in the world of nature, bodies which man uses as raw material in his efforts to produce goods for consumption.[16]

For Descartes, bodies[17] (i.e., all material things) are like machines composed of parts, and their nature lies exclusively in extension.[18] Such a "mechanistic" view of nature regards "bodies present in the world of nature" as "raw material" upon which man may exert his will. Descartes rejects the existence of formal and final causes[19] in

---

15   Karol Wojtyla, "Thomistic Personalism," *Person and Community: Selected Essays* (New York: Peter Lang, 2008), 169.

16   John Paul II, *Letter to Families*, no. 19.

17   In his work, Descartes uses the term "bodies" interchangeably with "corporeal or extended substance, material substance, and matter" (Daniel Garber, *Descartes' Metaphysical Physics* [Chicago: The University of Chicago Press, 1992], 64). For him, the human body will fall under this general classification of "bodies."

18   "I might consider the body of a man as a kind of machine equipped with and made up of bones, nerves, muscles, veins, blood and skin in such a way that, even if there were no mind in it, it would still perform all the same movements as it now does in those cases where movement is not under the control of the will, or, consequently, of the mind" (Descartes, *Meditations on First Philosophy*, VI, 58). For Descartes, the "true nature of matter or 'body considered in general' consists solely in extension" (John Cottingham, *Descartes* [Oxford: Blackwell Publishing, 1986], 82), that is, in having dimensions and occupying space.

19   In fact, it is Descartes's denial of substantial form that will ultimately make the notion of final cause inconceivable to him (see Etienne Gilson, *From Aristotle to Darwin and Back Again: A Journey in Final Causality, Species, and*

nature, claiming them to be impractical and irrelevant to science, the goal of which is to make man the master and possessor of nature.[20] If man were only to discover how the "machine" worked, by knowing efficient and material causes, then man could exert power over nature and impose his own order and ends upon it. Since Descartes does not view man as a single substance which is comprised of matter and form, but rather as two separate substances, mind and matter, he quite naturally considers the human body in terms of extension alone and consigns it exclusively to the realm of the mechanical cosmos.[21] As such, the human body has no intrinsic "end" either, but is an "object" in the natural world, which man can exploit with knowledge of efficient and material causes, and upon which he can impose his own order and ends. In fact, for Descartes and those that followed in his tradition, rationality is seen as "the power to construct orders."[22]

To John Paul II's mind, the consequences of this are disastrous. He continues in *Letter to Families*, no. 19:

> But everyone can immediately realize what enormous dangers lurk behind the application of such criteria to man. When the human body, considered apart from spirit and thought, comes to be used as raw material in the same way that the bodies of animals are used—and this actually occurs for example in experimentation on embryos and fetuses—we will inevitably arrive at a dreadful ethical defeat.[23]

John Paul asserts that the failure to view the human person as a composite substance, i.e., as "a person in the unity of his body

---

Evolution [San Francisco: Ignatius Press, 2009], 21). According to Gilson, Montaigne was the first to reject these and inspired Francis Bacon and Descartes (see *A History of Philosophy: Modern Philosophy, Descartes to Kant* [New York: Random House, 1963]).

20   In the Fourth Meditation, Descartes declares, "the customary search for final causes to be totally useless in physics" (Descartes, *Meditations on First Philosophy*, IV, 39). Descartes also believes that since God's nature is beyond human knowledge, so is knowledge of his purpose for his creation.

21   Ibid. Again, contemporary scholarship on Cartesian philosophy indicates that Descartes's own view may have been more complex than this.

22   Charles Taylor, *Sources of the Self: The Making of the Modern Identity* (Cambridge: Harvard University Press, 1989), 147.

23   John Paul II, *Letter to Families*, no. 19.

and his spirit,"[24] by identifying the human person as essentially a "mind" or "soul" somehow or another related to a body, which is viewed as mere extension, logically leads to a utilitarian view of the body. In other words, if the human body is viewed as an object among other objects in the observable universe, as "raw material" upon which man may exert his will, then its value is instrumental and not intrinsic. In such a case, the body is not viewed subjectively or personally.[25] Yet, if, as John Paul II claims, the person *is* his body and still the body is perceived as "merely an object" to be used by oneself or others, then *the person* in fact becomes "merely an object" to be used by oneself or others. To him, this leads to a "dreadful ethical defeat," and has far reaching consequences for bioethics and sexual ethics.

After pointing to Descartes who "gave the modern concept of man its distinctive dualistic character" and Modern Rationalism that makes a "radical contrast in man between spirit and body, between body and spirit,"[26] as well as posits a mechanistic view of nature in which "the human body, considered apart from spirit and thought, comes to be used as raw material," the Pope

---

24   Ibid. In the apostolic exhortation *On the Role of the Christian Family in the Modern World* (1981), no. 11, John Paul states that man is "an incarnate spirit, that is, a soul which expresses itself in a body and a body informed by an immortal spirit." In the encyclical *The Splendor of the Truth* (1993), no. 48, he asserts that the human person is a being "whose rational soul is *per se et essentialiter the form of his body*" and "exists as a whole—*corpore et anima unus*—as a person." In *Man and Woman He Created Them: A Theology of the Body*, John Paul II states that since the body is a "manifestation of the spirit" (45:2), "reveals man" (9:4), and "expresses a person" (7:2, 14:4), then man, in this sense, also "is" a body (2:4, 8:1) and is "that" particular body (55:2). The Pope goes on to say that masculinity and femininity are two "incarnations" or "two ways in which the same human being, created in the 'image of God' (Gen. 1:27), 'is a body'" (8:3).

25   "... [M]an no longer identifies himself subjectively, so to speak, with his own body, because he is deprived of the meaning and dignity that stem from the fact that this body is proper to the person" (John Paul II, *Man and Woman He Created Them: A Theology of the Body*, 59:3).

26   John Paul II, *Letter to Families*, no. 19. Again, there are some Cartesian scholars who suggest that such a characterization of Descartes fails to explain the complexities found in his writings. The views of such scholars will be treated in the chapter on Descartes. It is sufficient at this point to note that John Paul's point remains a viable (and even traditional) interpretation of Descartes's position.

immediately goes on to state, "Within a similar anthropological perspective the human family is facing the challenge of a *new Manichaeism*..." and to discuss how this New Manichaeism places body and spirit in "radical opposition" and results in the human person being reduced to "merely an *object*." With these words, John Paul is making a strong association of all that he has said thus far about Cartesian Rationalism with the New Manichaeism. First, his comments about the New Manichaeism are nestled right in the heart of his critique of Cartesian Rationalism. Second, the parallels between how John Paul describes this New Manichaeism and his critique of Cartesian Rationalism are striking, from the description of anthropological dualism to the human body being regarded as an object for manipulation and exploitation characteristic of a mechanistic view of nature. Third, the phrase "Within a similar anthropological perspective," is actually understated in the English translation of the text. For example, in the Latin translation,[27] the first part of this quote is *Simili quidem in anthropologico prospectu*. The word *quidem* means "certainly" or "indeed" and is a postpositive adverb, i.e., it is placed after the verb, adjective, or adverb which it modifies. In this specific case, *quidem* is placed after *simili*, which means "similar" or "like." Thus, *simili quidem* would mean "certainly like," which would denote a strong association of the anthropological perspective of the New Manichaeism with that of Descartes and Modern Rationalism and not a mere resemblance between them. The association is even stronger in the Italian, French, and German translations of this phrase. The Italian and French translate as, "In such an anthropological perspective,"[28] and the German as, "In the face of such an anthropological perspective."[29] In these cases, the anthropological perspectives of Cartesian Rationalism and the New Manichaeism either are identical, or there exists a causal relationship between them, namely, that the experience of a New

---

27 Lambert Greenan must be acknowledged for his assistance with the translation of the Latin.

28 Italian: *In una simile prospectiva antropologica*; French: *Devan tune pareille perspective anthropologique*. In Italian, when simile, which means "similar," follows the word it is modifying it becomes stronger, and thus the translation as "such." Francesco Pesce must be acknowledged for his assistance with the translations of the Italian, French, and German.

29 *In einer solchen anthropologischen Perspektive...*

Manichaeism is the result of the anthropological perspective of Cartesian Rationalism.

Finally, the phrase *vivere cogitur familia humana experientiam novi Manichaeismi*, which is rendered in the English translation as "the human family is facing the challenge of a new Manichaeism," is more literally translated as "the human family is *forced to undergo the experience* of a new Manichaeism..." This translation respects the passive voice of the verb *cogitur*. The human family is "forced": it is forced "to undergo" or "cope with" something (i.e., the experience of a New Manichaeism), because of something (i.e., an anthropological perspective strongly associated with or identical to that of Cartesian Rationalism). In the Italian, French, and German versions this phrase also reads passively as the human family "finds itself living the experience of," "comes to live the experience of," and "has presently/at this moment experienced" a "new Manichaeism."[30] It is interesting to note that in every case, the New Manichaeism is something that the human family is "experiencing" in a passive and receptive way. That is, the New Manichaeism can be said to be something "happening to" the human family that is the result of "a radically different way of looking at creation and the meaning of human existence" which it has received as an intellectual heritage from Cartesian Rationalism and which has formed the way contemporary men and women view the world and themselves.[31]

---

30 Italian: *la famiglia umana si trova a vivere l'esperienza di un nuovo manicheismo*; French: *la famille humaine en arrive à vivre l'expérience d'un nouveau manichéisme*; German: *erlebt die Menschheitsfamilie soeben die Erfahrung eines neuen Manichäismus.* In German, "erleben" is the verb for "to know," but "to know by experience."

31 The Pope seems to be suggesting that the errors of Cartesian Rationalism have led to the experience of a New Manichaeism. As a religion, Manichaeism is a "worldview," a "way of viewing reality" that manifests itself in certain "rites" and "behaviors." John Paul appears to insinuate that contemporary men and women are "raised" on this "radically different way of looking at creation and the meaning of human existence": they "inhale it" in the "air" of the culture, they have had it driven into them from their youth, it is their "worldview." From the point of view of ethics, they act a certain way and do not see any difficulties with those actions, because for them these actions simply "make sense" within the framework of their worldview. These ideas will be treated in more detail in Chapter 4 of this book when John Paul's use of the Manichaean label in the *Letter to Families* is compared to its characteristic use in Christian tradition.

LINKING THE NEW MANICHAEISM WITH
CARTESIAN RATIONALISM'S REJECTION OF
MYSTERY AND THE PHILOSOPHY OF BEING

John Paul does not stop with anthropological dualism and the mechanistic view of nature when drawing a strong association between the anthropological perspective of the New Manichaeism and Cartesian Rationalism. Upon considering the Pope's words about the "neo-Manichaean culture" that results from this anthropological perspective, one finds that John Paul connects the New Manichaeism with another alleged error of Cartesian Rationalism: the rejection of "mystery." When John Paul speaks of "mystery," he is implying the "mystery of being" and thus Thomas Aquinas's philosophy of being and the "notion of creation" which "characterizes the interior structure of *nearly all* the basic concepts"[32] in it. For Pope John Paul II, Cartesian Rationalism's rejection of mystery involves the "decisive abandonment" of Thomas's philosophy of being (*esse*), and thus the rejection of a truth of creation which must be acknowledged and of the God of Creation who is *Ens subsistens*[33] and *absolute uncreated Mystery*.[34] This link between the New Manichaeism and Cartesian Rationalism's rejection of mystery and the philosophy of being will more fully explain how it "provides a radically different way of looking at creation and the meaning of human existence."[35]

Immediately following his comments about how the New Manichaeism places a radical opposition between body and spirit, the Pope states:

> This neo-Manichaean culture has led, for example, to human sexuality being regarded more as an area *for*

---

32   Josef Pieper, "The Negative Element in the Philosophy of St. Thomas Aquinas," in *The Silence of St. Thomas* (South Bend, St. Augustine's Press, 1957), 47, 48.

33   John Paul uses this phrase in *Memory and Identity: Conversations at the Dawn of a Millennium* (New York: Rizzoli, 2005), 10, 12. He also refers to God as *Ipsum esse subsistens* in *Crossing the Threshold of Hope* (New York: Alfred A. Knopf, 1994), 51, which is related to *Ens subsistens* in that both describe God as Self-Subsisting Being. *Ipsum esse subsistens* emphasizes God as the very *Act of Existence Itself* by the use of the infinitive verb "to be" (*esse*).

34   John Paul II, *Crossing the Threshold of Hope*, 38.

35   John Paul II, *Letter to Families*, no. 19.

manipulation and exploitation than as the basis for that *primordial wonder* which led Adam on the morning of creation to exclaim before Eve: "This at last is bone of my bones and flesh of my flesh" (*Gen* 2:23). This same wonder is echoed in the words of the *Song of Solomon*: "You have ravished my heart, my sister, my bride, you have ravished my heart with a glance of your eyes" (*Song* 4:9).[36]

How John Paul saw the objectification of the body (or rather de-personalizing or de-subjectifying of the body) as linked to a mechanistic view of the world and leading to drastic consequences for bioethics and sexual ethics has already been discussed. In these lines, the Pope connects the New Manichaeism with the loss of a sense of wonder—wonder in the presence of creation, particularly in the presence of the person. To the mind of the Pope, this loss of wonder is due to the rejection of mystery[37] that is part of the legacy of Cartesian Rationalism. John Paul continues:

> ... Modern rationalism *does not tolerate mystery*. It does not accept the mystery of man as male and female, nor is it willing to admit that the full truth about man has been revealed in Jesus Christ. In particular, it does not accept the "great mystery" proclaimed in the *Letter to Ephesians*, but radically opposes it.[38]

If "wonder" is the proper response to "mystery," then *intolerance* of mystery leads to a *loss* of the sense of wonder. Rationalism, in its search for absolute certainty and its denial or doubt of whatever

---

36 Ibid.

37 There is a relationship between the notions of "wonder" and "mystery" and philosophical realism. Agreeing with both Plato and Aristotle, for example, Thomas Aquinas states that philosophy begins in wonder (*ST*, I–II, q. 41, a. 4, ad. 5) and his philosophy of being is permeated by a sense of wonder and mystery. Consider Randall B. Smith's article "'If Philosophy Begins in Wonder': Aquinas, Creation, and Wonder," *Communio* 41.1 [Spring 2014]: 92–111) and Kenneth L. Schmitz's book on the philosophy of being entitled *The Recovery of Wonder* (Kingston, ON: McGill-Queen's University Press, 2005) as two examples of this relationship. The work of Josef Pieper is also helpful in this regard. Wonder and mystery are also clear starting points of John Paul II's anthropology—see Carl Anderson and Jose Granados' *Called to Love: Approaching John Paul II's Theology of the Body* (New York: Doubleday, 2009), 2–11.

38 John Paul II, *Letter to Families*, no. 19.

cannot be proved, does not tolerate mystery.[39] Mystery, while not requiring one to abandon reason, involves an acceptance of that which transcends mathematical certainty. Rationalism does not accept the world and what is experienced through the senses as *prima facie* real (in fact, it engenders distrust in the senses), but rather only that which can be established "without doubt." This was the very point of Descartes's "method of doubt." Ultimately, Cartesian Rationalism holds an epistemological position contrary to the metaphysical realism that characterizes Thomas Aquinas's philosophy of being. Epistemologically, Thomas presumes human beings' "capacity to recognize and cognize both the essential nature of created things and the fact of their existence."[40] Thus, in accusing Rationalism of rejecting mystery, John Paul is highlighting its abandonment of Thomas's philosophy of being and metaphysical realism.[41]

In order to grasp this relationship more fully between the rejection of mystery, rejection of the "mystery of being," and the

---

39   It is interesting to note that Thomas Aquinas, referencing St. Augustine, accuses the Manichees of the same: "We should not, therefore, immediately reject as false, following the opinion of the Manicheans and many unbelievers, everything that is said about God even though it cannot be investigated by reason" (*SCG*, lib, I, cap. III).

40   Deborah Savage, "Metaphysical Realism as the Foundation of Environmental Stewardship and Economic Development," *Nova et Vetera* 10, no. 1 (2012): 237.

41   It seems likely that John Paul II was influenced in these ideas by his mentor in Thomism, Reginald Garrigou-Lagrange. For example, consider this quote from Garrigou-Lagrange's essay, "The Essence & Topicality of Thomism," trans. Alan Aversa, 2013 (Brescia: La Scuola editrice, 1946): Thomism "is a *realist doctrine* since it admits the primacy of being over knowledge, conceived as essentially relative to being; our intellectual knowledge indeed begins from the idea of being presupposed by all other ideas, and it takes place in judgment, the soul of which is the verb 'to be.' This realism does not diminish in anything the vitality and immanence of the act of knowing, but it affirms its value in relation to extra-mental being... Thomism is a *theocentric* doctrine that affirms the primacy of God, pure Actuality, over all creation, because actuality is more perfect than potentiality. There is more in what is than in what becomes. God is, thus, not universal becoming, but externally subsistent Being itself, infinitely more perfect in His fullness than all that participates in His perfections" (19-20). Also see *Thomistic Common Sense: The Philosophy of Being and the Development of Doctrine*, trans. Matthew K. Minerd (Steubenville: Emmaus Academic, 2021), of which the aforementioned essay is a summary and complement.

abandonment of Thomas's philosophy of being (*esse*) which John Paul II is forging here in *Letter to Families*, no. 19, one must move beyond the letter to consult other works in which he treats similar themes. Doing so not only reveals a similar line of reasoning on the part of the Pope, but also an elaboration of these themes. In his personal reflection, *Memory and Identity: Conversations at the Dawn of a Millennium*, John Paul likewise connects Cartesian Rationalism with errors in the areas of sexuality and bioethics by asserting that these errors are "profoundly rooted" in the history of European thought inspired by "the revolution brought about by the philosophical thought of Descartes."[42] The Pope considers this "revolution" precisely to be "the decisive abandonment of what philosophy had been hitherto, particularly the philosophy of Thomas Aquinas, and namely that of *esse* . . . "[43]

According to John Paul II, the abandonment of the philosophy of "*esse*" (being, to be, the act of existing) amounted to a change in

---

42 John Paul II, *Memory and Identity*, 7–8. The claim that his philosophy would lead to such errors likely would have shocked and offended Descartes. Descartes claimed to have designed his entire scientific/philosophical system in part as a new way of defending religious orthodoxy rather than undermining it (see his *Dedicatory Letter to the Theologians of the Sorbonne*, which prefaces the *Meditations* of 1640). This being said, it can be posited that, while Descartes may have thought himself a devout Catholic and defended his philosophy as being perfectly compatible with orthodoxy, his philosophical system was actually opposed to orthodoxy. As Peter Schouls states, "At least in practice Descartes's revolution in the sciences was accompanied by a revolt against the traditional Christian view of the place of man. For Descartes, man has the first word and the last word in the matter of determining what is and what is not to be accepted as truth" (*Descartes and the Enlightenment* [Montreal: McGill-Queen's University Press, 1989], 37–38).

43 John Paul II, *Memory and Identity*, 7–8. Descartes was not necessarily rejecting Thomas' philosophy of being consciously. He had received the Thomistic tradition via Suarez and often looked to him for his metaphysical concepts (see Desmond Clarke, *Descartes' Philosophy of Mind* [Oxford: Oxford University Press, 2003], 30), which scholars in the Existential Thomist line (like Etienne Gilson, Stefan Swieżawski, and John Paul II) believe to be a skewed version of Thomas. Reginald Garrigou-Lagrange saw Suarez as seeking a "middle way" between Aquinas and Scotus (cf. "The Essence & Topicality of Thomism," 24) and thus as obfuscating the fundamental distinctions of Thomism. Therefore, it is possible that Descartes held an incorrect view of Thomas' teaching on essence and existence.

"the direction of philosophizing,"[44] for "doubt"[45] and "the act of thinking" are placed as the starting point of philosophy instead of the "act of existing" and the principles of being.[46] That is, *cogito* is placed prior to *esse*. As John Paul indicates in *Memory and Identity*:

> The *cogito ergo sum* (I think therefore I am) radically changed the way of doing philosophy. In the pre-Cartesian period, philosophy, that is to say the *cogito*, or rather the *cognosco*, was subordinate to *esse*, which was considered prior. To Descartes, however, *esse* seemed secondary, and he judged the *cogito* to be prior.[47]

This contrast between the approaches of Descartes and Thomas Aquinas is also highlighted by John Paul in *Crossing the Threshold of Hope*, a book of answers to questions from Italian journalist Vittorio Messori, in which he states that Descartes "split thought from existence and identified existence with reason itself: '*Cogito, ergo sum*' ('I think, therefore I am')," but that for Thomas Aquinas "it is not *thought which determines existence, but existence, 'esse' which determines thought!*"[48]

While a full treatment of Thomas Aquinas's philosophy of being is beyond the scope of this book, at this point a brief summary of

---

44   There is little doubt that Descartes initiated a revolution in philosophy and beyond (see Schouls, *Descartes and the Enlightenment*, "Chapter 1: Escape from Bondage"). The prominence of Descartes' alleged abandonment of the philosophy of being in this revolution remains to be established and will be explored in the chapter on Descartes.

45   Contemporary Cartesian scholars emphasize that "doubt" was more a "method" employed by Descartes against skepticism than an indication of a real agnosticism or skepticism on his part. Bernard Williams, for example, calls the skepticism of the *Meditations* "preemptive" ("Introductory Essay to René Descartes," *Meditations on First Philosophy: With Selections from the Objections and Replies*, trans. John Cottingham [Cambridge: Cambridge University Press, 1996], xv). A reading of the *Meditations* which overstates Descartes's "skepticism" is not upheld by many leading Cartesian scholars. Some, like Daniel Garber and Desmond Clarke, will even suggest that Descartes's method and thought as a whole need to be interpreted and understood through the lens of Cartesian science.

46   Philosophies which accept the reality of being and the principles of being as "givens" are called "realist" philosophies and their adherents are said to ascribe to "metaphysical realism."

47   John Paul II, *Memory and Identity*, 7–8.

48   John Paul II, *Crossing the Threshold of Hope*, 38.

the main points in Thomas Aquinas's philosophy of being to which John Paul is alluding is warranted. These points are important not only for understanding John Paul's diagnosis of a New Manichaeism, but also for ascertaining to what extent his anthropology could be seen as a remedy for Cartesian Rationalism.[49]

The first point concerns Thomas's position that the fundamental orientation of all philosophy is things existing in extra-mental reality. For Thomas, the "first conceptions" of the intellect are "a being" and "an essence," that is, we first have a concept of a thing as having existence, and then of its kind or how it exists in its own particular way.[50] In Latin, there are two distinct terms for "being": *ens* and *esse*. *Ens* refers to "a being" or "a thing," something existing in reality. *Esse* refers to the "act of being" or "act of existing." Yet, since the letters "*ns*" at the end of a Latin word indicate the exercise of an activity,[51] the word *ens* itself implies that an activity is being exercised, and this activity is precisely *the activity of existing*. All other activities are based on this highest activity, for something cannot exist in a particular way unless it exists.[52] For Thomas, a "being" is primarily that which is divided into the "Ten Categories of Being" (i.e., *substance* and the *nine accidents* of quantity, quality, relation, place, time, position, state, action, and passion), so "nothing can be called a being unless it is something positive in reality."[53] This proposes the necessary

---

49   One way John Paul's anthropology can be seen as an antidote to Cartesian Rationalism is by demonstrating that, in some way, he seeks to return to the philosophy of being and to particular realist presuppositions. This will be investigated in Chapter 5 of this book.

50   In his *Summa Theologiae*, Thomas states, "The first act of the human intellect is to know being, a reality as the first and proper object of understanding, just as sound is the first and proper object of hearing, and as sight is the first and proper object of our eyes" (*ST*, I, q. 5, a. 2). See also Ronda Chervin and Eugene Kevane, *Love of Wisdom: An Introduction to Christian Philosophy* (San Francisco: Ignatius Press, 1988), 119.

51   Ronda Chervin and Eugene Kevane, *Love of Wisdom: An Introduction to Christian Philosophy*, 118.

52   Thomas "was the first to appreciate fully the supremacy of the act of existing over essence" and this "existentialist turn" was a genuine metaphysical reformation (Armand Maurer, "Introduction" in Thomas Aquinas, *On Being and Essence*, trans. Armand Maurer [Toronto: Pontifical Institute of Mediaeval Studies, 1968], 11).

53   Thomas Aquinas, *On Being and Essence*, I, 2, 30.

starting point and fundamental orientation for all philosophy: *things existing in extra-mental reality.*[54] Philosophy begins with *entia*, with beings that come to us in sense experience,[55] which are designated by the term *substances.*[56] A substance "is called 'essence' when considered as definable";[57] in fact, "the essence is what the definition says the substance is."[58] For this reason, philosophers often substituted the term "quiddity" for the term "essence." Quiddity refers to the "whatness" of a thing; to that which makes anything to be what it is. Aquinas remarks that essence is also called "form," since "form signifies the determination of each thing," as well as "nature," since nature is "the essence of a thing as directed to its specific operation."[59] Thus, it is clear that in accepting human beings' "capacity to recognize and cognize both the essential nature of created things and the fact of their existence,"[60] and in emphasizing the supremacy of the activity of existing over essence, Thomas holds an epistemological position fundamentally opposed by Cartesian Rationalism, which placed *cogito* as prior to *esse*, split thought from existence, and identified existence with reason itself.

---

54   It is important to note that knowledge of the "concept of being" is only possible for beings endowed with intelligence. This higher knowledge is distinct from the knowledge of the five senses. Therefore, the "science of being as being" (metaphysics) is preliminary to the "philosophy of knowledge" (epistemology), which is actually a consequence of it. The Cartesian revolution turns this upside down; in John Paul II's words, Descartes considered "*cogito*" prior to "*esse*."

55   For Thomas, all knowledge begins with sense experience, but the mind is not a passive receiver of sense impressions, but plays an active analyzing role through, for example, what Thomas calls separation.

56   Etienne Gilson, *The Christian Philosophy of St. Thomas Aquinas* (Notre Dame: Notre Dame University Press, 1994), 29. A substance is "an essence or quiddity existing by itself in virtue of its own act of being" (Gilson, *The Christian Philosophy of St. Thomas Aquinas*, 30). It is a substance that is the existing thing itself: that which is independent of its attributes/accidents and in which these attributes subsist.

57   F. C. Copleston, *Aquinas* (New York: Penguin Books, 1955), 87.

58   Gilson, *The Christian Philosophy of St. Thomas Aquinas*, 30. Essence refers to that which is common of all beings of a particular kind, all beings belonging to a particular genus and species.

59   Thomas Aquinas, *On Being and Essence*, I, 4, 31–32.

60   Savage, "Metaphysical Realism as the Foundation of Environmental Stewardship and Economic Development," 237.

The second point is that Thomas's philosophy of being is inextricably linked to the "notion of creation," which "characterizes the interior structure of *nearly all* the basic concepts" in it.[61] This is why John Paul sees the rejection of the philosophy of being as amounting to the rejection of a truth of creation, which must be acknowledged, and of the God of Creation, who is *Ens subsistens* and *absolute uncreated Mystery*. In *Memory and Identity*, the Pope sums the relationship between Thomas's philosophy of being and the "notion of creation":

> God as fully Self-sufficient Being (*Ens subsistens*) was believed
> to be the necessary ground for every *ens non subsistens, ens
> participatum*, that is, of all created beings, including man.[62]

Thomas held that "all existing being proceeds from God as its efficient, formal, and final cause."[63] For him, "nothing exists that is not *creatura*, except the Creator Himself" and "this createdness determines entirely and all-pervasively the inner structure of the creature."[64]

For all *creatura*, including "simple substances" like intelligences (angels), which are solely forms, their act of existing is other than their essence or quiddity or form. There can only be one being whose quiddity is its act of existing, only one reality that is pure act and subsistent being (*Ens subsistens*). And this is how Thomas moves to the reality of God. Since everything whose act of existing is distinct from its essence must have its act of existing from another, and "everything that exists through another is reduced to that which exists through itself as to its first cause," it stands to reason that "there must be a reality that is the cause of being for all other things, because it is pure being."[65] And this reality is God. In fact, for all other things their act of existence is "received" from God—from Pure Being (*esse tantum*) or Being

---

61 Pieper, "The Negative Element in the Philosophy of St. Thomas Aquinas," 47, 48.

62 John Paul II, *Memory and Identity*, 12.

63 Savage, "Metaphysical Realism as the Foundation of Environmental Stewardship and Economic Development," 238.

64 Pieper, "The Negative Element in the Philosophy of St. Thomas Aquinas," 47, 48. See also Savage, "Metaphysical Realism as the Foundation of Environmental Stewardship and Economic Development," 238–239.

65 Thomas Aquinas, *On Being and Essence*, IV, 7, 56–57.

Itself (*ipsum esse*)—and "therefore is limited and restricted to the capacity of the recipient nature."[66] That is, "God has no other essence or nature than being; he is being in all its purity (*esse tantum*). Creatures receive being as a participation of the divine being, their essence limiting the degree of this participation."[67]

For Thomas, every finite being "receives in particular fashion" that which belongs to God in "universal fashion."[68] All created being participates in the divine essence by way of similitude or imitation,[69] and it is this "special way in which the divine perfection is imitated that constitutes the special essence of a thing."[70] In addition, when something participates in some perfection, it participates in it from some source, which is the cause of the participated perfection in the "participating being."[71] Thus, God can be said to be to be the exemplar cause, as well as the efficient and final cause of all created *esse*.[72] In John Paul's words, God (*Ens subsistens*) is the "necessary ground" for of all created beings (*ens non subsistens, ens participatum*). According to Thomas, the divine ideas are "exemplar forms existing in the divine mind," and "although they are multiplied with respect to things, they are not really other than the divine essence, insofar as its likeness can be diversely participated in by diverse things."[73] Since things are "creatively thought" by God, they are

---

66 Ibid., V, 4, 62.

67 Armand Maurer, "Introduction," in Thomas Aquinas, *On Being and Essence*, 10. See also Savage, "Metaphysical Realism as the Foundation of Environmental Stewardship and Economic Development," 238-239.

68 This is from Thomas' commentary on Boethius' *De Hebdomadibus*, lect. 2, Leon. 50.271:71-73. See John Wippel, *The Metaphysical Thought of Thomas Aquinas* (Washington, D. C.: Catholic University of America Press, 2000), 96.

69 "Thomas refers to such entities as participating in the First Act, or the First *Esse*, or the First Being, and as he often adds, by similitude or by imitation. This does not imply that they have a part of God's being. It rather means that in every finite substantial entity there is a participated likeness or similitude of the divine *esse*, that is, an intrinsic act of being (*esse*) which is efficiently caused in it by God" (Wippel, *The Metaphysical Thought of Thomas Aquinas*, 121).

70 Pieper, "*The Negative Element in the Philosophy of St. Thomas Aquinas*," 66.

71 Thomas Aquinas, *De substantiis separatis*, Leon. 40. D46:11-15. See John Wippel, *The Metaphysical Thought of Thomas Aquinas*, 117.

72 Wippel, *The Metaphysical Thought of Thomas Aquinas*, 116.

73 "What is real is called true in so far as it realizes that toward which it is ordained in the mind of God" (Thomas Aquinas, *Disputed Question on Truth*, I, 2). See Pieper, "The Negative Element in the Philosophy of St.

true to the extent that they instantiate the idea in God's mind.[74] There is an archetypal pattern in the divine mind, and things are real or true or good or have being to the degree that they match that pattern. Truth, goodness, and being are "transcendentals," properties of being that apply to all things and "go beyond" the ten categories, i.e., substance and the nine accidents. While distinct, these transcendental properties are convertible. For example, because the good is that which all things desire, but a thing is desirable insofar as it is perfected, and a thing is perfected to the degree that it is actual, then a thing is good to the degree that it has being, and so "being" and "good" convert (ens et bonum convertuntur).[75] Thus, all finite, created being has a positive value, is "good," by virtue of its existence as an *ens participatum*. Ultimately, since God's essence is his existence, since he is Pure Act and Being Itself, since all perfections are subsumed in his very act of existing identifying him as the Absolutely Perfect Being, and since all creatures receive their being as a participated likeness or similitude of the divine *esse*, the transcendental concepts are found in creatures (*ens participatum*) to the degree that they have a participated likeness to God, limited by their particular essences.[76]

A third point is Thomas's view that while things have an essential nature and are intrinsically knowable or intelligible *precisely because* they are creatively thought and fashioned by God (which is why the philosophy of being underlies a realist metaphysics), it is also because things are creatively thought and fashioned by God that "we do not know substantial forms as they are in themselves,"[77] and "the essential grounds of things

---

Thomas Aquinas," 62.

74   Thomas Aquinas, *Disputed Question on Truth*, I, 2. See Pieper, "The Negative Element in the Philosophy of St. Thomas Aquinas," 62.

75   *ST*, I, q. 5, a. 1, in *Thomas Aquinas: Selected Writings*, 345.

76   It ought to be said that since these perfections exist in God in an absolute way, when they are found in created beings—including and especially the primary transcendental property of being—they can only be meant in an analogous way. God is and always remains Transcendent Being—God's mode of existing is unique and radically distinct from that of creatures. (See Ronda Chervin and Eugene Kevane, *Love of Wisdom: An Introduction to Christian Philosophy*, 166.)

77   Thomas Aquinas, *Disputed Question on Spiritual Creatures*, 11, ad. 3. See

are unknown to us."[78] This is another reason why John Paul II sees the rejection of mystery as related to the abandonment of Thomas's philosophy of being. While we can know being and the essence of things,[79] at the same time "the ultimate reality of things is something we can never finally penetrate, because we can never fully grasp these likenesses of the divine ideas precisely as likenesses."[80] The brightness of their illumination dazzles our human intelligence.[81] Thus, our knowledge reaches its boundary: "the boundary of mystery,"[82] a "fullness of being with which the intellect enters into a vital union and into which it plunges without exhausting it."[83]

There are two main consequences of this rejection of Thomas's philosophy of being and its corresponding "notion of creation" by Cartesian Rationalism. The first consequence is the rejection of the God who is *Ens Subsistens* (*Ipsum esse subsistens*) and *absolute uncreated Mystery*. This rejection is alluded to by the Pope right in *Letter to Families*, no. 19 immediately following his comments about the New Manichaeism, when he alleges that, at best, Cartesian Rationalism may allow for "a vague deism."[84] The second

---

Pieper, "The Negative Element in the Philosophy of St. Thomas Aquinas," 62.

78 Thomas Aquinas, *Disputed Question on Truth*, I, ad. 8. See Pieper, "The Negative Element in the Philosophy of St. Thomas Aquinas," 62.

79 "The intellect penetrates the essence, for the object of the intellect is 'what a thing is'" (*ST*, I–II, q. 31, a. 5).

80 Pieper, "The Negative Element in the Philosophy of St. Thomas Aquinas," 67. Pieper here is reflecting on *ST*, I, q. 15, a. 2, "Every creature has its own proper species according to which it participates in some way in the likeness of the Divine Essence. Therefore, as God knows His Essence as so imitable by such a creature, He knows it as the particular model and idea of that creature."

81 Pieper, "The Negative Element in the Philosophy of St. Thomas Aquinas," 70.

82 Josef Pieper, "On Thomas Aquinas," *The Silence of St. Thomas* (South Bend: St. Augustine's Press, 1957), 38.

83 Jacques Maritain, *A Preface to Metaphysics: Seven Lectures on Being* (London: Sheed and Ward, 1939), 4–5.

84 John Paul II, *Letter to Families*, no. 19. A question to be explored in the chapter on Descartes is whether or not Descartes's view leads to a deistic view of God. This view of God was prevalent among many Enlightenment thinkers. One non-deist Enlightenment thinker, Blaise Pascal, believed it did, stating, "I cannot forgive Descartes; in all his philosophy he did his best to dispense with God. But he could not avoid making Him set the world in

consequence is the rejection of "a truth of creation which must be acknowledged," [85] that is, that things have a given nature from the Creator, a substantial form and a final cause.

In *Memory and Identity*, John Paul states that, due to *cogito* being placed prior to *esse*: "God is reduced to an element within human consciousness" and can no longer be considered the "ultimate explanation of the human sum" or remain as Creator, as Self-sufficient Being (*Ens subsistens*).[86] In *Crossing the Threshold of Hope*, John Paul reflects:

> The author of *Meditationes de Prima Philosophia*, with his ontological proofs, *distanced us from the philosophy of existence*, and also from the traditional approaches of St. Thomas Aquinas which led to a God who is "autonomous existence," *Ipsum esse subsistens*. By making subjective consciousness absolute, Descartes moves instead toward *pure consciousness of the Absolute*, which is *pure thought*. Such an Absolute is not *autonomous existence*, but rather *autonomous thought*.[87]

So, according to John Paul II, the "author of the Meditations" effectively even if unintentionally "distanced us" from the

---

motion with a flip of His thumb; after that he had no more use for God" (*The Pensées*, Section 2, no. 77, trans. W. F. Trotter, https://sourcebooks.fordham. edu/mod/1660pascal-pensees.asp). Additionally, Charles Taylor in *Sources of the Self: The Making of the Modern Identity*, states that Descartes opened the "road to Deism" as well as "prepared the ground for modern unbelief" (157–158). Although this most likely was not Descartes's intention, John Paul would agree with Taylor's assessment that this is where Descartes's thought led.

85 John Paul II, *The Gospel of Life* (1995), no. 22.

86 John Paul II, *Memory and Identity*, 10. John Paul II is simply saying that since Descartes's arguments for God's existence are from the "idea" of God (which according to Descartes is innate and caused in us by God, since there needs to be "just as much being in the cause as in the effect"), and since, according to John Paul, these arguments ultimately fail to get us from the idea of God to the reality of God, all that Descartes winds up being left with is a "pure consciousness of the Absolute." Clearly, Descartes believed he broke from thought to reality where God was concerned. This is the sole reason he believes he can trust his "clear and distinct" ideas (because God is "no deceiver"). Nevertheless, according to John Paul (and even critics from Descartes's day), he does not adequately prove God's existence, and so is left without the certainty of God, and thus without the certainty of the existence of anything else, including his own body.

87 John Paul II, *Crossing the Threshold of Hope*, 51.

"philosophy of existence" (i.e., the philosophy of being or "*esse*") and led to the rejection of a God who objectively exists and is the "necessary ground" of all created beings including human beings, trading "He Who Exists" for "He Who Exists as a Thought in my Consciousness." While Descartes, as John Paul admits, "certainly cannot be blamed for the move away from Christianity"[88] that arose in the years after him, the Pope goes on to say, "it is difficult not to acknowledge that he created the climate in which, in the modern era, such an estrangement became possible."[89]

In *Crossing the Threshold of Hope*, when John Paul reflects upon the philosophy of the Enlightenment, which he believes Descartes's thought to have inspired,[90] in words that recall the reference to a "vague deism" in *Letter to Families*, no. 19, he explains that the "*rationalism of the Enlightenment put to one side the true God—in particular, God the Redeemer*," although it "*was able to accept a God outside of the world primarily because it was an unverifiable hypothesis*."[91] Consequently,

> ...*man was supposed to live by his reason alone, as if God did not exist*. Not only was it necessary to leave God out of the objective knowledge of the world, since the existence of a Creator or of Providence was in no way helpful to science, it was also necessary to act as if God did not exist, as if God were not interested in the world.[92]

This God, the "God of the deists," was "decidedly a God outside of the world."[93] In the rationalistic view of the Enlightenment, the human being puts himself in the place of God. He exists and operates as if there were no God, rejecting that things have substantial forms which are the source of their characteristic activity, or final causes which are the ends or purposes of that

---

88 Ibid.
89 Ibid. While this estrangement occurred gradually, John Paul laments, "...about 150 years after Descartes, all that was *fundamentally Christian* in the tradition of European thought *had already been pushed aside*" (*Crossing the Threshold of Hope*, 51).
90 See Schouls, *Descartes and the Enlightenment* (Montreal: McGill-Queen's University Press, 1989) for a definitive treatment of Descartes's influence on Enlightenment philosophy.
91 John Paul II, *Crossing the Threshold of Hope*, 53 (italics in the original).
92 Ibid.
93 Ibid.

characteristic activity, since both are considered impractical and irrelevant to science.[94]

Thus, Thomas's view of formal and final causality is another aspect of his philosophy of being that is important to comprehend in order to understand John Paul's diagnosis of a New Manichaeism and for ascertaining to what extent his anthropology could be seen as a remedy for it. For Thomas Aquinas, "form signifies the determination of each thing"[95] and the formal cause in composite substances is that which actuates the potency in matter to become a thing of a specific kind. In addition to composing a complete substance when instantiated in matter, substantial forms were held to be the source of the characteristic activity of different kinds of substances. For Thomas, final cause is the end or purpose of a being's characteristic activity. In fact, he considers final cause as the "first" among causes because things are only moved by an agent and "the agent only moves by intending an end."[96] Thomas uses the term "nature" to refer to "the essence of a thing as directed to its specific operation." That is to say, each substance has a "nature," a particular act of existing which actuates its essence and is revealed by its characteristic activity: *operare sequitur esse* (operation follows "being" or the "act of existing"). With respect to final cause, each thing that exists receives a particular act of existing (*esse*) that orients it to a characteristic activity directed towards some end or purpose (*telos*). In Thomas's philosophy of being, formal and final causes are fundamental, and these are roundly rejected by Cartesian Rationalism.

LINKING THE NEW MANICHAEISM WITH CARTESIAN RATIONALISM'S TENDENCY TO RELATIVISM AND UTILITARIANISM IN ETHICS

According to John Paul, because God is placed outside of the world, and formal and final causes are denied, "Man assumes the role as the creator of himself, his own history and civilization, and becomes the one who determines what is good and evil."[97]

---

94 Descartes declares "the customary search for final causes to be totally useless in physics" (*Meditations on First Philosophy*, IV, 39).

95 Thomas Aquinas, *On Being and Essence*, I, 4, 31.

96 *ST*, I–II, q. 1, a. 2, in *Thomas Aquinas: Selected Writings*, 486.

97 John Paul II, *Memory and Identity*, 10.

For the Pope, this amounts to a rejection of a "truth of creation," and ultimately leads to relativism and utilitarianism in ethics. It leads to relativism because John Paul recognized that from the tendency in the modern scientific and technological worldview to confuse the "order of existence" and the "laws that govern it" (which have their foundation in God) with the "biological order" (which "has man for its immediate author") it was a "short jump" to "claim autonomy in one's ethical views."[98] Once God is placed outside of the world, human beings become the ones who determine meanings and ends: the nature of things, including human nature, and even the nature of good and evil. Descartes's goal to make man the master and possessor of nature with "the power to construct orders"[99] (and, in effect, to determine the "truth" about creation) opens the door to exercising the same autonomy in ethics. "For Descartes, man has the first word and the last word in the matter of determining what is and what is not to be accepted as truth."[100] John Paul also sees the eviction of God from the world and the denial of formal and final causality as leading to utilitarianism. According to the late Pope, when *in theory* one denies a "truth of creation" (including substantial forms and ends in nature) and only accepts as true that which can be empirically verified, *in practice* production and efficiency become the standards. To his mind, this inevitably leads to "a civilization of production and of use ... a civilization in which persons are used in the same way things are used,"[101] and to human sexuality becoming an "area for manipulation and exploitation."[102] John Paul holds that the use of contraception, i.e., the intentional elimination of the possibility of children from the conjugal act, is one example of this, for it transforms the sexual act from one in which the persons involved are "co-creators of love" into one of mutual use whereby the persons reduce themselves to being mere "partners in an erotic experience."[103] He states that contemporary culture,

---

98   Wojtyła, *Love and Responsibility*, 57.
99   Charles Taylor, *Sources of the Self: The Making of the Modern Identity* (Cambridge: Harvard University Press, 1989), 147.
100   Schouls, *Descartes and the Enlightenment*, 38.
101   John Paul II, *Letter to Families*, no. 13.
102   Ibid., no. 19.
103   "When a man and a woman who have marital intercourse decisively

35

which in *Letter to Families* he describes as "neo-Manichaean," is marked by a pervasive "contraceptive mentality":[104] an attitude whereby procreation is regarded "as an obstacle to personal fulfillment"[105] rather than an intrinsic end of sexual union, and the child is viewed "not as a blessing, but as a danger from which to defend oneself"[106] and as "an enemy to be avoided at all costs."[107]

For John Paul II, the mechanistic view of the world and anthropological dualism discussed earlier in this chapter are actually *consequences* of the abandonment of Thomas's philosophy of being and the corresponding rejection of the Creator and the created order. In his encyclical letter *The Gospel of Life*, John Paul explains that a prevalent "technical and scientific way of thinking" (rooted in Cartesian Rationalism) leads to Nature (including human beings) being reduced to mere matter and "subjected to every kind of manipulation," because it has "removed all reference to God" and "rejects the very idea that there is a truth or creation which must be acknowledged, or a plan of God for life which must be respected."[108] Included in this rejection of "a truth of creation" is the rejection of human nature itself, specifically its hylomorphic structure. Descartes's movement away from the philosophy of being ultimately causes a "great anthropological shift in philosophy."[109] In *Memory and Identity*, reflecting on the connection between what he termed the "ideologies of evil"[110] and the Cartesian heritage, John Paul asks:

---

preclude the possibility of paternity and maternity, their intentions are thereby diverted from the person and directed to mere enjoyment: 'the person as co-creator of love' disappears and there remains only the 'partner in an erotic experience.' Nothing could be more incompatible with the proper ends of the act of love" (Wojtyła, *Love and Responsibility*, 234). See also John Paul II, *Man and Woman He Created Them: A Theology of the Body*, 47:1–48:5.

104 John Paul II, *The Gospel of Life*, no. 13.

105 Ibid.

106 John Paul II, *The Role of the Christian Family in the Modern World*, no. 6.

107 John Paul II, *The Gospel of Life*, no. 13.

108 Ibid., no. 22.

109 John Paul II, *Crossing the Threshold of Hope*, 51.

110 With regard to the "legal extermination of human beings conceived but unborn" and the legal recognition of "homosexual unions as an alternative type of family with a right to adopt children," John Paul remarks: "It is legitimate and even necessary to ask whether this is not the work of another ideology of evil, more subtle and hidden, perhaps, intent upon exploiting human rights themselves against man and against the family" (11).

What is the root of these post-Enlightenment ideologies? The answer is simple: it happens because of the rejection of God qua Creator, and consequently qua source determining what is good and what is evil. It happens because of the rejection of what ultimately constitutes us as human beings, that is, the notion of human nature as a "given reality"; its place has been taken by a "product of thought" freely formed and freely changeable according to circumstances.[111]

At the root of the rejection of the reality of human nature,[112] according to the Pope, is the rejection of God: "When the sense of God is lost, the sense of man is also threatened and poisoned."[113] This is why John Paul laments in *Letter to Families*, no. 19: "with regard to his deepest, metaphysical dimension contemporary man remains to a great extent a *being unknown* to himself..."[114]

All of these reflections lead to the conclusion that for John Paul II the rejection of mystery by Cartesian Rationalism and the loss of a sense of wonder in the neo-Manichaean culture it inspired (all of which he mentions in *Letter to Families*, no. 19) evoke the rejection of Thomas's philosophy of being with its corresponding "notion of creation" and of a realist metaphysics. Because John Paul sees Descartes and his tradition as denying the capacity of human beings to know "the essential nature of created things and the fact of their existence,"[115] and thus as denying the capacity to

---

111   John Paul II, *Memory and Identity*, 12.
112   This will eventually find particular expression in the work of Jean-Paul Sartre. Sartre rejected the idea of a "universal human nature" holding that human nature is not determined by a pre-existing essence, but is "nothing else but what he makes of himself." For Sartre this rejection of human nature is likewise rooted in the rejection of God: "There is no human nature, since there is no God to conceive it" (See Sarte's essay, "Existentialism and Human Emotion," Cf. Pieper, "The Negative Element in the Philosophy of St. Thomas Aquinas," 52).
113   John Paul II, *The Gospel of Life*, no. 22. As the Second Vatican Council concisely states: "Without the Creator the creature would disappear... But when God is forgotten the creature itself grows unintelligible" (Vatican II, *Pastoral Constitution on the Church in the Modern World*, no. 36).
114   John Paul II, *Letter to Families*, no. 19.
115   Savage, "Metaphysical Realism as the Foundation of Environmental Stewardship and Economic Development," 237.

know the formal and final causes of created things and the end towards which they are ordered, the late Pope sees in Cartesian Rationalism a fundamental rejection of the "notion of creation," of a "truth about creation," and of the Creator who is *Ens subsistens* and *absolute uncreated Mystery*. These rejections lead to a mechanistic view of nature with the human body consigned to the realm of pure materiality, a sharply dualistic view of the human person, and a tendency towards relativism and utilitarianism. The New Manichaeism is strongly associated or identified with all of these aspects of Cartesian Rationalism in *Letter to Families*, no. 19.

COMPARING THE LABEL'S USE IN THE *LETTER TO FAMILIES* WITH *LOVE AND RESPONSIBILITY* AND THE *THEOLOGY OF THE BODY*

It is important to recognize that John Paul II utilized the Manichaean label in other works apart from the *Letter to Families*. A brief comparison between these other uses and the one in the letter will serve to clarify further John Paul's diagnosis of a New Manichaeism. The comparison will be endeavored through an investigation of the two texts in which he uses the label most prominently: in *Love and Responsibility*, published in 1960 as Karol Wojtyła, and the *Theology of the Body*.

In *Love and Responsibility*,[116] Wojtyła references Manichaeism in two contexts: in his denunciation of a rigorist/puritanical interpretation of the sexual urge and in his reflections on the value of virginity. In reference to the former, he states that the "rigorist" or "puritanical" interpretation of the sexual urge, which condemns sexual pleasure and enjoyment as evil and considers all that is "carnal" as "evil and unclean in itself," is a "reversion to the Manichean tradition" and falls "into the very error which the teaching of the Gospels and of the Church, properly understood, seeks to exclude."[117] Under this rigorist/puritanical interpretation, the so-called "evil" of sexual pleasure is tolerated solely because of the good of procreation. Similarly, John Paul claims that the case of a prudish person who "is prepared to condemn all, even the most natural, manifestations of sex and sexuality" and the case of

---

116 It is interesting to note that Papal biographer George Weigel calls *Love and Responsibility* "an antidote to Manichaeism" (Weigel, *Witness to Hope*, 142).
117 Wojtyła, *Love and Responsibility*, 59.

those who hold "the belief that sex merely gives the opportunity for sexual release and does not open the way to love between people" both "smack of Manichaeanism."[118] In reference to virginity, Wojtyła insists that its great value, including its "superiority" to marriage, cannot be found in a skewed understanding of the superiority of the spirit over the body and matter, which could be "easily confused with the Manichean antithesis between spirit and matter."[119] From these examples, it is clear that John Paul uses the Manichaean label to refer to an opposition between spirit and matter which considers all things bodily as evil or unclean and includes the condemnation of sex and sexuality. John Paul highlights the incompatibility of this anthropology and its corresponding ethical conclusions with that of the Gospel.

In the *Theology of the Body*, a work in which many of the themes found in *Love and Responsibility* are furthered and theologically developed, Manichaeism is referenced in similar ways. First, in Chapter Two, "Christ Appeals to the Human Heart," John Paul expressly states that authentic Christian tradition does not condemn the body and has nothing in common with Manichaeism, and he insists that Christ's words about "looking with lust" and "adultery in the heart" cannot be given a Manichaean interpretation as if the body and sex were "anti-values."[120] Neither can the Christian condemnation of pornography/pornovision be understood this way.[121] Second, in Chapter Three, "Christ Appeals to the Resurrection," John Paul makes clear that the authentic tradition of the Church about "continence for the kingdom of heaven" (celibacy) and even its "superiority" to marriage does not even imply "sliding... towards Manichean positions,"[122] and in no way can be construed as a condemnation of the body, marriage, and sex.[123] Thus, John Paul uses the Manichaean label in the *Theology of the Body* to identify, by way of analogy, certain anthropological and ethical errors, specifically those that would deny the essentiality of the body in the overall structure of the human person, would

---

118 Ibid., 188.
119 Ibid., 254. In this, Pope John Paul II is not denying the soul's superiority to the body, but only that a "skewed understanding" of its superiority is problematic.
120 John Paul II, *Man and Woman He Created Them: A Theology of the Body*, 36:3, 41:4, 44:5–6, 45, 49:6, 55:3.
121 Ibid., 62:5.   122 Ibid., 78:6.   123 Ibid., 82:6, 83:3, 85:5.

identify the body as a source of evil and sin, and thus reject all things bodily, particularly sex and marriage.

While he does relate Manichaeism to body-spirit dualism and to certain attitudes about sexuality, what distinguishes his diagnosis of a New Manichaeism in the *Letter to Families* is that John Paul connects Manichaeism with the Cartesian tradition and does not refer at all to an attitude that views the body, sex, or anything carnal as evil or unclean in itself. This is his main thrust in *Love and Responsibility* and the *Theology of the Body*, for, as the previous analysis has shown, in these works he likens a certain way of perceiving the body and sex that regards the body as the source of evil, temptation, and lust, and all sexual desire or pleasure as inherently sinful with the Manichees' contempt for the body and abjuration of sex due to their belief in its diabolical origin. Rather, in *Letter to Families*, the Pope uses Manichaeism to describe a worldview that sees the universe as comprised of two distinct substances, mind (the "thinking thing") and matter (pure extension), wherein "mind" is associated with human identity, and "matter"—which is essentially value-free and only seen in terms of its instrumental or utilitarian value—with the human body. The body, viewed as pure extension, thus becomes an object of manipulations. According to the Pope, this view of the body is clearly exemplified in contemporary attitudes towards sexuality and sexual activity.

However, it is on this last motif that there may be subtle points of contact between the Pope's use of the Manichaean label in the *Letter to Families* and his uses in *Love and Responsibility* and the *Theology of the Body*. In *Love and Responsibility*, he suggests that the rigorist/puritanical interpretation of the sexual urge which "stops short" of Manichaeism by affirming that "marriage is permissible for the good of the species," but thereby "lapses" into utilitarianism by seeing the very essence of marriage as using "a person for the objective end of procreation."[124] In the *Theology of the Body*, John Paul discusses that a Manichaean attitude would lead to a negation of human sex or "at least to their 'mere' toleration within the limits of the 'need' marked off by procreation."[125] Thus, we can see that in *Love and Responsibility* and the *Theology of the Body*, Karol Wojtyła/John Paul II did indeed link Manichaeism

---

124   Wojtyła, *Love and Responsibility*, 59.
125   John Paul II, *Man and Woman He Created Them: A Theology of the Body*, 45:3

and utilitarianism, and that his uses of the label in these works and in *Letter to Families* coincide in this manner.

Nevertheless, when one compares John Paul's use of the Manichaeism label in the *Letter to Families* and his use in *Love and Responsibility* and the *Theology of the Body*, one can discern much that is "new" about the New Manichaeism. His use of the label in the letter does not include a certain way of perceiving the body and sex that regards the body as the source of evil, temptation, and lust, and all sexual desire or pleasure as inherently sinful, whereas his uses in *Love and Responsibility* and the *Theology of the Body* do. Yet, his uses of the label in *Love and Responsibility* and the *Theology of the Body* do not suggest a rejection of the Creator, the goodness of creation, and the created order as the cause of these Manichaean views nor a mechanistic view of the material cosmos, whereas his use of the label in the letter does. Thus, we can see how, as Christopher West proposed, "the ancient Manichaean devaluation of the body takes on a new face"[126] in the New Manichaeism. In it, the body becomes an object of manipulation in contrast to being viewed as intrinsically evil and corrupt.

CONCLUSION

This analysis of John Paul II's *Letter to Families*, no. 19 has identified the specific problematic features of Cartesian Rationalism that John Paul is diagnosing as a "New Manichaeism" and which make up its overall structure:

1. Anthropological dualism,
2. A mechanistic view of nature,
3. The rejection of the philosophy of being and its corresponding "notion of creation,"
4. The tendency towards relativism and utilitarianism in ethics, especially in sexual ethics and bioethics.

Since, according to John Paul, Descartes posited that man is comprised of two separate and distinct substances—mind (the "thinking thing") and matter (pure extension)—and saw the person as identified with the mind and the body as "mere matter," he associates the New Manichaeism with Descartes's anthropological dualism and to the "radical contrast in man between spirit

---

126   West, *Theology of the Body Explained*, 13.

and body, between body and spirit,"[127] which he makes. Also, since John Paul held that for Descartes bodies are like machines composed of parts ("raw material" whose nature lies exclusively in extension) and the human body is viewed likewise, he associates the New Manichaeism with Descartes's mechanistic view of nature. Additionally, because John Paul believed that in placing *cogito* prior to *esse*, Descartes reduced God "to an element within human consciousness," such that God can no longer be considered the "ultimate explanation of the human sum" or as Self-sufficient Being,[128] and paved the way for a "vague deism" in which man puts himself in the place of God, exists and operates as if there were no God, rejects created things as having essential natures (i.e., denies formal and final causes and a "truth of creation" to be acknowledged, even of human nature), and thus assumes the role as the one who determines what is good and evil,[129] the Pope associates the New Manichaeism with Descartes's rejection of Thomas Aquinas's philosophy of being and its corresponding "notion of creation." Finally, because John Paul held that Descartes sought to make man the master and possessor of nature with "the power to construct orders" (and, in effect, to determine the "truth" about creation) and Descartes's thought as leading to the trend to place God outside of the world and to deny formal and final causality (all of which leads to the rejection of a "truth of creation" and of human nature), he associates the New Manichaeism with the tendency towards relativism. And since, for John Paul, when one denies a "truth of creation" production and efficiency become the standards leading to "a civilization of production and of use ... a civilization in which persons are used in the same way things are used,"[130] and in which human sexuality becomes "an area *for manipulation and exploitation*,"[131] he also associates the New Manichaeism with the tendency to utilitarianism.

Having thus analyzed *Letter to Families*, no. 19 and elucidated the association between the New Manichaeism and Cartesian Rationalism, the structure of the New Manichaeism has been

---

127 John Paul II, *Letter to Families*, no. 19.
128 John Paul II, *Memory and Identity*, 10.
129 Ibid., 10.
130 John Paul II, *Letter to Families*, no. 13.
131 Ibid.

established. Now this work seeks to place Cartesian Rationalism "under the microscope." By looking more closely at these features of Descartes's philosophy, through an examination of Descartes's own thought and writings with the assistance of contemporary Cartesian scholarship, we can offer a more precise diagnosis of the spiritual disease identified by John Paul II.

CHAPTER 2:

The Origins of the
New Manichaeism

INTRODUCTION

As previously stated, commentators on John Paul II's anthropology have posited that his anthropology is built in opposition to the Cartesian paradigm. However, these commentators do not provide significant treatment of the specific areas of Descartes's philosophy that were of concern for John Paul II or look to contemporary studies of Descartes to do so. Neither do they associate these maladies of Descartes with John Paul's diagnosis of a New Manichaeism. A fuller treatment of these specific features of Descartes's philosophy will foster a greater understanding of Pope John Paul II's diagnosis and the remedy he proposes through his anthropological project.

DESCARTES'S DUALISM

According to John Paul, Cartesian Rationalism endorses a form of anthropological dualism, which makes a "radical contrast in man between spirit and body" by positing that man is comprised of two separate and distinct substances, mind (*res cogitans*) and matter (*res extensa*). Such a dualist view rejects the hylomorphic view that man is a single composite substance comprised of form (soul) and matter (body). The person is primarily identified with his or her mind, as "a thing that thinks." In the *Letter to Families*, John Paul offers a vigorous defense of hylomorphism and laments that the denial of this truth has led our contemporary "neo-Manichaean" culture to a fundamental misunderstanding of what it means to be a human being, as well as to disastrous ethical errors.

In the traditional interpretation of Descartes, he holds a form "substance dualism" in which the body and soul are two separate and distinct substances, rather than the body-soul unity constituting a single composite substance of matter and form. This is the main interpretation of Descartes which will be treated, and is the one which matches John Paul's understanding of Descartes's position. However, some contemporary Cartesian scholars have proposed that Descartes's dualism may not be as clear cut as originally suspected, suggesting that Descartes is inconsistent on this issue and at times seems to indicate the existence of a third substance, namely, the "close union of soul and body." This interpretation refers to Descartes as a "trialist" instead of as a dualist. This position also will be considered in brief due to its contemporary appeal, even though one does not find allusion to it in John Paul's works.[1]

Descartes is very concerned with the separability of the mind and body, for he believed establishing this to be required to prove the immortality of the soul,[2] which he himself states as a purpose of his work. However, it may be that what was more important for Descartes was to establish that the mind and body were totally different kinds of substances with different kinds of modes, in order to justify his mechanistic view of the physical world. Thus, a critical issue for what is typically referred to as the Real Distinction Argument is Descartes' notion of substance. This notion, as it turns out, bears some similarity to the Scholastic one. For example, he defines substance as a thing "that so exists that it needs nothing else in order to exist."[3] A mode exists in and through something else; a substance exists through itself. Modes inhere in substances—a substance has its own existence, unlike a mode. Descartes's view of substance differs from the Scholastics, however, insofar as he states the essence of a substance consists in its principal attribute: "there is one principal property for each substance, which constitutes its nature and essence and to which all the other ones are referred."[4] In other words, all other

---

1 A minority of scholars, most notably Paul Hoffman, suggest that more credence ought to be given to Descartes occasional use of hylomorphic language and speculate that Descartes may have actually accepted the hylomorphic view. It would seem however that this interpretation does not represent the generally held position of scholars today, which either categorize Descartes as a dualist or trialist and, in both cases, as one who rejects hylomorphism.

2 For Descartes, mind and soul are interchangeable terms, for he does not admit divisions within the soul, but that it is one thinking substance.

3 Descartes, *Principles of Philosophy* (Radford, VA: Wilder Publications, 2008), I, 51.   4 Ibid., I, 53.

properties of a substance are modes or expressions of the principal attribute and presuppose it. It is the principal attribute that makes a substance a being in its own right as opposed to a being in something else, i.e., a mode. According to Descartes, the principal attribute of matter is extension and the principal attribute of mind is thought. Since thought is a principal attribute and not a mode for Descartes, mind is a complete substance. Mind is not a mode of extension, i.e., of the body, because we can doubt the existence of the body while being certain of the existence of the mind: "we can clearly apprehend substance apart from the mode which we say differs from it; while, on the other hand, we cannot conceive this mode without conceiving the substance itself."[5] In her esteemed work on Descartes's dualism, Marlene Rozemond highlights that a major concern for Descartes was in fact to demonstrate that since thought cannot presuppose or be presupposed by extension it cannot be a mode of the body, but rather must be a principal attribute or some mode of a principal attribute different from extension.[6] But, since a substance can have only one nature (as constituted by the principal attribute which determines and unifies all its properties and modes), and since it is only a substance that can exist in its own right, it follows that mind and body, whose principal attributes are thought and extension respectively, are really distinct substances and can exist one without the other. Thus, there is a radical and real distinction between the incorporeal and corporeal, between the soul and the body, between mind and matter.

Additionally, Descartes regards "the mind not as part of the soul, but as the whole soul, which thinks,"[7] and he sees the intellect as the essence of and equated with the mind. All operations that the Scholastics ascribed to the soul other than intellectual ones he believed could be accounted for mechanistically, and so he removed from the soul those functions the Scholastics held human beings to have in common with animals and restricted the soul to those activities that demonstrate its independence from the body. And while Descartes agreed with the Scholastics that sensation and imagination are dependent on the body, he claims

5   Ibid., I, 61.
6   Marlene Rozemond, *Descartes's Dualism* (Cambridge, MA: Harvard University Press, 1998), 21.   7   Ibid., 47.

that these belong to the mind.[8] Regarding sensible qualities, he holds that these are mere sensations in the mind (though, according to Rozemond, they "constitute a new type of mental mode," "a special subspecies of thought" which results from the union of body and soul,[9]) and he demonstrates this by utilizing skeptical arguments to undermine trust in the senses. Ultimately, according to Descartes, our ideas about sensible qualities are confused and obscure (which fails his criterion of only holding as certain ideas which are clear and distinct), and the existence of such qualities are not necessary for explanatory purposes; mechanistic explanations will suffice. Regards imagination, Descartes holds that it is dependent on the power of intellection. Yet, since it involves images, it (like sensation) must result from the union of body and soul. As will be seen, sensation will be the primary gateway for those who support a trialist interpretation of Descartes. In any case, this reassignment of which activities belonged to the soul went to serve Descartes's project of expanding the scope of mechanistic science and defending the immortality of the soul.

Though Descartes agreed with the Scholastics on the separability of the soul from the body, he disagreed with them on the nature of the soul. As mentioned, he did not view the soul as the principle of life, but of thought, and he explained mechanistically most of the functions attributed to the soul by the Scholastics. For Descartes, there is no sense in which the soul demands union with the body. He did not hold the Scholastic view that the soul was an "incomplete substance" that could only become complete by union with the body or that the body required the soul to exercise some of its functions. "Descartes rejects out of hand the possibility of a single thing, a single substance (as opposed to a composition of two distinct substances) that is both thinking and extended."[10] He saw the body and soul each as complete substances in themselves, which do not by their nature belong to a composite. As Rozemond explains, in Descartes's view "when we consider the body alone we simply perceive nothing in it because of which it desires to be united to the soul; just as we perceive nothing in the soul because of which it must be united with the body..."[11]

---

8   Ibid., 55.   9   Ibid., 173.
10   Daniel Garber, *Descartes' Metaphysical Physics*, 88.
11   Rozemond, *Descartes's Dualism*, 157. While Descartes did refer to the

In fact, for him, it is because they are substances that they must be complete. While Descartes states that "the nature of man" is "a combination of mind and body,"[12] he often expresses himself in a way that suggests that the human identity is really associated with the mind alone. For example, in the Second Meditation, he states, "I am, then, in the strict sense only a thing that thinks; that is, I am a mind, or intelligence, or intellect, or reason."[13] Similarly, in the Sixth Meditation, Descartes comments:

> My essence consists solely in the fact that I am a think-
> ing thing. It is true that I may have (or anticipate, that
> I certainly have) a body very closely joined to me. But
> nevertheless, on the one hand I have a clear and distinct
> idea of myself, in so far as I am simply a thinking, non-
> extended thing; and on the other hand I have a distinct
> idea of body, in so far as this is simply an extended, non-
> thinking thing. And accordingly, it is certain that I am
> really distinct from my body, and can exist without it.[14]

In neither case does Descartes state that his "mind" is joined to a body to make "him," but that there is a body that is closely joined to "him" and that he is simply a "non-extended, thinking thing." In fact, nowhere in his writings does Descartes identify *himself* with his body, even if he considers himself to be "very closely joined to it and, as it were, intermingled with it" so that "I and the body form a unit."[15] Yet examples abound where he identifies himself with his soul or mind, and even these statements point to such a view. Additionally, while Descartes believes he has "taken sufficient care that no one would think...that the man is only a mind using a body,"[16] and that "I am not merely present in my body as a sailor is present in a ship,"[17] he also states that he "might consider the body of man as a kind of machine equipped with and made up of bones, nerves, muscles, veins, blood and skin in such a way that, even if there were no mind in it,

body and the mind as "incomplete" in relation to the human being, Roze-mond states that this "does not at all entail that the human being is a single individual as opposed to an aggregate" (159).

12   Descartes, *Meditations on First Philosophy*, VI, 61.
13   Ibid., II, 18.   14   Ibid., VI, 54.   15   Ibid., VI, 56.
16   Rozemond, *Descartes's Dualism*, 158.
17   Descartes, *Meditations on First Philosophy*, VI, 56.

it would still perform all the same movements as it now does in those cases where movement is not under the control of the will or, consequently, of the mind.[18] Likewise, in his *Discourse on Method* he states that "the body is like a machine" and goes to great lengths to describe it in mechanistic terms.[19]

It is commonly acknowledged that Descartes rejected the notion of substantial forms. Since he believes that such forms were accepted "for no other reason than that they are thought necessary to explain the causes of natural phenomena,"[20] and since to him such phenomena can be explained mechanistically these forms were "simply useless." Considering how Descartes understands such forms and what their rejection means for his dualism is important. To him, a substantial form is "some substance joined to matter and composing some merely corporeal whole with it, and which, not less or even more than matter, is a real substance, or a thing subsisting per se, since it is said to be act, matter mere potency."[21] Descartes rejects the notion of substantial forms as applied to corporeal entities other than human beings, for human beings are not merely "corporeal wholes," and he dismisses the Scholastics idea that the human soul, while unique, is just one among many substantial forms. For Descartes, so intent on demonstrating the real distinction of thinking substances from extended ones in order to advance mechanism and demonstrate the immortality of the human soul, the Scholastic view of substantial forms being applied to non-human entities confuses the distinction between the corporeal and the incorporeal, between the physical and the mental, and between animals and humans. Therefore, according to Descartes, it jeopardizes the argument for the immortality of the soul. This is why he will state that the human mind is "a real substantial form" and "the only substantial form."[22] However, an important comment needs to be made about Descartes's application of the term "substantial form" to the human soul. While Descartes considered the soul a substantial form, he did not hold that the soul "informs" the body in the hylomorphic way in which

---

18 Ibid., VI, 58.
19 Descartes, *Discourse on Method and Related Writings*, trans. Desmond Clarke (London: Penguin Books, 2003), V, 40. See also *Principles of Philosophy*, I, 71.
20 Rozemond, *Descartes's Dualism*, 115.
21 Ibid., 123.   22 Ibid.

the Scholastics understood[23]—as soul and body constituting one composite substance—but rather wished to identify the soul with its principal attribute of thought and emphasize its incorporeality.[24] Even when Descartes at times uses Scholastic language in stating that the soul is "substantially united" to the body, he seems to be speaking phenomenologically, i.e., what the experience of being embodied is like, and not metaphysically, i.e., what the nature of that union is.[25] Descartes never calls the human being, the mind-body composite, a substance.

Those scholars who would claim that Descartes's dualism is less clear, like the well-respected John Cottingham, emphasize certain Cartesian texts that they believe to posit sensation as a third type of mode corresponding to a third type of substance, i.e. the union of mind and body (as modes of thought pertain to the mind and modes of extension pertain to the body). [26] This is often referred to as "trialism." In addition to texts already cited that indicate Descartes's view that the mind is "very closely joined" to the body "and, as it were, intermingled with it" so that "I am the body form a unit,"[27] proponents of Cartesian trialism find justification in Descartes's definition of a "thinking thing" as "a thing that doubts, understands, affirms, denies, is willing, is unwilling, and also which imagines and has sensory perceptions,"[28] highlighting not only that the last two characteristics of imagination and sensation are set apart from the other modes listed (as if they belonged in a special category), but that Descartes's later treatment of sensation and imagination seems to identify them specifically as modes of the mind-body union, which appears as a

---

23 "The body, as Descartes conceives it, is not such that it can accommodate the soul. It cannot, so to speak, be penetrated by the soul; it can only remain in external contact with it" (William Barrett, *Death of Soul: From Descartes to the Computer* [New York: Doubleday, 1986], 19–20).

24 Descartes also had political reasons for use of this phrase since the Lateran Council had just issued a decree affirming that the soul was a substantial form.

25 Bernard Williams, *Descartes: The Project of Pure Enquiry* (New York: Pelican Books, 1978), 280. Williams believes this is clear in Descartes denial that he is a pilot of a ship.

26 Although, proponents of trialism admit that Descartes is inconsistent on the issue.

27 Descartes, *Meditations on First Philosophy*, VI, 56.   28 Ibid., II, 19.

third substance alongside mind and body. Proponents of a trialist interpretation also discuss Descartes's "three grades of sensory response" as corresponding to these three substances. The first grade is the purely physical corresponding to the body, the second grade is the purely intellectual corresponding to the mind, and the third grade is the sensation corresponding to the union of body and mind.[29] Take, as an example, the case of hunger. The bodily response would be the fall in blood sugar, the contraction of the stomach, etc.; the mental response would be the mental judgment that my body needs food or the decision to eat; and the response resulting from the union of body and soul would be "that indefinable 'I-know-not-what tugging' sensation we call the feeling of hunger."[30] This third grade of sensory response is said to be quite distinct from the first two grades, since one could have the sensation without forming a judgment about the body requiring food and one could form the judgment that one needed food without having the sensation. It is this distinctness which those who propose a trialist interpretation emphasize when they suggest that sensation is a third type of mode resulting from a third type of substance, namely, the union of body and soul.

However, if every substance has a principal attribute, it is not clear what the principal attribute of this third category of substance would be. Neither is it clear how the union of mind and body would be really distinct and independent from the mind or the body. If mind and body are complete substances and are really distinct and do not by nature belong to a composite, how can their union be a complete substance? Alternatively, sensations can simply be considered as a mode of thought that is dependent on the mind-body union, and Descartes himself never directly calls the mind-body union (or human being) a substance. His reflections on sensation make clear that he believed the mind and body were closely united and that this union explained interaction and the possibility of sensation, but, as Marlene Rozemond understands it, such reflections do not demonstrate "that he regarded the resulting entity as *unified* in so strong a sense as to constitute a genuine unity and a substance."[31] These criticisms aside, even

---

29 John Cottingham, *Descartes* (Oxford: Blackwell Publishing, 1986), 128.
30 Ibid., 128–129.
31 Rozemond, *Descartes's Dualism*, 213.

proponents of trialism will strongly attest to Descartes's rejection of hylomorphism.[32] In fact, he considered hylomorphism as a foundation of Scholastic thought, the very thought which he sought to supplant, and so hylomorphism was the most obvious target of his philosophical anthropology.[33]

When John Paul II describes the New Manichaeism in *Letter to Families*, no. 19, he states that it places body and spirit "in radical opposition." The "real distinction" which Descartes wanted so much to demonstrate became a real opposition according to John Paul, because thought and extension were so radically defined. According to Descartes, since a substance can have only one nature (as constituted by the principal attribute which determines and unifies all its properties and modes), and since it is only a substance that can exist in its own right, it follows that mind and body, whose principal attributes are thought and extension respectively, are really distinct substances and can exist one without the other. In spite of Descartes's language indicating that the soul and body are "intermingled" or "substantially united," in his attempt to describe mechanistically most of what was traditionally attributed to the soul, he created a radical division. And while Descartes considered the soul a substantial form, he did not hold that the soul "informs" the body in the hylomorphic way in which the Scholastics understood, that is, as soul and body constituting one composite substance, but rather wished to identify the soul with its principal attribute of thought and emphasize its incorporeality.[34] "The body, as Descartes conceives it, is not such that it can accommodate the soul. It cannot, so to speak, be penetrated by the soul; it can only remain in external contact with it."[35] For Descartes, body and soul do not by their nature belong to a composite: there is nothing in the body that because of which it desires to be united to the

---

3 2   Garber, *Descartes' Metaphysical Physics*, 103, 105. This third notion—the union of mind and body—is not like the other two of thought and extension, for "it corresponds to a distinct aspect of a thing's nature, and not to a distinct type of thing" (John Cottingham, *Cartesian Reflections: Essays on Descartes' Philosophy* [New York: Oxford University Press, 2008], 186).

3 3   Garber, *Descartes' Metaphysical Physics*, 94–95.

3 4   Descartes also had political reasons for use of this phrase since the Lateran Council had just issued a decree affirming that the soul was a substantial form.

3 5   Barrett, *Death of Soul*, 19–20.

soul, and nothing in the soul that because of which it must be united with the body.[36] This is why John Paul states that due to the New Manichaeism, "the body does not receive life from the spirit, and the spirit does not give life to the body." The human being is not a being "whose rational soul is *per se et essentialiter the form of his body*"[37] and "exists as a whole—*corpore et anima unus*—as a person."[38] Rather, the person is primarily identified with his or her mind, and the body is described like a machine. Descartes at best sees the person as an aggregate, but certainly not as a composite. Because the human body is no longer viewed personally and subjectively, John Paul states that human beings, whose bodies have been de-personalized or objectified, cease "*to live as a person and a subject*" and instead become merely objects.

DESCARTES'S MECHANISM

In *Letter to Families*, no. 19, after discussing the anthropological dualism he associates with Cartesian Rationalism, the Pope immediately highlights a broader, "cosmic" form of dualism likewise associated with Descartes. As has been shown, for Descartes, the world is essentially divided into two types of substances: mind (the "thinking thing") and matter (pure extension). In considering the views of our "neo-Manichaean culture," John Paul states that "the separation of spirit and body in man has led to a growing tendency to consider the human body, not in accordance with the categories of its specific likeness to God, but rather on the basis of its similarity to all the other bodies present in the world of nature."[39]

An important goal of Descartes's project was to replace the Aristotelian-Scholastic view of the physical world with his own mechanistic view. As was seen in the discussion about the "real distinction" between soul and body, for him all other properties of a substance are modes or expressions of its principal attribute and presuppose it. It is the principal attribute that makes a substance a being in its own right as opposed to a being in something else,

---

36 Rozemond, *Descartes's Dualism*, 157. While Descartes did refer to the body and the mind as "incomplete" in relation to the human being, Rozemond states that this "does not at all entail that the human being is a single individual as opposed to an aggregate" (159).

37 John Paul II, *The Splendor of the Truth*, no. 48.

38 Ibid.   39 John Paul II, *Letter to Families*, no. 19.

i.e., a mode. According to Descartes, the principal attribute of matter is extension, i.e., having dimensions and occupying space. When Descartes uses the term "bodies" in a general sense, he is simply referring to extended things. Bodies can be understood without particular shapes and sizes and so these are not essential, but rather are "modes" of extension ("modes" being Descartes's favored term for non-essential ways of being a particular substance). Thus, all that is in the body is comprehended through extension as the principal attribute, and all other properties are to be referred to that attribute.[40] That is, "everything that can really be attributed to body as such must be some way or another of being an extended thing."[41]

For Descartes, all properties of body are ultimately and broadly geometrical, that is, as being extended in length, breadth, and height.[42] Corporeal things exist, but not "altogether as they are comprehended by sense," since the "comprehension of the senses is in many ways very obscure and confused."[43] All that can be clearly and distinctly understood about corporeal things is that which is "included in the object of pure mathematics."[44] For Descartes, an advantage of matter being identified with extension is that it can "enjoy the simplicity, precision and certainty of geometrical demonstration."[45] Sensible qualities—like color or heaviness— find no place in Descartes's understanding of the physical world; since they are not capable of being measured, our ideas of them are confused and obscure, and to him, they do not really exist in bodies, but rather in the mind. He seeks to engender distrust in the senses, in particular calling into question that extended

---

40   Descartes seems to paint a rather simple picture, but his mechanistic view of the physical world is a bit more complex. "Though not all accidents of body are modes of bare extension, ways of being extended *simpliciter*, they must all be ways of being an *extended substance*. That is to say, all accidents must be the sort of thing that could pertain to a purely geometrical object" (Garber, *Descartes' Metaphysical Physics*, 68).

41   Garber, *Descartes' Metaphysical Physics*, 69.

42   Descartes, *Principles of Philosophy*, II, 1; Garber, *Descartes' Metaphysical Physics*, 76; Cottingham, *Descartes*, 83.

43   Descartes, *Principles of Philosophy*, II, 1.

44   Ibid. Of course, what is "clear and distinct" is the criterion of Descartes's accepting anything as certain.

45   Cottingham, *Descartes*, 83.

things resemble our sense perceptions,[46] as a way to advance his mechanistic view of the physical world, since only mechanistic qualities are clearly and distinctly perceived.

A key example Descartes uses is that of wax.[47] He considers wax fresh from a honeycomb having a certain taste, smell, color, size, shape, hardness, temperature, etc. When put to the fire, all of these change, but it is still the same piece of wax. As a result, Descartes states that none of these attributes were in the wax. All that remains is something extended, flexible, changeable. Thus, only these pertain to the nature of the wax. While not employed primarily for this purpose, according to Daniel Garber, the widely-regarded scholar of Descartes's "metaphysical physics" and mechanistic worldview, the wax example gives a "foretaste of the full doctrine of the body"[48] in the *Meditations*, which is that bodies are only extended things having length, breadth, and depth. And so, bodies are known through the intellect alone, and not through sense perception or imagination. Descartes wants to establish that what belongs to bodies are geometrical properties alone, and that the sensations we usually attribute to bodies, e.g., color, are not really in bodies at all, but are in the mind: "sensations we call tastes, smells, sounds, heat, cold, light, colors, and the like...in truth are representative of nothing existing out of the mind..."[49]

In addition, according to John Cottingham, Descartes has essentially a "monistic" understanding of corporeal substance.[50] To him "the world, that is the whole universe of created substance, has no limits to its extension" and "occupies all imaginable space."[51] The various shapes that corporeal substance can take are all modes of a principal attribute—extension. So, for Descartes, "the universe is a single, indefinitely modifiable, infinitely extended thing."[52] While it is not necessary to go into the details of Cartesian physics

---

46 According to Descartes, the tendency to trust the senses can be traced back to childhood.

47 Descartes, *Meditations on First Philosophy* II, 20–22.

48 Garber, *Descartes' Metaphysical Physics*, 78.

49 Descartes, *Principles of Philosophy*, I, 71; Descartes also states, "what is called 'having sensory perception' is...simply thinking" (*Meditations on First Philosophy* II, 21–22.; cf. Garber, *Descartes' Metaphysical Physics*, 83).

50 Cottingham, *Descartes*, 84. "Of corporeal substance"—not like Spinoza's monism, which ascribed to a "single substance" view.

51 Ibid., 84–85.   52 Ibid., 85.

here, it is important to note that, to Descartes's mind, individual things—whether a horse, a tree, or a chair[53]—are not substances in their own right, but are simply "local modifications of a single extended substance."[54]

The essence of the human body, like all bodies in the universe, is extension. It is merely a modification of a single extended substance, a "cluster" of "accidental properties, or modes...of one all-encompassing, incorruptible extended substance."[55] Thus, like all corporeal substance, it is entirely explainable via geometrical and mathematical models. "This body is not the physical body, our physical body, as we know it in our daily intimacy with it. It is the body of physics—that is, of the science of physics; a piece of matter, and particularly as Descartes conceived matter."[56]

It is clear why Descartes's view of the human body would pose particular concerns for John Paul II. For Descartes, the human body is considered as pure extension without substantial form, like all other bodies in the corporeal universe. It is simply a modification of a single extended substance somehow or another "related" to the soul, but not forming a composite with it. Thus, the human body is not considered on the basis of its specific likeness to God but its similarity to all the other bodies present in the world of nature, "bodies which man uses as raw material in his efforts to produce goods for consumption."[57] As merely a modification of a single extended substance, the human body is "raw material" indeed. According to John Paul, viewing the human body in this way, in the same categories that other bodies in nature are viewed, has led our contemporary "neo-Manichaean" culture to accept using the human body in the same way that the bodies of animals are used, as happens with experimentation on embryos and fetuses. This is why he believes such a view ends in "a dreadful ethical defeat."[58]

DESCARTES'S REJECTION OF THE PHILOSOPHY OF BEING

According to John Paul, the New Manichaeism is associated with another error of Cartesian Rationalism, that is, with the rejection

---

53   Ibid., 84.   54   Ibid., 85.
55   Georges Dicker, *Descartes: An Analytic and Historical Introduction* (Oxford: Oxford University Press, 2013), 298.
56   Barrett, *Death of Soul: From Descartes to the Computer*, 20.
57   John Paul II, *Letter to Families*, no. 19.   58   Ibid.

of "mystery." As has been seen, for John Paul, Cartesian Rationalism's rejection of mystery involves the "decisive abandonment" of Thomas's philosophy of being, and thus is a rejection of creation as such, of a truth of creation which must be acknowledged, and of the God of Creation who is *Ens subsistens*[59] and *absolute uncreated Mystery.*[60] The Pope states that Cartesian Rationalism does not start from certain "realist presuppositions," does not tolerate mystery, provides a radically different way of looking at creation, and, at best, admits a "vague deism."

It was an expressed goal of Descartes to supplant the Aristotelian-Scholastic worldview with his own, one that took into account the discoveries of the "new science," rejected a simplistic, common sense view of the world, and sought the certainty and precision of mathematics in the pursuit of knowledge. According to the highly regarded Etienne Gilson, Descartes clearly held to the position that "in our search for the direct road towards truth, we should busy ourselves with no object about which we cannot attain a certitude equal to that of the demonstrations of arithmetic and geometry."[61] Rationalism, in its search for absolute certainty and denial or doubt of whatever cannot be proven, does not tolerate mystery. Mystery, while not requiring one to abandon reason, involves an acceptance of that which lies beyond it. Getting to what can without doubt be known was the very point of Descartes's "method of doubt."

Descartes is often identified with "methodical doubt." While it is commonly believed that this method is an example of his skepticism, Descartes really, although somewhat ironically, employed doubt as a means to refute skepticism. "Methodical doubt" was meant to eliminate the argument of the skeptics, like Montaigne, that absolute certainty cannot be attained and, in a sense, to beat them at their own game.[62] While doubt "introduces and forms the enquiry," this "eventually makes way for a systematic vindication of knowledge, and an orderly reconstruction of it."[63] This said, by use of this method of doubt Descartes will move from

---

59 John Paul II, *Memory and Identity*, 10, 12.

60 John Paul II, *Crossing the Threshold of Hope*, 38.

61 Etienne Gilson, *The Unity of Philosophical Experience* (San Francisco: Ignatius Press, 1999), 104–105.

62 Etienne Gilson, *A History of Philosophy: Modern Philosophy*, 61.

63 Williams, *Descartes: The Project of Pure Enquiry*, 33.

the mind to things (or rather, from the mind to God to things). In the movement from mind to things, "Cartesian metaphysics generates three existential claims: I am, I exist (the Cogito); God exists (divine veracity); corporeal things exist (the foundations of physics)."[64] It is this movement from the mind to things instead of from things to the mind that has earned Descartes his title as the Father of Modern Rationalism and is the basis of John Paul's accusation that Descartes changed the direction of philosophizing and rejected "realist presuppositions," specifically, those of Aquinas's philosophy of being. Descartes rejects that the "first conceptions" of the intellect are "a being" and "an essence" (i.e., that we first have a concept of a thing as having existence, and then of its kind or how it exists in its own particular way), and consequently, that the senses put us in direct contact with external reality. This leads to the rejection of God as *Ens Subsistens* and the necessary ground for every *ens contingens/ens participatum*, and the existence of "a truth of creation which must be acknowledged,"[65] including a truth about human nature.

In his *Discourse on Method*, Descartes lays down the "four rules" of the Method. First, he describes why he has come to the decision to "take on the task of guiding himself."[66] He states how, in his search for certain knowledge, all his various studies (save mathematics) have yielded unsatisfactory results, how philosophy (in spite of being practiced by the best minds) contains nothing that is indubitable, and how his travels showed him that reasonable people everywhere can hold quite different ideas.[67] Thus, he concluded that "our convictions result from custom and example very much more than from any knowledge that is certain."[68] Descartes, instead, seeks the certain knowledge of mathematics. He seeks to "reconstruct knowledge" starting from "indubitable first principles." And so, Descartes commits never to accept anything as true unless it appeared so clearly and distinctly to his mind that he had no opportunity to cast doubt

---

64   Jean-Marie Beyssade, "The idea of God and the proofs of his existence," *The Cambridge Companion to Descartes*, ed. John Cottingham (Cambridge: Cambridge University Press, 1992), 183.

65   John Paul II, *The Gospel of Life*, no. 22.

66   Descartes, *Discourse on Method*, II, 15.

67   Ibid., II, 9, 14–15.

68   Ibid., II, 15.

on it, to avoid prejudice and jumping to conclusions, to reflect first on the objects that are simplest and easiest to know and to move "as if by steps" to knowledge of the most complex (subdividing each problem into its smallest components), and finally to make a review so complete that nothing could have been omitted.[69]

Consistent with this method, Descartes rejects as false anything in which he could imagine the slightest doubt in order to see if anything would remain which could be considered certain and indubitable. This rejection necessarily included rejecting what the senses tell us, since the senses sometime deceive us. Descartes seeks to engender distrust in the senses and states that the "chief and most common mistake" made by human beings is to judge that one's ideas resemble or conform to that which exists "outside" oneself.[70] For example, it is common to believe that "the heat of a fire comes from something other than myself, namely the fire by which I am sitting."[71] He states that his natural impulses cause him to do this, and that this error has been engrained in him from childhood. But, ultimately, these impulses are not trustworthy and at times push us in the wrong direction. Descartes's skeptical arguments are the way he seeks to "wean us from our belief in sensible qualities"[72] and this is an expressed aim of the First Meditation.[73] He sees sensible qualities as inherently confused and obscure, and as ultimately unreliable. Thus, Cartesian Rationalism does not accept the world and what is experienced through the senses as *prima facie* real, but only that which can be proved with absolute certainty. Even when he becomes convinced, through God's guarantee, that corporeal things exist, he cautions that they may not exist as the senses perceive them, and, in fact, do not.[74] To Descartes, the essence of a thing cannot be known through the senses, but only with the intellect, and this is one of the main functions of his wax example. He simply does not believe that the senses get us to the essential properties of material things.[75]

For Descartes, the rejecting of anything in which one could imagine the slightest doubt[76] led to a necessary first principle:

---

69 Ibid., II, 16.   70 Descartes, *Meditations on First Philosophy* III, 26.
71 Ibid.   72 Rozemond, *Descartes's Dualism*, 137.
73 Cottingham, *Descartes*, 31.   74 Ibid., 79.   75 Ibid., 81.
76 This also included rejecting as false all arguments he had previously accepted as demonstrations since people can err in reasoning. Additionally,

"I think, therefore I am," for in every case above, it was necessary that he, who was thinking, was something. While he could pretend he had no body or the existence of objects outside of him were illusions, from the very fact that he was thinking of doubting these things, it was evidently true that he existed.

However, "having thus extracted the mind from its world, Descartes is hard put to get it back in."[77] He requires the existence of God to help him to do this. Demonstrating with certainty the existence of anything outside of him—the material world including his own body—will require the existence of a benevolent God, who is "no deceiver," who would not lead human beings astray by allowing them to err in those things which they so clearly and evidently perceive as real. So, according to Jean-Marie Beyssade and his study of the place of God in Descartes's philosophy, "Descartes' whole system of scientific knowledge depends on our assured knowledge of God."[78]

In order to demonstrate such assured knowledge of God, Descartes must "generate the idea of God by means of a construction that operates in parallel with the proof of his existence."[79] That is, he must demonstrate that the idea of God, like the idea of the self, is innate and does not require corporeal causes. Only being sure of his existence as a "thinking thing," Descartes cannot employ a teleological argument beginning with God's effects in the world. So, he rather assesses all of the ideas he finds within himself, and finds the idea of "a supreme God, eternal, infinite, omniscient, omnipotent and the Creator of all things that exist apart from him."[80] Since he believes it to be self-evident that "there must be at least as much reality in the efficient and total cause as in the effect of that cause,"[81] he himself cannot be the cause of this idea of God. He states, "All the attributes represented in my idea of God are such that, the more I carefully concentrate on them, the less probable it seems that the idea I have of them could have originated from

Descartes decided to pretend that nothing that had ever entered his mind was truer than the illusions of his dreams.

77 Barrett, *Death of Soul: From Descartes to the Computer,* 17.
78 Beyssade, "The idea of God and the proofs of his existence," 174.
79 Ibid., 178.
80 Descartes, "Second Replies," *Meditations on First Philosophy: With Selections from the Objections and Replies,* trans. John Cottingham (Cambridge: Cambridge University Press, 1996), 84.   81 Ibid.

me alone."[82] On the contrary, the cause must be a "thinking thing" that really possesses the perfections found in the idea, which is God. And so, God necessarily exists, since this idea of God could not exist unless God did. Additionally, Descartes will state that "existence can no more be separated from the essence of God than the fact that its three angles equal to two right angles can be separated from the essence of a triangle."[83] As a classic expression of the ontological argument, Descartes alleges that supreme perfection implies existence. Also, Descartes argues that he did not create himself, for if he were self-creating he would have certainly given himself the perfections he has in his idea of God. So, for Descartes, God's existence is *a priori* or self-evident since 1) the idea of God that he has must have a thinking thing with such perfections as its cause, 2) possessing such perfections implies existence, and 3) if he himself were self-creating he would have given himself the very perfections, which he knows he does not possess.

Of course, Descartes's version of the ontological argument is contestable for the very reasons that Thomas Aquinas put forth against the ontological argument in the *Summa* (and that Caterus puts to Descartes in the first objections, which, in Cottingham's view, Descartes does not seem to adequately answer),[84] namely, that while the idea of a supremely perfect being implies existence, it does not follow that such a being necessarily exists in extramental reality. Additionally, Descartes's very method can be said to have made his arguments for God's existence problematic. This is the so-called Cartesian Circle: he relies on clear and distinct ideas to prove God and yet requires God to validate his clear and distinct ideas. Some allege that Descartes's way out of the circle was to posit that there is certain self-evident knowledge, like "two plus three is five," that does not require God's guarantee. However, Descartes even calls such "certain" knowledge into question in the First and Third Meditations. Also, if the very perfections which constitute Descartes's idea of God (which he is convinced he did not/could not generate) he recognizes as imperfections in himself, is it not possible that he is merely extrapolating to the perfection from his perceived imperfection, which means that he had ideas of imperfections prior to the idea of God (and it must

---

82 Descartes, *Meditations on First Philosophy*, III, 31.
83 Ibid., V, 46.   84 Cottingham, *Descartes*, 61.

be remembered that God's existence will be required to guarantee such ideas)? According to Cottingham, Descartes's response to this objection seems to fail.[85] If Descartes fails to prove God's existence, he cannot prove the existence of the physical world, even his own body, nor can he guarantee any knowledge that is not "clear and distinct," even perhaps any certain knowledge beyond the Cogito. Thus, once he has called the external world into question and requires God to guarantee its existence, Descartes seems to have a difficulty in getting back to it or in proving God under the confines of his own method. Though he believed himself to be successful in proving God's existence and securing certain knowledge of the world, for without these he would have had no foundation for his physics, it could be said that Descartes is ultimately left alone with his consciousness, and a God that is "reduced to an element within human consciousness."[86]

> The road Descartes constructed back from the extreme point of Doubt ... essentially goes over a religious bridge ... the collapse of the religious bridge has meant that his most profound and most long-lasting influence has not been in the direction of the religious metaphysics which he himself accepted. Rather, philosophy after Descartes was driven to search for alternative ways of getting back from the regions of skepticism and subjective idealism in which it was stranded when Cartesian enquiry lost the Cartesian road back.[87]

Additionally, Descartes holds that God not only creates the world, but conserves it in being. At first, it may not seem that far from the view of Aquinas and his philosophy of being. However, there is a profound difference between their two notions of continual creation, because there is a profound difference in how they understand the being of things. As Gilson clarifies, "The Thomist God conserves the being of a world of substantial forms and essences... But, on the contrary, in Cartesianism, there are no substantial forms anymore."[88] In addition to composing a complete

85   Ibid., 55.   86   John Paul II, *Memory and Identity*, 10.
87   Williams, *Descartes: The Project of Pure Enquiry*, 162.
88   Etienne Gilson, quoted in Daniel Garber, *Descartes Embodied: Reading Cartesian Philosophy through Cartesian Science* (Cambridge: Cambridge University Press, 2001), 196.

substance when instantiated in matter, substantial forms were held to be the source of the characteristic activity of different kinds of substances (like neighing to a horse, or heating to a fire). Form is the principle of actuality: a thing being the kind of thing it is. In the absence of forms, Descartes must come up with another explanation for certain characteristic behaviors. On one level, he does so mechanistically. However, mechanical explanations will require knowledge of the relevant causes of motion, and for this Descartes turns to God as the cause of motion in the way that substantial forms were for the Scholastics. Though it seems as if he never denied finite causes of motion and that God only enters in to give a "divine shove" when such finite causes are not available, God is the "universal and primary [cause of motion], which is the general cause of all motions there are in the [physical] world."[89] And so, as Daniel Garber states, "Descartes' account of God as cause of motion is deeply (and obscurely) intertwined with his account of God as sustainer of the world."[90] In this sense, Garber holds, one might at least be able to call Descartes a "quasi-occasionalist."[91]

It is commonly held that Descartes rejected final causes. In great measure, this is due to his rejection of substantial forms. If the form, which is what makes a thing the kind of thing it is, is eliminated, then the final cause, which is the end or purpose of a being's characteristic activity, goes away as well. Descartes did not hold that individual substances have essences or natures, but rather that they are different modifications of extended substance. This contradicts Aquinas's philosophy of being, particularly his view of *ens participatum*, i.e., that all created being participates in the Divine Essence by way of similitude or imitation and that it is this "special way in which the Divine Perfection is imitated that constitutes the special essence of a thing."[92] Additionally, Descartes not only considered final causes to be "totally useless to physics"[93] and to the cause of forming a practical philosophy

---

89   Descartes, *Principles of Philosophy*, II, 36. See Garber, *Descartes Embodied*, 198.

90   Garber, *Descartes Embodied*, 198

91   Ibid., 218. "Quasi" since occasionalists did not typically make room for any other causes of motion than God, and Descartes does.

92   Pieper, "The Negative Element in the Philosophy of St. Thomas Aquinas," 66.

93   Descartes, *Meditations on First Philosophy*, IV, 39.

by which we could "make ourselves...the lords and masters of nature,"[94] but fundamentally impious since positing final causes would be the equivalent to believing oneself "capable of investigating the impenetrable purposes of God."[95] He stated that "we cannot pretend that certain of God's purposes are more out in the open than others: all are equally hidden in the inscrutable abyss of his wisdom."[96] Descartes seems to have held a view of God that might be characterized as "voluntaristic,"[97] for he holds that God's power is so absolute that "nothing binds him to bring about this or that state of affairs, or make some or other proposition true."[98] Descartes wrote to Arnauld that "he should never say of anything that it cannot be brought about by God" even that he "cannot make a mountain without a valley, or that one and two should not be three."[99] And to Mesland he declares, "God cannot have been determined to make it true that contradictories cannot be true together, and therefore...he could have done the opposite."[100] However, for Aquinas, "there does not fall under the scope of God's omnipotence anything that implies a contradiction."[101] In fact, Thomist critics of Descartes's Cogito argument

---

94   Descartes, *Discourse on Method*, VI, 44. For Descartes, "...since the efficient cause [cause mécanique] is the only one that gives us a grip on nature, it is the only one worth knowing" (Etienne Gilson, *From Aristotle to Darwin and Back Again: A Journey in Final Causality, Species, and Evolution* [San Francisco: Ignatius Press, 2009], 23.

95   Descartes, *Meditations on First Philosophy*, IV, 39.

96   From the Fifth Replies. See Cottingham, *Descartes*, 98.

97   Though possibly not the extreme voluntarism of William of Ockham, for example.

98   Paul Sperring, "Descartes, God and the Eternal Truths," *Richmond Journal of Philosophy* 10 (Summer 2005).

99   From Descartes' Letter to Arnauld (29 July 1648). See Sperring, "Descartes, God and the Eternal Truths."

100   Descartes, Letter to Mesland (2 May 1644).

101   Thomas Aquinas, *ST*, I, q. 7, a. 2; I, q. 25, a. 4. Even if what Descartes meant by such a statement was that "prior to" God's creative acts he is absolutely free and that "after" God ordains such truths, the immutability of God's will and the unity of his intellect and will make him "bound" by them to conserve creation in the manner in which he first created it (see Sperring, "Descartes, God and the Eternal Truths"; Margaret J. Osler, "Divine Will and Mathematical Truth," *Descartes and His Contemporaries: Meditations, Objections, and Replies*, ed. Roger Ariew and Marjorie Grene [Chicago: The University of Chicago Press, 1995], 152), this difference with Aquinas philosophy of

demonstrate the impossibility of moving to *ergo sum* from *cogito* without pre-supposing that the first object of the intellect is being or accepting the Principle of Non-contradiction upon which his *Cogito* argument depends.[102]

It has been proposed that Descartes's thought opened the "road to Deism" as well as "prepared the ground for modern unbelief."[103] The Enlightenment thinker Blaise Pascal stated, "I cannot forgive Descartes; in all his philosophy he did his best to dispense with God. But he could not avoid making Him set the world in motion with a flip of His thumb; after that he had no more use for God."[104] Pascal's perceptions were understandable, for "while the Cartesian universe certainly does not dispense with God, the conception of God which it invokes is an austere and in many respects impersonal one."[105] That such an impersonal and deistic view of God became prevalent during the Enlightenment is well attested,[106] and Descartes's work was a seminal, if not a direct, inspiration for Enlightenment philosophy.[107] Descartes's philosophical system, rooted in the advances of the Scientific Revolution, served generally to replace "theologically sanctioned ideas about Man, God, and the universe" with "secular, mechanistic conceptions which stood independent of any theological sanction."[108] Descartes's system so fundamentally diverged from the Aristotelian-Scholastic way

---

being still stands since for Aquinas the first object of the intellect is being and the principles of being.

102   See Reginald Garrigou-Lagrange's "The Thomistic Critique of the Cartesian Cogito," which was published in French in 1937 and in Spanish in 1950. A new English translation has been published in Reginald Garrigou-Lagrange, *Philosophizing in Faith: Essays on the Beginning and End of Wisdom*, trans. Matthew K. Minerd, (Providence: Cluny Media, 2019), 261–272.

103   Charles Taylor, *Sources of the Self*, 157–158.

104   Blaise Pascal, *The Pensées*, sect. 2, n. 77, trans. W. F. Trotter, https://sourcebooks.fordham.edu/mod/1660pascal-pensees.asp.

105   Cottingham, *Descartes*, 100.

106   Jonathan I. Israel, *Radical Enlightenment: Philosophy and the Making of Modernity 1650–1750* (New York: Oxford University Press, 2001), 12.

107   For example, "Descartes and the *philosophes* were at one on the point that a person's cultural context burdens him with the kind of prejudice which seems to make progress nigh impossible. They were agreed, furthermore, that it was especially early education that riveted prejudice to the mind... And most agreed that this bondage to prejudice was 'unnatural'" (Schouls, *Descartes and the Enlightenment*, 65).

108   Israel, *Radical Enlightenment*, 14.

of viewing the world that it "inevitably entailed the subordination of theology and Church authority to concepts rooted in mathematically grounded philosophical reason," even if this was neither Descartes's nor his followers' intentions.[109] The "Cogito" effectively "emancipates reason from all restraints of piety."[110]

As has been previously mentioned, Descartes held that human beings cannot know God's ultimate purposes. He saw the world "as arising inevitably, and without any direct reference to the needs of man, simply as a result of the immutable laws of matter and motion."[111] It seems that, for Descartes, God establishes the world and its laws and is needed to impart initial motions to the various parts of matter, even if God does continually conserve the world in being.[112] This last point may distinguish Descartes from the deistic views that followed him, which held that the world, once set in motion, would continue until God annihilated it;[113] they viewed God's conservation of the universe merely as a choice not to destroy it, whereas Descartes believed that God continually creates so that the world is like "a movie show of still frames."[114] But though Descartes considered God to be benevolent (as such is necessary to guarantee his clear and distinct ideas), Descartes rejected the idea that a benevolent God created everything in nature for the sake of man out of a special care for his welfare,[115] and thus presents an impersonal God more akin to the God of the deists. And since he has committed to only accepting as true that which he judges to be so, one can understand how in short order one finds a demand to construct a "reasonable Christianity" (i.e., a "version" of the Christian faith "which could be apprehended by human reason"[116]), which would downplay biblical revelation and Church authority, reject

---

109   Ibid.
110   Hiram Canton, "The Origins of Subjectivity: An Essay on Descartes," as cited in Schouls, *Descartes and the Enlightenment*, 60. Schouls states, "It is not Descartes the notably pious man, but Descartes the free thinker when philosophizing, who helped shaped the modern mind" (61).
111   Cottingham, *Descartes*, 100.   112   Ibid., 99.
113   Williams, *Descartes: The Project of Pure Enquiry*, 149.
114   A description of Gilson's view of the consequences of Descartes' rejection of forms and belief that God must be the cause of motion as it relates to God's conservation and continual creation by Daniel Garber, *Descartes Embodied*, 196.   115   Cottingham, *Descartes*, 98.
116   Dorinda Outram, *The Enlightenment* (Cambridge: Cambridge University Press, 2013), 122.

creation as traditionally understood, deny the intervention of a providential God in human affairs, dismiss the possibility of miracles, and rebuff the notion of a reward or punishment in an afterlife.[117]

In the *Discourse*, Descartes states that he approaches his enquiry with the intention of coming to purely mechanistic explanations of natural phenomena as if God "did nothing else except lend his ordinary cooperation to nature and allow it to act in accordance with the laws that he had established."[118] Apart from the world owing its existence to God, Descartes finds nothing in nature that cannot be explained quite easily by means of the principles he discovered.[119] The mechanistic conception of the world put forth by Descartes will be further advanced (at the same time as "corrected") by later rationalists, like Spinoza, who will "define motion as integral, not as external, to substance," and thus, "provides the first germ of the idea that the creation and evolution of living and inanimate bodies is a natural process inherent in the properties of nature."[120] By Descartes's mechanistic worldview being thus developed, God is edged out from the world. Therefore, it can be reasonably suggested that Descartes "prepared the ground" for modern atheism,[121] as well as for a scientific rationalism, which states that "the laws science

---

117 Spinoza is famous for his rejection of miracles. And of course, there is Locke's *The Reasonableness of Christianity*. This search to discover what is "universal" in Christian belief, and corresponding interest in comparative religions, led to "an increasing uncertainty about the status of Christianity to that of other religions" and "to the study of religion as a human creation," for example, as found in David Hume's *Natural History of Religion* (Outram, *The Enlightenment*, 123). One reaction to these new challenges was Deism. Another was to "return to a view of religion which emphasized faith, trust in revelation, and personal witness to religious experience" as was found in Methodism and Pietism, as well as the "Great Awakening" in the North American British Colonies (Outram, *The Enlightenment*, 126–127).

118 Descartes, *Discourse on Method*, V, 31.   119 Ibid., VI, 46.

120 See Jonathan Israel's writings on the relationship between Spinoza and Descartes.

121 Schouls adds that Descartes's assertion that "the only ground for doubt of the absolute trustworthiness of reason ... is the supposed existence of an evil genius" and his subsequent rejection of this ground, effectively removes God from philosophy, for in rejecting the evil genius (who is supposed to be supremely powerful, that is, God), he has rejected God. "Thus, whether or not God exists, we can trust reason" (61). According to Jonathan Israel, Spinoza was a main influence (even over Hobbes) on modern atheism in the early Enlightenment (*Radical Enlightenment*, 603).

demonstrates through experiment and mathematical calculation are universally valid and the sole criterion of truth."[122] "We need not wait for either 'the English'... or for the *philosophes* to see deism practiced in philosophy,"[123] for its foundations can be found right in the work of Descartes, the Father of Modern Rationalism.

Since "in our search for the direct road towards truth, we should busy ourselves with no object about which we cannot attain a certitude equal to that of the demonstrations of arithmetic and geometry,"[124] Descartes cannot tolerate mystery. Through methodical doubt, Descartes "changed the direction of philosophizing," as John Paul suggests, because he moved from the mind to things instead of from things to the mind, i.e., he considered *cogito* as prior to *esse*. He rejects the reality of being and the principles of being as the starting point of philosophy, denies "the capacity to recognize and cognize both the essential nature of created things and the fact of their existence,"[125] and the corresponding notion that the senses put us in direct contact with external reality by making us aware of concrete individual qualities of material objects. Instead, Descartes holds the senses as thoroughly unreliable and denies that they put us in touch with the true nature of things, which he demonstrates most vividly in his example of the wax. The world God creates, according to Descartes, is mechanistic, one of pure extension; it is not a world of substantial forms with intrinsic ends. Thus, as John Paul states, Cartesian Rationalism "provides a radically different way of looking at creation": one that rejects a "truth of creation which must be acknowledged" and a created order, since, according to Descartes we cannot know God's purposes. While Descartes believes that God creates and conserves nature, he does not understand creation in terms of all created being participating is Supreme Being and as receiving their specific essences from him, which are their unique modes of participation. Rather, Descartes's God is remote and human beings cannot know his purposes in creation. He requires God to validate the existence of his "clear and distinct ideas," and thus accomplish his goal to establish certain foundations; however, he

122   Israel, *Radical Enlightenment*, 244.
123   Schouls, *Descartes and the Enlightenment*, 62.
124   Gilson, *The Unity of Philosophical Experience*, 104-105.
125   Savage, "Metaphysical Realism as the Foundation of Environmental Stewardship and Economic Development," 237.

cannot use the world to prove God's existence and must approach this from pure consciousness and the idea of God. He is ultimately unsuccessful in this, and thus in his thought, "God is reduced to an element within human consciousness" and can no longer be considered the "ultimate explanation of the human sum,"[126] as John Paul alleges. Descartes even will not accept "realist presuppositions" about human nature, e.g., that "man is a rational animal," for to him such presuppositions will merely lead to more difficult questions that would be unanswerable according to his method of doubt.[127] And so, by turning to Descartes's works one can see more clearly what John Paul II means when he associates Cartesian Rationalism's rejection of "mystery" with the rejection of the philosophy of being and the corresponding "notion of creation," which "characterizes the interior structure of *nearly all* the basic concepts"[128] in it.

DESCARTES'S ETHICS

John Paul identifies in Cartesian Rationalism a tendency towards relativism and utilitarianism in ethics, which he believes in our contemporary "neo-Manichaean" culture manifests itself most vividly in the areas of sexual ethics and bioethics. The Pope indicates that since Cartesian Rationalism does not start from certain "realist presuppositions" and involves the "decisive abandonment" of Thomas's philosophy of being, it denies a truth of creation which must be acknowledged, provides a radically different way of looking at creation, and opens the "road to Deism." Since formal and final causes are removed from Descartes's conception of the world, man can become the master and possessor of nature by imposing his will and purposes on it via knowledge of efficient and material causes. There is no inherent "created order," but man has "the power to construct orders" (and, in effect, to determine the "truth" about creation). John Paul saw a "short jump" from this autonomy to "claiming autonomy in one's ethical views."[129] And when in *theory* one denies a "truth of creation" and only accepts as true that which can be proved with mathematical certainty; in *practice*, production and efficiency become

---

126   John Paul II, *Memory and Identity*, 10.
127   "But what is man? Shall I say 'a rational animal'? No..." (Descartes, *Meditations on First Philosophy* II, 16).
128   Pieper, "The Negative Element in the Philosophy of St. Thomas Aquinas," 47, 48.   129   Wojtyła, *Love and Responsibility*, 57.

the standards. To John Paul II's mind, this inevitably leads to "a civilization of production and of use ... a civilization in which persons are used in the same way things are used,"[130] to "the tendency to use the human body as raw material,"[131] and "to human sexuality being regarded more as an area *for manipulation and exploitation.*"[132]

Though Descartes himself never produced a treatise in ethics or himself thought that he succeeded in developing a complete moral science,[133] much can be divined about his moral philosophy from his writings. It seems clear that Descartes himself was neither a relativist nor utilitarian in the traditional sense. However, one discovers hints of these ethical approaches in his own method and rejection of formal and final causes, all of which can be said to have "prepared the ground" for these approaches to morality. According to Peter Schouls, a scholar of Descartes's influence on the Enlightenment, for Descartes, "man has the first word and the last word in the matter of determining what is and what is not to be accepted as truth,"[134] and it was, "Descartes the free thinker when philosophizing who helped shaped the modern mind."[135]

In Descartes's famous analogy, he stated that the whole of philosophy is like a tree: "the roots are metaphysics, the trunk is physics, and the branches emerging from the trunk are all the other sciences, which may be reduced to three principal ones, namely, medicine, mechanics and morals."[136] Thus, a "highest and most perfect moral system"[137] would "presuppose a complete knowledge of the other sciences";[138] that is, it "will require an understanding of our nature as 'thinking things' distinct from the material world, and a fully developed physics of matter in motion, plus an understanding of the mechanical operations of the material world."[139]

---

130   John Paul II, *Letter to Families*, no. 13.
131   Ibid., no. 19.   132   Ibid.
133   Thomas Sorell, "Morals and Modernity in Descartes," *The Rise of Modern Philosophy: The Tension between the New and Traditional Philosophies from Machiavelli to Leibniz*, ed. Thomas Sorell (Oxford, UK" Clarendon Press, 1993), 276. See also John Marshall, *Descartes's Moral Theory* (Ithaca, NY: Cornell University Press, 1998), 1.
134   Schouls, *Descartes and the Enlightenment*, 38.   135   Ibid., 61.
136   Descartes, *Principles of Philosophy*, Preface to French Edition, 12.
137   Ibid.   138   Sorell, "Morals and Modernity in Descartes," 284.
139   Roger Ariew, *Descartes and the First Cartesians* (Oxford, UK: Oxford University Press, 2014), 152.

Descartes believed that the system he would raise from sure foundations would yield practical benefits that would make for a better life: it would enable human beings to become "lords and masters of nature" and lead to "the invention of innumerable devices which would facilitate our enjoyment of the fruits of the earth and all the goods we find there."[140] It would lead to medical discoveries that would prolong life and preserve health, the latter of which Descartes considered the "foremost good" and "foundation for all other goods in this life."[141] Morals, for Descartes, is "the science of good living."[142] He plainly stated that he was looking to develop a practical philosophy that would be "very useful for life" in place of the speculative philosophy of the Scholastics.

When embarking on his method of doubt, Descartes senses the need to establish a "provisional morality" that would guide his choices since while calling all beliefs into doubt, including moral ones, he will undoubtedly need to take decisions. The general view of this provisional morality is that it would only remain in place until the formation of Descartes's metaphysics and physics. The "final morality," the tenets of which could affirm or deny the provisional one, "would be proven or founded on Cartesian phi- losophy,"[143] i.e., morality will ultimately be based on his method. As the respected Cartesian scholar Roger Ariew attests, there is a parallel between epistemology and morals in Descartes's philosophy, and in both cases, Descartes proceeds in a purely rationalistic way, in which religion is "bracketed aside."[144]

Yet, by "provisional" Descartes may have meant to indicate that our moral opinions may always be improved, for he "does not speak of finding definitive opinions, but of finding 'better opinions.'"[145] He considered certainty in morals not to be attainable in the same way as certainty in metaphysics or physics. For Descartes, "there is no infallible moral canon—for metaphysical reasons,"[146] and

---

140   Descartes, *Discourse on Method*, VI, 44.
141   Ibid.
142   Marcelo de Araujo, *Scepticism, Freedom and Autonomy: A Study in the Moral Foundations of Descartes' Theory of Knowledge*, (Berlin, Germany: Walter de Gruyter GmbH & Co., 2003), 184.   143   Ibid.
144   Ariew, *Descartes and the First Cartesians*, 149.
145   de Araujo, *Scepticism, Freedom and Autonomy*, 184.
146   Ibid., 171. There are no simple moral natures to which we can reduce moral problems, and thus we cannot put forth universally applicable moral

"we cannot expect to establish, on solely rational grounds, what is morally good in every circumstance of life."[147] If morals is "the science of good living," what constitutes a good life is "always susceptible to revision,"[148] and we may well change our opinion about what is worth pursuing in the face of new information. So, while Descartes's morality is rationalistic in approach, and he holds that one's judgments should not be influenced by prejudice or by any authority other than the authority of one's own reason, it also takes a modest approach to moral knowledge. Descartes does not offer specific courses of action in particular circumstances in his discussion of morals, but rather a general approach to making the best moral judgments one can make at any given time in any given situation. As John Marshall, commentator on Descartes's moral theory, summarizes: "It would not be far wrong to interpret Descartes's moral theoretical project to be that of working out a way for us to live well and happily in the face of uncertainty, an uncertainty that, owing to our finitude, is not fully eliminable."[149]

This belief in the "uncertainty" of moral knowledge can be seen elsewhere in Descartes's works. For example, in undertaking his methodical doubt, Descartes acknowledged that "reasonable individuals and peoples differ about how to live well and happily, and we should concede that we ourselves are no more qualified to dismiss their opinions as absolutely false then they are of ours."[150] While he may have been optimistic about the possibility of establishing a "perfect moral science," by his own admission he never did so. One reason Descartes himself gives for his sparseness on the topic of morality is that he held that no one, other than sovereigns, had the right to concern themselves with regulating the morals of other people.[151] He limits the role of philosophy, it would seem, in the area of determining specific moral rules and believes that, while sovereigns have the responsibility to establish laws for the ordering of society, the ultimate responsibility for determining the

---

rules for action like can be developed for geometry, like Euclid's *Elements*, or metaphysics, like Descartes's *Meditations* (173).
147 Ibid., 179   148 Ibid., 184.
149 Marshall, *Descartes's Moral Theory*, 5.   150 Ibid., 24.
151 Donald Rutherford, "Descartes' Ethics," *The Stanford Encyclopedia of Philosophy* (Spring 2013 Edition), ed. Edward N. Zalta, http://plato.stanford.edu/archives/spr2013/entries/descartes-ethics/.

best course of action lies with each person. He ultimately describes the virtue that leads to "contentment" as "the firm and constant resolution to do everything *we judge to be best* and to use all our power of mind to know these,"[152] and not in the objective "rightness" of the action itself. If a person has made the best decision she possibly can based on what reason tells her, then she should have "peace" or "satisfaction" of mind and avoid "regret" or "remorse," even if the decision proves incorrect. Although there seems to be a similarity between Descartes's and the Aristotelian-Scholastic goal of "happiness" through the pursuit of virtue, once again one can recognize Descartes's characteristic refashioning of Scholastic terms. For Descartes, virtue does not lie in acting in accordance with the nature of things in terms of formal or final causes, i.e., by acting in consort with a being's characteristic function or its end, for he does not recognize these causes or that one can know God's purposes in creating things. Rather, he sees virtue in general as a "firm and constant resolution" to act according to one's best judgments (i.e., as primarily in one's well-founded intentions), and thus holds in particular esteem the virtue of generosity, which disposes us "to use our free will well," to treat "others as objects of our esteem since they likewise possess a free will," and impels us "to realize, as much as we can, the general welfare of all people."[153] It is in the possession of free will that human beings are most like God according to Descartes.[154] In fact, he states that God's will "does not seem any greater than mine when considered as will in the essential and strict sense."[155] Neither the power of understanding nor the power of willing are in themselves to blame for error;

---

152 Ariew, *Descartes and the First Cartesians*, 155, my italics.

153 Descartes, *Discourse on Method*, VI, 44. Descartes views that because all human beings possess free will, and thus are capable of self-determination and have the potential to better themselves, all have dignity and should be held in esteem. This seems like an idea that is later taken up and developed by the Personalists, of which Karol Wojtyła/John Paul II was one.

154 Descartes, *Meditations on First Philosophy*, IV, 40. Descartes states: "Free will is in itself the noblest thing we can have, since it makes us equal to God and seems to exempt us from being his subjects; and so its correct use is the greatest of all the goods we possess." One uses free will correctly when one follows Descartes's three rules.

155 Descartes, *Meditations on First Philosophy*, IV, 40. That is, in its ability to affirm or deny, to pursue or avoid.

error is not due to a defect in these faculties *per se*. Error comes in judgment, specifically, when I extend the will to cases in which I do not perceive the truth with sufficient clarity and distinctness. However, since "God has given each of us a light for distinguishing what is true from what is false,"[156] Descartes believes that one can by and large trust his own judgments when his knowledge is sufficiently clear.[157] In any event, a person should not be content with the views of others unless they have been personally examined and found worthy. This is why we see that in the "post-method" formulation of his morality,[158] Descartes alters the first "rule" of his "provisional" or "pre-method" morality from "obeying the customs of his country and following the faith in which he had been raised" to "always use his mind as well as possible to discover what he should do in all the circumstances of life."[159]

The three rules of Descartes's "post-method" or "mature" morality are found in a Letter to Elizabeth (August 4, 1645) and can be summarized as "deliberate well, have a firm and constant resolution to carry out what our reason commends, and keep in mind that if we do so we shall always have all the goods that are truly in our power."[160] Descartes's understanding of the passions, which are treated mechanistically in his treatise *Passions of the Soul*,[161] relates to all three.[162] Regarding sound deliberation, "since the passions

---

156 Descartes, *Discourse on Method*, III, 22.
157 Descartes, *Meditations on First Philosophy*, IV, 40–41.
158 This is often called his "final morality," but shouldn't be confused with the "perfect moral science" which he never completed.
159 Ariew, *Descartes and the First Cartesians*, 155.
160 Marshall, *Descartes's Moral Theory*, 97.
161 Interestingly, in a distinction similar to Karol Wojtyła's "man acts" and "something happens in man," Descartes views volitions (free choices) as those things the soul does and passions as those things that happen to the soul, though for Wojtyła these will be defined a bit differently. See Chapter 5 of this book.
162 It is important to note that Descartes did not view his treatise on the passions as a moral treatise, but a scientific one. He seeks to provide a mechanistic view of these passions in particular against those who "have based their classification on a distinction they draw, within the soul's sensitive part, between the two appetites they call 'concupiscible' and 'irascible'" (Descartes, *Passions of the Soul*, 68), namely, the Scholastics. In Descartes's mechanistic view, the principal and most common causes of the passions are objects that stimulate the senses (Descartes, *Passions of the Soul*, 51). Descartes states that

tend to exaggerate the value of what they represent to us as good, we must correct for this deceptive appearance if we are to judge well."[163] Regarding firm and constant resolution, by understanding the passions "we can best cope with obstacles to steadily adhering to what we judge to be best."[164] Regarding the acceptance of one's lot, a proper understanding of the causes and effects of the passions empowers us "to become so thoroughly masters of our desires that our happiness cannot be held hostage to events not entirely within our power."[165] In all cases, Descartes seems to betray an expressly "mind over matter" view: by the proper mechanistic understanding of the passions one can likewise become the "master of possessors of nature" by becoming the "master of one's desires,"[166] and thus best follow Descartes's "three rules" and reach "contentment."[167] Nevertheless, the passions, while not uniformly beneficial, are good because they "dispose our soul to want the things that nature decides are useful to us."[168] Thus, "the good" seems to be identified with "what is useful," particularly, what is useful for a better life. It is interesting to note the rationalistic/naturalistic slant, for Descartes indicates that it is "nature" that "decides" what is useful.

What ought to become clear in these brief reflections is that "the focus of Cartesian morality is the actor rather than the action, just as the focus of the Cartesian enterprise in general is on the

---

their practical purpose is to "dispose our soul to want the things that nature decides are useful to us, and to persist in this volition" and that "the agitation of the spirits that normally causes the passions also disposes the body to move in ways that help to bring about those useful things" (Descartes, *Passions of the Soul*, 52). This is why, according to Descartes, "a list of the passions requires only an orderly examination of all the various ways—ways that are important to us—in which our senses can be stimulated by their objects" (Descartes, *Passions of the Soul*, 52), and it is just this that his treatise seeks to provide.

163   Marshall, *Descartes's Moral Theory*, 98.   164   Ibid.

165   Ibid. This refers to unintended and unforeseen consequences of one's actions, for example.

166   Even the suppression of feelings of regret and remorse when one has made the best choice possible at the time, even if one later discerns it to have been the wrong choice.

167   Many scholars see in Descartes an attempt to wed Stoicism (firm resolution, mastery of the passions) and Epicureanism (pleasure, contentment). See Ariew, *Descartes and the First Cartesians*, 155; Marshall, *Descartes's Moral Theory*, 65, footnote 11.

168   Descartes, *Passions of the Soul*, 52.

knowing subject rather than the known object."[169] Descartes's ethics does not center on "right conduct" or on "devising some decision procedure for particular acts," but rather is characterized by "the discovery of a complete personal pathway."[170] According to John Marshall, it is a subjectivist view, even if not relativistic or "value subjectivist."[171] One must act on what one discerns to be the best, so long as his or her firm resolution is to discover the best and to act decisively upon it. Though it could be said that Descartes's ethics is eudemonistic, the "contentment" it is after is the consequence of one's personal judgment about the most useful and beneficial ends for oneself and others. Descartes's mechanistic system sought to encourage the manipulation of nature via knowledge of causes and effects in order to promote the greater good of humanity and a more enjoyable earthly existence for all. This would include, it must be recalled, the manipulation of the human body. While Descartes may have believed in objective values, they are such not because God has written his law into the nature of the things he creates, and this law is discernable by the intellect,[172] but because we recognize certain inclinations in our nature as beneficial to us, and a benevolent God would not allow such to deceive us, even if they can at times exaggerate the good.[173] As John Marshall observes, it could be suggested that Descartes's held a view that "the value of some good depends on a subject's desiring it,"[174] and that it is the

---

169   V. Morgan, *Foundations of Cartesian Ethics*, 100, as cited in de Araujo, *Scepticism, Freedom and Autonomy*, 164.

170   Cottingham, "Partiality and the Virtues" in *How should I live? Essays on the Virtues*, ed. R. Crisp, 70. See de Araujo, *Scepticism, Freedom and Autonomy*, 165.

171   Marshall admits that while values are not constituted entirely from the passions, and thus Descartes cannot be said to hold to "straightforward value subjectivism," there are "more sophisticated subjectivist views" that can be used as suitable models for this part of the Cartesian theory of value" (*Descartes's Moral Theory*, 124).

172   Since Descartes rejects formal and final causes, there is no "natural law" for Descartes as the Scholastics, and particularly Aquinas, understood it. For Descartes, our minds cannot penetrate the essence of a thing as it relates to that thing's specific activity.

173   According to Marshall, "Divine benevolence plays the same role with respect to the passion-based value judgments as it does with respect to sensory-based judgments about the existence of external objects" (*Descartes's Moral Theory*, 121).

174   Marshall, *Descartes's Moral Theory*, 124.

enjoyment of the possession of some good that is the criterion for that thing being a true good.[175]

Additionally, Descartes's modest approach to moral knowledge (which lacks mathematical certainty and is always open to revision and "better opinions"), his recognition that reasonable individuals and peoples differ about how to live well and happily, and his belief that no one has the right to concern themselves with regulating the morals of other people can be seen as a precursor to a moral agnosticism. In fact, certain commentators[176] see Descartes's distinction between knowledge that can be known with certainty, like that of mathematics and physics, and that which cannot, like that of ethics and religion to be definitively entrenched by Immanuel Kant and summed up in his famous statement, "I had to do deny knowledge in order to make room for faith."[177] For Kant, questions about religion and ethics are beyond the competence of theoretical reason. These same commentators see the Positivism of Auguste Comte[178]—which held that the only authentic knowledge is that

---

175   Ibid.

176   See Barrett, *Death of Soul*, 51–58; Waldstein, "Introduction," *Man and Woman He Created Them: A Theology of the Body*, 44–55; Rhonda Chervin and Eugene Kevane, *Love of Wisdom: An Introduction to Christian Philosophy*, 248. Barrett's "Map of the Modern World" has Kant synthesizing the Rationalist and Empiricist strains in continental philosophy and then traditions such as Idealism, Phenomenology, and Positivism as stemming from Kant in various ways. For Barrett, this whole development is "bracketed" by the overarching tendency towards scientific rationalism.

177   Immanuel Kant, *Critique of Pure Reason*, BXXX. For Kant, questions about religion and ethics are beyond the competence of theoretical reason. In these questions one can at best act "as if God were to exist," and say "I am morally certain that God exists," not even "it is morally certain that God exists." Kant's "turn to the subject" completed Descartes's: all being is reduced to "being an object for consciousness." Even God is an object of consciousness for Kant (Waldstein, "Introduction," 45, 47). The person knows only phenomena—how these phenomena are gathered and appear to us as natures is not founded on reality but our own cognitive structure; what things are like "in themselves" is beyond our knowledge (Byrne, *Religion and the Enlightenment*, 210). In the tradition of Descartes, Kant does not recognize ends in nature, but for him "man *imposes* his models upon nature; he *compels* nature to answer his questions; he does not merely submit, but seeks a position of *command*" (Barrett, *Death of Soul*, 74). Kant's moral philosophy is rooted in the autonomy of the person and sees true morality as "self-legislative."

178   Comte, who is considered the first "philosopher of science" in the modern sense of the term, saw the scientific method as replacing metaphysics

which is based on sense experience, and positive verification—as one of the philosophies finding inspiration in Kant (and thus as traceable back to Descartes). John Paul II warns that Positivism leads to agnosticism in theory and utilitarianism in practice.[179] If, as the Positivists allege, the only genuine knowledge is that which is experienced through the senses and can be verified by the scientific method, then at best one can claim that if God or the soul do exist, one cannot *know* that they do. Thus, the only way to proceed is the way of efficiency, of bringing about the "best" results, which is the basis of utilitarian thinking.[180]

While Descartes himself cannot be classified as proponent of utilitarianism, one can see how his goal to develop a practical philosophy that would "facilitate our enjoyment of the fruits of the earth and all the goods we find there," promote the "general welfare" and "contentment" through the discernment of what is most useful and beneficial, and views the physical world (including the human body) mechanistically—as "raw material" without intrinsic ends and upon which human beings can impose their own ends—would set the stage for the utilitarian thinkers of the Enlightenment.

For John Paul II, as is indicated in his comments about the New Manichaeism, relativism and utilitarianism have particularly devastating consequences for sexual ethics and bioethics. Sexuality becomes an area for manipulation as opposed to evoking a "primordial wonder" in the face of God's creation and the truth of creation. Bioethics becomes an area for the body, like the bodies of embryos and fetuses, to be used as "raw material." While one finds no expressed mention of sexuality or bioethics in Descartes's

---

in the history of thought. The connection between positivism and utilitarianism is more than theoretical: Comte, was good friends with John Stuart Mill, the British philosopher and major proponent of utilitarianism who wrote a book that bears it as a title and who considered himself a follower of Comte.

179   Karol Wojtyła will, however, benefit much from Kant, especially his critique of utilitarianism and his formulation of the categorical imperative that one should "So act as to treat humanity, whether in your own person or in that of any other, always at the same time as an end, and never merely a means," which bears striking similarity to what Wojtyła will call the Personalistic Norm.

180   Though it should be noted that this would have been an unintended consequence for Kant who wrote a strong critique of utilitarianism and tried to safeguard against it in his moral philosophy (John Paul II, *Crossing the Threshold of Hope*, 201-203).

moral writings, his dualistic views, his mechanistic view of the body, his rejection of ends and purposes in nature, his paving the road for Deism (for a God who is remote from his creation), and preparing the ground for modern unbelief as well as for relativism and utilitarianism in ethics, could all be said to have helped to set the foundations for the contemporary approaches to sexual ethics and bioethics with which John Paul had particular concern.[181]

CONCLUSION

These reflections have helped to expose the seriousness of the Cartesian philosophy's maladies John Paul II associates with a New Manichaeism in *Letter to Families*, no. 19. The "real distinction" between soul and body, which Descartes wanted so much to demonstrate in positing thought and extension as radically separate substances, became a real opposition according to John Paul. In Descartes's attempt to describe mechanistically most of what was traditionally attributed to the soul, he produced a radical division. He did not hold that the soul "informs" the body as in hylomorphism. Descartes, at best, sees the person as an aggregate, never as a composite. The person is primarily identified with his or her mind, as a "thinking thing." The human body is like a machine, and simply a modification of a single extended substance which is somehow or another "related" to the soul. The body cannot accommodate or be penetrated by the soul. Thus, the human body is no longer viewed personally and subjectively, but rather in the same categories of other bodies in nature are viewed. For John Paul, this fundamentally conflicts with the irreducibility of the person.

Descartes changes the direction of philosophizing through his methodical doubt, moving from the mind to things instead of from things to the mind. Being fixed on mathematical certitude, he demonstrates an intolerance for mystery. He rejects the reality of being and the principles of being as the starting point of philosophy, and denies that the senses put us in direct contact with external reality and enable us to cognize the being and essence of

---

181   Michael Waldstein shows how this philosophical foundation may have informed Immanuel Kant's view that while nature may have implanted the mutual sexual inclination of man and woman toward one another for the purpose of begetting children, such an intention is not required for marriage to be legitimate (Waldstein, "Introduction," 57).

things. According to Descartes, the world God creates is one of pure extension; it is not a world of substantial forms with intrinsic ends. Descartes's God is remote, and human beings cannot know his purposes in creation. Descartes does not understand creation in terms of all contingent beings participating in Supreme Being and as receiving their specific essences from him, which are their unique modes of participation. Though Descartes requires God to validate the existence of his "clear and distinct ideas," he is ultimately unsuccessful in proving God's existence from pure consciousness and the idea of God, which his system demands. Thus, "God is reduced to an element within human consciousness" and can no longer be considered the "ultimate explanation of the human sum,"[182] as John Paul suggests.

Not only could it be said that Descartes set the foundation for Deism, but also for relativism and utilitarianism. While not establishing a "perfect moral science" or writing a treatise on moral philosophy, Descartes's writings indicate a subjectivist turn in moral decision making, even though he could not be considered strictly a relativist. For Descartes, man has the first word and the last word in the matter of determining what is and what is not to be accepted as truth. He seems to limit the role of philosophy in the area of determining specific moral rules and believes that, while sovereigns have the responsibility to establish laws for the ordering of society, the ultimate responsibility for determining the best course of action lies with each person. He ultimately describes the virtue that leads to "contentment" as "the firm and constant resolution to do everything *we judge to be best*"[183] and not in the objective "rightness" of the action itself. For Descartes, virtue does not lie in acting in accordance with the nature of things in terms of formal or final causes, i.e., by acting in consort with a being's characteristic function or its end, for he does not recognize these causes or that one can know God's purposes in creating things. There is no inherent "created order," but man has "the power to construct orders" (and, in effect, to determine the "truth" about creation). John Paul saw a "short jump" from this autonomy to "claiming autonomy in one's ethical views."[184] And while Des-

---

182   John Paul II, *Memory and Identity*, 10.
183   Ariew, *Descartes and the First Cartesians*, 155, my italics.
184   Wojtyła, *Love and Responsibility*, 57.

cartes himself cannot be classified as proponent of utilitarianism, one can see how his goal to develop a practical philosophy that would facilitates "our enjoyment of the fruits of the earth and all the goods we find there," promotes the "general welfare" and "contentment" through the discernment of what is most useful and beneficial, and views the physical world (including the human body) mechanistically—as "raw material" without intrinsic ends and upon which human beings can impose their own ends—would set the stage for the utilitarian thinkers of the Enlightenment. When in *theory* one denies a "truth of creation" and only accepts as true that which can be proved with mathematical certainty, in *practice* production and efficiency become the standards.

Though Descartes never advocated a permissive view of sexual ethics, his dualistic views, his mechanistic view of the body, his rejection of ends and purposes in nature, his paving the road for Deism, and his preparing the ground for modern unbelief as well as for relativism and utilitarianism in ethics, could all be said to have helped to set the foundations for the contemporary approaches to sexual ethics and bioethics with which John Paul had particular concern. In the absence of formal and final causes in nature and in the face of a "reasonable Christianity" which would downplay biblical revelation and Church authority, one can understand how a movement away from viewing procreation as an intrinsic end of marriage and sex might follow.

Now this work must turn to exploring the relationship between these maladies of Cartesian Rationalism, that John Paul diagnosed as a New Manichaeism, and Manichaean tradition itself. How is the New Manichaeism related to the beliefs and practices of the ancient Manichees, specifically those related to John Paul II's anthropological and ethical concerns? Such an exploration will serve to clarify how the late Pope's anthropology can be seen as a remedy to Descartes and to so-called "Manichaean" views and attitudes, and provide greater support for his diagnosis of a New Manichaeism infecting the human family.

CHAPTER 3

The Relationship of the New Manichaeism to Manichaean Tradition

INTRODUCTION

Now that the ills of Cartesian Rationalism and their relationship to the New Manichaeism have been established, clarified, and elaborated, an evaluation of how the New Manichaeism is related to Manichaean beliefs and practices becomes necessary. In Christian tradition and in John Paul II's view, Manichaeism is an ancient dualist heresy[1] that "sprang up in the Orient from Mazdean dualism"[2] with Mani from Babylonia in the latter part of the third century, and then "attempted to enter the terrain of Christianity."[3] What is it about the New Manichaeism diagnosed by John Paul II that is expressly Manichaean?

First, it must be made clear that this study of Manichaean beliefs and practices is not being approached as a historian, but as a philosopher and theologian. This is the way that John Paul II himself approached Manichaeism, and is the approach relevant to his anthropological concerns. Second, this chapter will only treat the Manichaean views of creation, anthropology, and sexual

---

1 Manichaean studies have undergone a kind of renaissance in the last decades, principally due to the novel insights of scholars like Jason BeDuhn and Philip Mericki who have suggested that Manichaeism has been historically mischaracterized, especially in its traditional understanding as a Gnostic dualist Christian heresy. Their views are at odds not only with the traditional understanding of Manichaeism, but with the work of modern scholars of Manichaeism who have earned tremendous respect, like Henri Charles Puech and Julien Ries.

2 John Paul II, *Man and Woman He Created Them: A Theology of the Body*, 44:5. This is a reference to the Zoroastrian cosmogony which played such a major role in the development of Mani's own and displays John Paul II's knowledge of the pre-Christian roots of Manichaeism.

3 Ibid. John Paul II believed that the port of entry was, in fact, the theology and ethos of the body.

ethics[4] for these are the areas which find closest relationship with those aspects of the Cartesian Rationalism that John Paul strongly associates with the New Manichaeism. Additionally, it will look primarily to the tradition on Manichaeism associated with the work of Henri-Charles Puech and Julien Ries since these scholars, considered even by current scholars of Manichaeism as the "touchstone of received wisdom in the study of Manichaeism,"[5] are the ones John Paul II uses to support his own commentary on Manichaeism.[6] However, some points from more recent views on Manichaeism will also be brought into the discussion, especially when they offer an alternative view to the traditional one associated with Puech and Ries and alluded to by John Paul. Specifically, the positions of Jason David BeDuhn will be discussed for his work regarding Manichaean attitudes towards the material world in general and the human body in particular. Though John Paul II's statements on Manichaeism and the New Manichaeism predate BeDuhn's work, his work is important to consider, because it challenges the traditional understanding of Manichaeism as a Gnostic Christian heresy. By analyzing possible challenges to the Pope's analogical use of the Manichaean label in *Letter to Families*, no. 19,

---

4   While Manichaean ethics in general might be summed up in the word "abstain," due to its disdain for all things material and bodily, this is not where the New Manichaeism finds a relationship with Manichaean ethical practice. Rather, as will be seen, it is in the case of the more lax attitudes towards the sexual practices of the Auditors that the relationship becomes evident. As has been said many times, John Paul sees sexuality's becoming an area for manipulation and use as a quintessential consequence of the New Manichaeism.

5   Jason David BeDuhn, *The Manichaean Body in Discipline and Ritual* (Baltimore, MD: The Johns Hopkins University Press, 2000), 211.

6   We gain the greatest insight into John Paul's understanding of Manichaeism from a section and lengthy footnote in *Man and Woman He Created Them: A Theology of the Body*, 44:5 in which he offers a general description of the ancient religion. His description is based on the work of Henri-Charles Puech and Julien Ries, which he himself cites. It is reasonable to conclude that the Pope had a broader understanding of Manichaeism than the few points his brief summary in the *Theology of the Body*, 44:5 and its footnote would indicate. Since this summary flows from what many would consider to be some of the best scholarship on Manichaeism available at the time, one can speculate with some confidence that John Paul's understanding of Manichaeism was informed by and consonant with that scholarly tradition. This seems to place John Paul's view in the mainstream of the "traditional (Gnostic) interpretation" of Manichaeism.

and thus to his diagnosis of a New Manichaeism infecting the human family, this diagnosis indeed can be tested and confirmed.

THE MANICHAEAN VIEW OF CREATION

John Paul states that Manichaeism held "the *dualism* of two coeternal principles radically opposed to each other," the Light (Spirit) and the Darkness (Matter). Before creation, there existed a time of original separation between the two co-eternal principles.[7] The "Father of Greatness" dwelt in the Realm of Light, while the Prince of Darkness (or *Hyle*, i.e., "Matter") dwelt in the Realm of Darkness. John Paul II describes the nature of the Darkness as "... concupiscence, an evil appetite for pleasure, an instinct of death, comparable if not identical with sexual desire, with 'libido.' It is a force that attempts to attack the Light: it is disordered movement, bestial, brutal, and semi-conscious desire."[8] According to Manichaean belief, the Realm of Darkness mounted an assault against the Realm of Light. The Father of Greatness then brought forth an initial creation (something he would not have been inclined to do otherwise), the Primal Man, as a strategy to counteract the Darkness. The Primal Man and his sons sacrificed themselves and were devoured by the sons of Darkness. Thus, "the darkness is placed at the mercy of the divine,"[9] as a part of the Primal Man's own light and substance (Soul or Living Soul) was devoured by and mixed with the Darkness (or Matter). The Darkness became "poisoned but addicted to the Light elements it swallowed,"[10] and

---

7   In fact, there are three "times" or "epochs." As described by John Paul II, there are: "the 'initium [beginning]' or primordial separation; the 'medium' or present mixture; and the 'finis [end],' which consists in the return to the original division, in a salvation that implies a complete break between spirit and matter" (John Paul II, *Man and Woman He Created Them: A Theology of the Body*, 44:5). It is interesting to note here that John Paul II divides Part I of the *Theology of the Body* into three chapters that parallel these three "times" or epochs: Christ Appeals to the Beginning (Original Man), Christ Appeals to the Human Heart (Historical Man), and Christ Appeals to the Resurrection (Eschatological Man).

8   John Paul II, *Man and Woman He Created Them: A Theology of the Body*, 44:5, footnote.

9   H. C. Puech, *Le Manichéisme: son fondateur-sa doctrine*, 77. "L'Obscurité et la met désormais à la merci du divin."

10   Yuri Stoyanov, *The Other God: Dualist Religions from Antiquity to the Cathar Heresy* (New Haven, CT: Yale University Press, 2000), 109.

it is so melded with the Light that it cannot survive without it. The ultimate goal of this strategy is the eventual separation of the Light from the Darkness, of the Living Soul from Matter, which will result in the "final death" of the Darkness.[11]

This cosmic battle wound up leading to further creations. The scorched skins of the sons of Darkness were spread across the sky, thus creating the ten heavens; their bones were dispersed, thus creating the mountains; and their flesh and excrement were thrown down to the land, thus creating the eight earths. Then, from the Light that had not suffered from contact with the darkness, the sun and the moon were created, and from the Light which the combination had affected only in a weak way, came the stars. "Manichaean pessimism has here devised the extreme imaginative expression of a negative view of the world: all the parts of nature that surround us come from the impure cadavers of the powers of evil."[12]

As creation progresses in the Manichaean myth, the process by which things are brought into being becomes more shocking, for creation itself becomes the weapon of war in the battle between the Light and the Darkness,[13] and the primary strategy in the

---

11   H. C. Puech, *Le Manichéisme: son fondateur-sa doctrine*, 78. " ...ce serait pour elles la mort définitive."

12   Hans Jonas, *The Gnostic Religion, 3rd Edition* (Boston: Beacon Press, 2001), 224. Historians generally have turned away from Jonas's "history of religions" approach that interpreted Gnosticism (including Manichaeism) as an independent worldview, seeing him as "constructing" religions with which even the fathers of the Church would have been unfamiliar (see *The Cambridge History of Christianity, Volume 1: Origins to Constantine*, ed. Margaret M. Mitchell and Frances M. Young [Cambridge: Cambridge University Press, 2006], 247). This present enquiry is not taking a historical approach to Manichaeism, but rather seeking to draw a relationship between certain beliefs of those thus named (upon which scholars generally agree) and those aspects of Cartesian Rationalism that John Paul II strongly associates with the label "New Manichaeism."

13   Cardinal Carlo Maria Caffarra (1938–2017), commenting on Fatima visionary Sr. Lucia words to him that the "decisive battle" between the Kingdom of God and the Kingdom of Satan will be over marriage and the family, stated that Satan is building an anti-creation in which he deconstructs and reconstructs the meaning human life, masculinity and femininity, sex and procreation, and marriage and the family. What we are witnessing in our time is this battle between God's creation and Satan's anti-creation (https://voiceofthefamily.com/cardinal-caffarra-we-are-no-longer-witnesses-but-deserters-if-we-do-not-speak-openly-and-publicly/). This is interesting

effort to either release or entrap the Light or Living Soul. The Father of Greatness initiated a new creation, the Messenger, which used its beauty to seduce the evil archons. In its "radiant nudity" the Messenger appeared in the sun in a female form to the male archons and in a male form to the female archons.[14] He so aroused the male archons that in their burning lust they ejaculated the light which they had consumed along with their sin/sperm. The sin/sperm fell to the earth, and the portion that fell on the land caused five trees to germinate and grow, and from these trees all vegetative life stemmed with the light elements trapped therein. The female archons, "pregnant from the beginning on account of their own nature,"[15] looked upon the beauty of the Messenger and their fetuses were aborted and fell to the earth, creating the animal kingdom.[16] The animals also imprisoned elements of the Light or Living Soul. Again, the "Manichaean pessimism" is evident in that all plant life derives from the evil seed of the male archons and the animal kingdom from the aborted fetuses of the female archons, with concupiscent desire as the root cause on all accounts.

Yet, this pessimism may not be as absolute as first perceived, for while matter and creation is evil, nevertheless, the cosmos was constructed in such a way as to allow for the efficient release of the Light from its entrapment in matter. Jason David BeDuhn alleges that while it is true that in Manichaean cosmogony the material cosmos was created either by the Prince of Darkness or as a defensive and strategic response by the Father of Greatness to the onslaught of the Darkness, the physical cosmos was not seen in exclusively negative terms by the Manichees.[17] First, the cosmos itself was fashioned by the Realm of Light, albeit reluctantly, and was so constructed as to have different regions, each with differing levels of blended Light and Darkness, as well as with

---

in view of fact that for the Manichees creation itself was a weapon of war in the battle between the Light and the Darkness.

14   H. C. Puech, *Le Manichéisme: son fondateur-sa doctrine*, 80. "Dans sa nudité radieuse, et comme 'Vierge de Lumière' il apparaît dans le Soleil, tantôt sous forme féminine aux démons males, tantôt sous forme masculine aux démons femelles."

15   Michel Tardieu, *Manichaeism* (Chicago, IL: University of Illinois Press, 2008), 80.

16   Jonas, *The Gnostic Religion*, 226.

17   BeDuhn, *The Manichaean Body in Discipline and Ritual*, 92.

the means for redeeming the light elements.[18] Thus, though the locale of the Light's entrapment, the entire cosmos is structured as a great machine which functions to liberate the Light from that entrapment. There are even certain fruits, vegetables, and grains that contain greater amounts of Light that are released when eaten and digested in the stomachs of the Manichaean Elect.

Manichaean attitudes towards creation are also evidenced in the discipline and practice of the Manichees. The extreme ascetical practices of the Manichees are to be understood "principally as the outcomes of the negative attitude toward the world conveyed by Mani's teachings,"[19] including the cosmsogenic myths. This asceticism was lived out differently depending upon the particular Manichee's place within the Manichaean hierarchy, for the Manichees were divided into the Elect (Perfect) and the Auditors (Hearers), with the Elect living a rigorous asceticism and the Auditors a more relaxed one.[20] According to H. C. Puech, "Abstinence within the limits set by necessity for maintaining life is the only means to redemption."[21] In fact, the Elect "are redeemed by virtue of their total asceticism."[22] Abstention characterizes the Elect's contact and interaction with the world: " ... the entire ethic consists in a single commandment: abstain, in order to acquire and preserve purity, a largely negative commandment... [T]he break with matter is here renunciation, withdrawal, removal."[23] While the total fulfillment of such a discipline entails the negation of life itself, there was permitted a certain concession from the ideal of "absolute divorce from the world," given the body's imperfectability and need for nourishment.[24]

---

18 Stoyanov, *The Other God: Dualist Religions from Antiquity to the Cathar Heresy*, 110.

19 BeDuhn, *The Manichaean Body in Discipline and Ritual*, 214.

20 Ibid., 65. This division is variously attributed to Buddhist or Marcionite influences (Stoyanov, *The Other God: Dualist Religions from Antiquity to the Cathar Heresy*, 112).

21 H. C. Puech, "The Concept of Redemption in Manichaeism," *The Mystic Vision*, (Princeton, NJ: Princeton University Press, 1968), 297.

22 Ibid., 309.   23 Ibid., 292.

24 Ibid., 295. Wolfgang Lentz stated, "Even the ideal of starvation as the only manner of death corresponding to real wisdom lies not far from the ordinances of the Elect." Samuel Lieu concurs: "Taken to its logical conclusion, strict observance of these Manichaean ethical principles would result in starvation and the eventual extinction of the human race" (as quoted by BeDuhn, *The Manichaean Body in Discipline and Ritual*, 213).

The view that the practical consequence of Manichaean cosmological-soteriological schema amounts to a rejection of the world is shared by Julien Ries. For Ries (as for Puech) *gnosis* is the sole means of salvation in Manichaeism. This *gnosis* or "fundamental, ineffable mystery" is that of the Living Soul "held prisoner in matter, the mystery of the soul of the world, which implicates the attitude of man in its regard."[25] As John Paul puts it, Manichaeism "contains and brings to maturity the characteristic elements of all 'gnosis'" and "the concept of a *salvation* that is realized only through *knowledge* ('gnosis') or self-understanding," a salvation which "implies a complete break between spirit and matter."[26] This is why for Ries, the doctrine of the Three Seals, which holds central importance in Manichaeism and in the discipline of the Manichaean Elect in particular, is "grafted" upon the mystery of the entrapped Light or Living Soul in Matter.[27] He characterizes the doctrine as "a veritable compendium of gnostic ethics."[28] The Three Seals as described by John Paul II correspond closely to Ries's account:

> The elect constitute the group of the perfect, whose virtue has an ascetical character, namely, practicing the abstinence commanded by the three "seals": the "seal of the mouth" prohibits all cursing and commands abstinence from meat, from blood, from wine, and all alcoholic drinks, as well as fasting; the "seal of the hands" commands respect for all the life (the "light") that is enclosed in bodies, in seeds, in trees, and prohibits the gathering of fruit. The tearing

---

25 Julien Ries, "La doctrine de l'âme du monde et des trois sceaux dans la controverse de Mani avec les Elchasaites," *Codex Manichaicus Coloniensis* (Consenza: Marra editore, 1986), 174, as cited in BeDuhn, *The Manichaean Body in Discipline and Ritual*, 121.

26 John Paul II, *Man and Woman He Created Them: A Theology of the Body*, footnote to 44:5. Cf. Julien Ries, "La doctrine de l'âme du monde et des trois sceaux dans la controverse de Mani avec les Elchasaites," Codex Manichaicus Coloniensis (Consenza: Marra editore, 1986), 174, as cited in BeDuhn, *The Manichaean Body in Discipline and Ritual*, 121.

27 BeDuhn, *The Manichaean Body in Discipline and Ritual*, 121.

28 Julien Ries, "La doctrine de l'âme du monde et des trois sceaux dans la controverse de Mani avec les Elchasaites," *Codex Manichaicus Coloniensis* (Consenza: Marra editore, 1986), 169, as cited in BeDuhn, *The Manichaean Body in Discipline and Ritual*, 38.

of plants, and the taking of the life of men or animals; the "seal of the womb" commands total continence.[29]

The Three Seals correspond to the Five Commandments that must be observed by the Elect.[30] In fact, Ries believed them to overlap so considerably that "he proposed synthesizing them into a single system."[31]

Jason David BeDuhn, however, does not understand the doctrine of the Three Seals or the Five Commandments solely as a condemnation and utter rejection of the world. He holds that, for the Manichees, one does not remove himself from the world simply because the material world is so detestable, but because by doing so the Manichaean Elect becomes a productive "salvational machine" for use during the daily ritual meal. He explains:

> Manichaean disciplinary regimens, therefore, incorporate not only means of personal purification, but also techniques of exorcizing, demarcating, and sealing a holy site. Within the sacred space of their corrected and perfected bodies, the Elect conduct the principal salvational rite of the Manichaean tradition: the daily ritual meal. [32]

The Manichaean Auditors played their own crucial role in the Manichaean salvific economy through the practice of almsgiving,

---

29   John Paul II, *Man and Woman He Created Them: A Theology of the Body*, 44:5, footnote.

30   Tardieu, *Manichaeism*, 63. The First Commandment, called "Truth," in a general way prohibits lying but in a particular way requires complete assent to the *gnosis* revealed by Mani, and bears resemblance to the Seal of the Mouth. The Second Commandment, called "Non-violence," prohibits any activity that could injure the Light elements in all things, thus corresponding to the Seal of the Hands. The Third Commandment is called "Behavior in Accordance with Religion" and corresponds precisely with the absolute rejection of sexual relations and sensual pleasure associated with the Seal of the Breast. The Fourth Commandment, known as "Purity of the Mouth," being concerned with dietary laws that imposed strict vegetarianism as well as rigorous protocols associated with the ritual meal and with moderation in speech corresponded to the Seal of the Mouth. Finally, the Fifth Commandment, called "Blessed Poverty," enjoins complete destitution upon the Elect so they might be entirely devoted to preaching and prayer; to the spreading of the gnosis and the salvific work of the liberation of the Light.

31   BeDuhn, *The Manichaean Body in Discipline and Ritual*, 45.

32   Ibid., 125.

which provided for the daily ritual meal. In following the Three Seals in a faithful manner according to their state as Auditors, in their provision for the Elect, and in their preparation of the ritual meal, the Auditors hoped that, upon their death, their soul[33] would be transmigrated into the body of a Manichaean Elect or into melons and cucumbers whose Light is released through consumption by the Elect in the daily ritual meal.[34]

Thus, in Jason BeDuhn's view, the created world has a certain value for the Manichees as a "salvation machine" and the codes of behavior served to maximize the effectiveness of the liberation process. As he explicates:

> The codes of behavior sanctioned by Manichaean author-
> ity regulated individual action with explicit reference to
> the goal of the ritual meal... Manichaean anthropol-
> ogy and cosmology modeled a universe that enabled the
> alms-service and ritual meal to function for salvational
> effect, and this ritual system was the central soteriological
> operation of the religion.[35]

THE NEW MANICHAEISM'S MECHANISM AND
REJECTION OF THE PHILOSOPHY OF BEING
AND THE MANICHAEAN VIEW OF CREATION

In the *Letter to Families*, Pope John Paul II strongly associates Cartesian Rationalism's rejection of the philosophy of being and its corresponding "notion of creation," and its subsequent rejection a truth of creation which must be acknowledged and of the God of Creation who is *Ens subsistens*, with the New Manichaeism being experienced by the human family. The traditional interpretation of Manichaean cosmogony likewise stands in stark contradiction with Thomas Aquinas's philosophy of being and with the "notion of creation" that "characterizes the interior structure of *nearly all* the basic concepts" in it. Manichaeism certainly would not

---

33   Unlike in the Gnostic interpretation of Manichaeism, for BeDuhn the "soul" referred to here, whether ascending to heaven or reincarnated in human or vegetable form, is not a "personal" soul, but merely that part of the Living Soul which is entrapped in that particular material prison.
34   BeDuhn, *The Manichaean Body in Discipline and Ritual*, 103. A higher form of life is always one from which the Light can more readily be released.
35   Ibid., 209.

acknowledge the intrinsic goodness of creation as *ens participatum* or of the Creator as *Ens subsistens*, or hold that "being" and "the good" are convertible. Thus, the Manichees would reject that all finite, created being has a positive value (i.e., is "good") by virtue of its existence as an *ens participatum*. They would not accept that, all creatures receive their being as a participated likeness or similitude of the divine *esse*, or that the transcendental concepts are found in creatures (*ens participatum*) to the degree that they have a participated likeness to God, limited by their particular essences. Instead, among the Manichees there is a fundamental rejection of the intrinsic goodness of creation as *creatura*. It holds a form of dualism in which the entire cosmos is separated into two substances: Spirit, which is intrinsically good, and Matter, which is intrinsically evil. The Prince of Darkness himself is named *Hyle* (Matter). The cosmos is created either as a war strategy of the Father of Greatness or is the direct result of the work of the Prince of Darkness in an attempt to entrap the Light elements. This is why, in classic Gnostic style, the Manichees rejected the God of the Old Testament—"*He Who Is*" or Being Itself[36]—for they identified him with the Prince of Darkness. As previously discussed, according to the Manichaean myth, all the parts of nature that surround us do not come from Supreme Being but the impure cadavers of the powers of evil. All plant life derives from the evil ejaculate of the male archons, and the animal kingdom springs from the aborted fetuses of the female archons, with concupiscent desire as the root cause. The goal of Manichaean life is to free the Light elements, the Living Soul, embedded in matter, so at last the evil substance can be discarded. The way to accomplish this separation is through a rigorous asceticism—a denial of all things bodily in man. The Three Seals and the Five Commandments guide the Manichaean Elect on the path of total abstention and divorce from the world. The only concession made is for cases of absolute necessity, i.e., for what is required to sustain life. It is in this context that the daily ritual meal is situated, in the traditional view. It is a meager allowance

36   In his footnote to *Man and Woman He Created Them: A Theology of the Body*, 2:5 referencing Etienne Gilson, John Paul states that while the revelation of God's name as "I am he who am" in Exodus 3 constitutes an object of reflection for many philosophers, it was St. Thomas who "bridged the gap" that separated "the being of essence" from "the being of existence" with his proofs of God's existence.

that maintains life at its basic level, yet can also serve as a vehicle to liberate the Light from the confines of certain fruits, vegetables, and grains by means of the disciplined bodies of the Manichaean Elect. The Auditors are called to observe a more relaxed version of these disciplinary practices, but find their main role in providing for the Manichaean Elect and especially for the daily ritual meal.

In John Paul's identification of Cartesian mechanism with the New Manichaeism, one finds another important connection between the New Manichaeism and ancient Manichaeism: a utilitarian view of the material cosmos. According to the Manichees, all matter is evil, but it may prove *useful* as a vehicle of liberation. In the Manichaean view, creation's only possible "positive" value is a utilitarian one: it has been constructed in such a way as to provide mechanisms for the liberation of the Light elements. Its only value comes from its efficacy as a salvation machine. Manichaeism divided the cosmos into two substances, drawing a radical opposition between matter and spirit. While the New Manichaeism, with its association with Cartesian Rationalism, does not consider matter to be intrinsically evil like ancient Manichaeism did, it does regard matter as "raw material" that is essentially value-free, and divides the cosmos into two substances: mind (the "thinking thing") and matter (pure extension). In the New Manichaeism, the universe too is a great machine which only need be properly understood, through the attainment of a kind of "scientific gnosis," in order to be manipulated and exploited for desirable ends. The "practical materialism"[37] which results from the rejection of the Creator in the New Manichaeism may be likened to ancient Manichaeism in that the Manichees viewed the material cosmos in a mechanistic way, seeing its value solely in terms of utility and production.

MANICHAEAN ANTHROPOLOGY

Since Manichaeism essentially tells the story of "the fallen soul which is imprisoned in matter and is liberated by knowledge,"[38] John Paul states that the Manichees *"saw the source of evil*

---

37   John Paul II, *The Gospel of Life*, no. 23.
38   Ibid. Cf. H. C. Puech, "The Concept of Redemption in Manichaeism," 313–314; Ries, "La doctrine de l'ame du monde et des trois sceaux dans la controverse de Mani avec les Elchasaites," Codex Manichaicus Coloniensis, 180, as cited in BeDuhn, *The Manichaean Body in Discipline and Ritual*, 217.

in matter, in the body, and therefore condemned all that is bodily in man."[39] In the Manichaean creation story, the appearance of the Messenger and its effect on the archons caused the Prince of Darkness to grow afraid. He thus devised a plan to concentrate a large portion of the Light in a creation of his own, as a type of counter-attack to the divine creation. The Prince of Darkness created two demons—one male, a son named Ashaqlan, and one female, a daughter named Namrael—and charged them to execute this plan. Ashaqlan devoured all the aborted fetuses of the archons in order to ingest the totality of the light they contain, and then mated with his sister Namrael, and from her the first two human beings, Adam and Eve, were born.[40] So, as Puech states, "the human race is born in a series of repugnant acts of cannibalism and sexuality"[41] and bears the stigma of this "diabolical beginning" in the body and the libido, which cause man to reproduce and thus imprison indefinitely the Light or Living Soul, which human generation transfers from body to body.[42] Especially evil is the human body and its tendency towards copulation and procreation, the main mode of luminous entrapment. Now that the greatest part of the Light has been entrapped in Adam, it is he and his progeny who become the central object of the liberating process and the new battleground in the struggle for the Light.[43]

Adam is created oblivious to the Light within him; he is "blind and deaf, unaware and adrift," his "accursed body fallen with unconsciousness" as in a dream *(torpor).*[44] The Father of Greatness, therefore, sent a savior, Jesus the Splendor, to awaken Adam

---

39 John Paul II, *Man and Woman He Created Them: A Theology of the Body,* 44:5.

40 H. C. Puech, *Le Manichéisme: son fondateur-sa doctrine,* 80.

41 Ibid., 81. The incestuous nature of the sexual acts warrants particular mention. "Notre espèce naît donc d'une suite d'actes répugnants de cannibalisme et de sexualité."

42 Ibid., 81. "Elle garde les stigmates de cette origine diabolique le corps, qui est la forme animale des Archontes; la libido, le désir qui posse l'homme à s'accoupler et à se reproduire à son tour, c'est-à-dire, conformément au plan de la Matière, a maintenir indéfiniment dans sa captivité l'âme lumineuse que la génération transmet, 'transvase', de corps en corps."

43 One could argue that rivaling views the human person and of what it means to be a human being is the contemporary battleground as well.

44 Ibid., 81. " Le Matière a fait Adam aveugle et sourd, inconscient et égaré, oublieux de sa lointaine origine divine. Son âme, solidement liée au corps maudit, a littéralement 'perdu connaissance' tombée 'sans connaissance'."

from his unconscious state or "deep sleep," to reveal to him his true nature and that of the physical cosmos, and to make him conscious of the plight of the imprisoned light in all matter. Jesus the Splendor made Adam eat from the Tree of Life,[45] and upon consuming its fruit Adam received full knowledge (*gnosis*) of the plight of the imprisoned Light and corruption of matter. He tore out his hair, beat his breast, and cried out, "Woe, woe upon the maker of my body and upon the one who has shackled my soul and upon the rebels that have enslaved me!"[46] This negative view of the human body finds expression in Mani's declaration that the body "is defiled and molded from a mold of defilement."[47] As previously mentioned, according to Puech, Manichees "are redeemed by virtue of their total asceticism";[48] abstention characterizes the Manichaean ideal of contact and interaction with the world. Since the human body is intrinsically evil it must be denied. "Taken to its logical conclusion, strict observance of these Manichaean ethical principles would result in starvation and the eventual extinction of the human race."[49] Yet, a meager amount of food was permitted as a concession in order to sustain life. Every form of sensual pleasure was sinful—even the touch of linen or the taking of baths.[50]

The traditional interpretation of Manichaeism holds that Manichees believed in a metaphysical person—the *grev* (self, ego, "soul," or inner essence) of the Turfan fragments or "living self" or "luminous self" of the Manichaean hymns[51]—that is identified with the Light imprisoned in the human body. The Manichaean belief in the transmigration of souls is yet another demonstration of the Manichaean disregard for the body and discloses their non-identification of the body with the "self." For example, in following the Three Seals in a faithful manner according to their state, the Auditors hoped that, upon their death, their soul would be transmigrated into the body of a Manichaean Elect or into melons and

---

45   Due to this, it was a common Christian accusation that the Manichees equated Jesus the Splendor with the serpent in the Hebrew myth.

46   This is a quote from Theodore Bar Konai's Scholia as cited in Tardieu, *Manichaeism*, 80.

47   From the *Cologne Mani Codex* 81.2-82.13, as cited in BeDuhn, *The Manichaean Body in Discipline and Ritual*, 97.

48   H. C. Puech, "The Concept of Redemption in Manichaeism," 309.

49   BeDuhn, *The Manichaean Body in Discipline and Ritual*, 213

50   Tardieu, *Manichaeism*, 65.   51   Jonas, *The Gnostic Religion*, 123.

cucumbers whose Light is released through consumption by the Elect in the daily ritual meal.[52]

Jason BeDuhn, however, argues for a nuanced alternative to the traditionally accepted view of Manichaean attitudes towards the human body. While BeDuhn admits that Mani's declaration that the human body "is defiled and molded from a mold of defilement"[53] has become the "classic statement of Manichaean anthropology,"[54] BeDuhn continues:

> But because the forces of evil modeled humanity on a divine form, the human body also possesses the structures necessary to function as a salvational machine. The liberating struggles in the larger universe are replayed in exact mimesis within the individual body (*Kephalaion* 70). By mastering the body, the Manichaean duplicates the victories of light in its battle for control of the cosmos, and establishes anatomical 'posts' corresponding to those which govern the universe.[55]

This is what, in BeDuhn's view, led St. Augustine to observe that " ... if the foods prepared from grain and fruits come to the holy ones, that is, to the Manichaeans, whatever is bright and divine in them is purified, that is, made perfect in every way, through their chastity, prayers, and psalms, in order that it may be returned to its own kingdoms without any trouble due to defilement."[56]

According to BeDuhn, this way of understanding Manichaean discipline and the daily ritual meal also makes clear that the human body has value. The body is not, as the traditional view associated with Puech and Ries alleges, merely something to be rejected by means of absolute abstinence, withdrawal, and immobility. "Mani does not conclude, as has been suggested, that the body is therefore a hopeless case. Rather, he declares that 'genuine purity'

---

52   BeDuhn, *The Manichaean Body in Discipline and Ritual*, 103. A higher form of life is always one from which the Light can more readily be released.

53   From the *Cologne Mani Codex* 81.2–82.13, as cited in BeDuhn, *The Manichaean Body in Discipline and Ritual*, 97.

54   BeDuhn, *The Manichaean Body in Discipline and Ritual*, 97.

55   Ibid. See also Michel Tardieu, *Manichaeism*, 89–90.

56   Augustine of Hippo, *De moribus Manichaeorum*, 15.36. *The Works of Saint Augustine: The Manichean Debate*, ed. Boniface Ramsey (Hyde Park, NY: New City Press, 2006), 85.

comes through separation of the two opposing forces within the body."[57] In fact, BeDuhn's analysis of the data leads him to the conclusion that Mani had a more "materialist" view of the manner in which the Light was entrapped in and released from the body: "The body is itself a duality, a mixture of good and evil. So the demarcation of purity cannot occur between the body and the world... but must be drawn within the body between its positive and negative components..."[58] In fact, the disciplinary practices are meant to reorder the body for the purposes of the Light's liberation, and it is this "reformation of the body's congenital defectiveness" that "forms the centerpiece of divine revelation and action."[59] Manichaean asceticism operates to reform the bodies of the Elect from "instruments of entrapment of the divine soul into machines of liberation for the divine soul."[60] Thus, the Elect could—through eating certain fruit, plants, and grains—separate the divine substance from the evil substance and liberate it through their prayers and hymns.

> ...the disciplinary regimens are said to correct and perfect the deficient human body, rending it into an instrument that can actively assist in the liberation of the Living Self from its 'mixture' in the universe... The rescue of the Living Self constitutes the principal purpose the Manichaeans themselves express for performing the ritual meal.[61]

Hence, BeDuhn rejects an overly spiritualized or psychological interpretation of the Manichaean understanding of the salvation process. According to BeDuhn, it had much more to do with the metabolism of the reformed bodies of the Manichaean Elect.

---

57 BeDuhn, *The Manichaean Body in Discipline and Ritual*, 121.
58 Ibid., 98–99. BeDuhn emphasizes that Mani was a "physician" whose analyses of the body's structure and function corresponded closely to the medical knowledge of his time: "Manichaean discourse on the body is a chemical, elemental physiology. The soul is a byproduct—or rather the essential product—of metabolic processes. In saying this, the Manichaeans were very much in line with the leading medical thought of the day" (*The Manichaean Body in Discipline and Ritual*, 223-224).
59 Ibid., 99.
60 From an interview with Jason BeDuhn in Miguel Conner, *Voices of Gnosticism: Interviews with Elaine Pagels, Marvin Meyer, Bart Ehrman, Bruce Chilton and Other Leading Scholars* (Dublin: Bardic Press, 2011), 120.
61 BeDuhn, *The Manichaean Body in Discipline and Ritual*, 166.

The offerings presented to the Manichaean Elect were cooked in their stomachs as opposed to being burned in a temple. In fact, the Manichaean body acted as a temple:

> The divine substance, the Living Self, that the whole world tramples on and profanes in ordinary life, finds in the disciplined bodies of the Elect the properly prepared temple where it can be offered and returned to its heavenly home. [62]

While other traditions focus on temple worship and sacrifice in their discourse, Manichees center on the processes of digestion. Thus, "...in Manichaeism the body served as not only the actor but also the arena of salvation... the bodies of the Elect were treated as implements employed in the ritual meal."[63]

Likewise, BeDuhn rejects the traditional view that Manichaeism represents a classic form of "spirit-matter dualism." In fact, he alleges that the distinction between matter and spirit is not the main one in Manichaean thought, but rather the distinctions between Light and Darkness, Good and Evil. BeDuhn believes that labeling Manichaeism as a type of "spirit-matter dualism" involves a misreading of the sources, which, according to him, actually demonstrate that "Manichaeans were thoroughgoing materialists."[64] For the Manichees, the body is a "not a 'real existence,' but a temporary conglomeration of incongruous substances";[65] it is "not a monad separable from the world," but "itself a duality, a mixture of good and evil."[66] The soul, according to BeDuhn's interpretation, "is a substance besides others in the body and in the world, impacting upon and in turn impacted by them."[67] In contradiction of the traditional interpretation of Manichaeism, BeDuhn states that the soul does not possess an immutable identity, for "the human soul is not a discrete, eternal monad, but simply a fragment or piece of the same soul substance that pervades the

---

62   Ibid., 125.   63   Ibid., 164-165.

64   Jason BeDuhn, "The Metabolism of Salvation: Manichaean Concepts of Human Physiology," *The Light and the Darkness: Studies in Manichaeism and Its World*, ed. Jason BeDuhn and Paul Mirecki (Boston, MA: Brill Academic Publishers, 2001), 5.

65   BeDuhn, *The Manichaean Body in Discipline and Ritual*, 223.

66   Ibid., 99.

67   BeDuhn, "The Metabolism of Salvation: Manichaean Concepts of Human Physiology," 5.

entire universe and all living things in it."[68] Humans can be said more precisely to have a certain quantity of soul substance than an individual soul.[69] Additionally, this soul substance is so mixed in with the body that it is not possible to discuss the soul as distinct from physiology. Thus, "when we look closely, Manichaean discourse about the soul and concern with its salvation turns out to be very much 'a something about the body.'"[70] According to BeDuhn, the only "soul" that the Manichaean Elect possesses is one that he "forms" within himself by "collecting" all the soul substance (which is identical with the Living Soul or Light) from throughout his body and "sealing" it in its ideal form.[71]

According to BeDuhn, Manichaean beliefs about transmigration must be understood in light of this view of Manichaean anthropology. He holds that for the Manichees humans "do not experience metempsychosis at their death, that is, their intact souls do not transmigrate to other bodies. Rather, the separable divine elements are reprocessed into new forms through 'transfusion' (metaggismos)."[72] The soul substance is passed on congenitally by "evil procreation." There is no "individual salvation" in Manichaeism. Rather, there is an "absolute identity" between the self and the Living Soul.[73] It is in the liberation of the Living Soul that the Manichaean Elect redeems himself.[74] This redemption is "finalized at the point of death, when the evil substance is discarded."[75]

---

68 Ibid., 8.

69 For Manichees, it is the sheer amount of divine material in the human that allows a level of consciousness to emerge, not the existence of an individual human personality. See BeDuhn, "The Metabolism of Salvation: Manichaean Concepts of Human Physiology," 5.

70 BeDuhn, *The Manichaean Body in Discipline and Ritual*, 233.

71 In the Manichaean Elect one witnesses a microcosmic replaying of the redemption of the Primal Man: "Individual Manichaeans, like the Primordial Man, must 'collect' their 'limbs,' that is, assemble separate identifiable traits into a complete 'soul' or self" (BeDuhn, *The Manichaean Body in Discipline and Ritual*, 223). As Michel Tardieu states, "The microcosm repeats the macrocosm" (Tardieu, *Manichaeism*, 89).

72 Ibid. In fact, BeDuhn states that available evidence indicates that Manichees held a traducian theory of soul, i.e., the substance "that will constitute a soul in the individual is biologically inherited from that individual's parents, whose reproductive elements in turn derive from the food they eat."

73 BeDuhn, *The Manichaean Body in Discipline and Ritual*, 232–233.

74 Ibid.

75 BeDuhn, *The Manichaean Body in Discipline and Ritual*, 251.

Taken altogether, if BeDuhn's materialist interpretation is correct, the concepts that typically characterize "spirit-matter dualism" do not neatly apply to Manichaean anthropology.

THE NEW MANICHAEISM'S ANTHROPOLOGICAL DUALISM AND MANICHAEAN ANTHROPOLOGY

John Paul II held that Descartes's anthropological dualism splits "the human being into an extended substance (the body) and a thinking substance (the soul), which are related to one another in a parallel way and do not form an undivided whole or one substantial *compositum humanum*." [76] Thus, Descartes rejected the hylomorphic view that man is a single composite substance comprised of form (soul) and matter (body), i.e., that man's essence "embraces both form and matter," [77] since it is through form that matter, as the principle of individuation, becomes an "actual being" existing as a "particular thing." Consequently, John Paul II recognized that Descartes's anthropology "lacks a sufficient basis for including the body, the organism, within the structural whole of the person's life and activity," [78] and rejects what ultimately constitutes us as human beings. In the *Letter to Families*, the Pope strongly identifies this placing of spirit and body into radical opposition with the New Manichaeism being experienced by the human family.

Reflecting upon the preceding summary of Manichaean anthropology leads one to the conclusion that the Manichees also clearly rejected hylomorphism. This rejection remains even if, as BeDuhn holds, Manichaeism does not represent a classic form of "spirit-matter dualism." Whether there exists a "self" which is identified with the Living Soul or no true "self" at all but only portions of Light substance, there is nonetheless a denial of man as a composite substance in which "the soul is the form of the body." If the Manichees, as those who employ the traditional Gnostic interpretation of Manichaeism suggest, held that there exists a metaphysical person—the *grev* (self, ego, "soul," inner essence)—then hylomorphism has been rejected in favor of a type of substance dualism. If the Manichees, as BeDuhn suggests, held that the body is "itself a duality, a mixture of good and

---

76 Wojtyła, "Thomistic Personalism," 169.
77 Thomas Aquinas, *On Being and Essence*, II, 1, 35.
78 Wojtyła, "Thomistic Personalism," 169.

evil";[79] that the soul is not a discrete, eternal monad" [80] with an immutable identity but "a substance besides others in the body,"[81] and that this "soul substance" is so mixed in with the body that it is not possible to discuss the soul as distinct from physiology, then hylomorphism has still been rejected. In fact, in this case, there is no distinctive human nature whatsoever. If BeDuhn's interpretation is correct, then Manichaeism would not be representative of spirit-matter dualism (also known as "mind-body dualism"), for indeed there is no "self" (i.e., "soul" or "mind") at all. The only "self" that the Manichaean Elect possesses is one that he "forms" within himself by "collecting" all the soul substance from throughout his body and "sealing" it in its ideal form. Humans exhibit certain powers typically associated with the soul or the mind (e.g., intelligence and will), simply because more of the Light substance inhabits them. This view is still tantamount to rejecting human nature as a "given reality,"[82] specifically as a composite substance; a being "whose rational soul is *per se et essentialiter the form of his body*"[83] and "exists as a whole—*corpore et anima unus*—as a person."[84]

A question follows, however, as to whether or not the Manichees asserted that the body and soul are substantially distinct. According to the traditional view, Manichaeism is a representation of "spirit-matter dualism," yet even more precisely of "substance dualism." Even though the Manichees did not make use of this term "substance," in the traditional understanding of Manichaeism the Light and Darkness, manifested in spirit and matter, are diametrically opposed and essentially different, bearing nothing in common. The tradition likewise recognizes in Manichaean thought a sharp division between spirit and matter, the former being intrinsically good and the latter intrinsically evil. So, according to the traditional view culminating in the work of Puech and Ries, it appears that the Manichees did view the body and soul as substantially distinct.

However, can one arrive at the same conclusion in light of more current Manichaean studies, like those of Jason David BeDuhn? If the body is not a "real existence" but a hodgepodge of different

---

79 BeDuhn, *The Manichaean Body in Discipline and Ritual*, 99.
80 BeDuhn, "The Metabolism of Salvation: Manichaean Concepts of Human Physiology," 8.
81 Ibid., 5.   82 John Paul II, *Memory and Identity*, 12.
83 John Paul II, *The Splendor of the Truth*, no. 48.   84 Ibid.

substances, some good and some bad, and the soul is merely a substance among others in the body, then Manichaeism would defy definition as a form of "spirit-matter dualism." Because of this, BeDuhn goes so far as to label the Manichees as "materialists." He posits that the Manichees believed the "soul" (or rather portions of Light substance or Living Soul) to occupy the same space as the body, to permeate the body and be totally blended with it.[85] In light of this, it seems that contemporary scholarship on Manichaeism debunks any charge of substance dualism. Nevertheless, there is no doubt that the Light and the Darkness, which current scholars identify as the real dichotomy in Manichaeism, are substantially different. Even if both are identified with the body on some level, they remain essentially distinct in kind. In fact, the whole Manichaean project was to release the Light substance from the other substances in the body by a proper ordering of the body's "congenital defectiveness."[86] If one were to accept that Manichees were "materialists" and that their view of salvation was soma-centric, then their particular form of substance dualism would not be between body and soul, but between the Light substance and the other substances that make up the body.

This being acknowledged, when one considers the way in which the different Light elements are trapped by the forces of Darkness in the anatomical structures of the body, the Manichaean view is more similar to substance dualism than first thought. Consider the following passage about from Mani's *Kephalaion*, 38:

> He constructed the body. Its [soul he] took from the five
> shining gods. [He] bound it in the five limbs of the body.
> He bound mind in bone, thought in nerve, insight in
> artery, intellect in flesh, reasoning in skin.[87]

The divine qualities or limbs which constitute the soul trapped in the five limbs of the body are all associated with powers typically attributed to the soul characteristic of substance dualism: mind,

---

85   BeDuhn, "The Metabolism of Salvation: Manichaean Concepts of Human Physiology," 9. Cf. Jason David BeDuhn, *Augustine's Manichaean Dilemma* (Philadelphia: University of Pennsylvania Press, 2010), 324, footnote 81. The Stoics were materialists conceiving the soul as "divine fire."

86   BeDuhn, *The Manichaean Body in Discipline and Ritual*, 99.

87   *Kephalaion*, 38, as cited in BeDuhn, *The Manichaean Body in Discipline and Ritual*, 93.

thought, insight, intellect, and reasoning.[88] Along with these entrapments, the forces of Darkness add an evil and corrupted counterpart of the same attribute: sin-mind, sin-thought, etc. It is these divine qualities or limbs that the Mind of Light,[89] the divine agent operating in the Manichaean Elect, releases from the five limbs of the body while adding virtues to strengthen the reformed body against future assaults. Thus, even if BeDuhn's interpretation of the data is correct, one can recognize a similarity between the descriptions of the soul substance mixed within the five limbs of the body and the powers of the soul as understood in classic formulations of substance dualism.

Additionally, when one reflects upon Manichaean anthropology one finds among the Manichees the rejection of the body as having positive intrinsic value (or any intrinsic value at all) and instead viewing the body solely in terms of its instrumental and utilitarian value. It is clear that for the Manichees, the material body was viewed as part of the material cosmos, which was evil in nature. The human body may have had greater value only insofar as it could become a most effective means of the Light's liberation. The value of the body, like the value of the physical cosmos at large, is exclusively instrumental and utilitarian. According to the Manichaean scriptures, the body is a "thing" [90] or "implement" [91] employed for efficiency and production in the ritual meal. Manichaean asceticism operates to reform the bodies of the Elect from "instruments of entrapment of the divine soul into *machines* of liberation for the divine soul."[92] In fact, the body only becomes useful to the degree that it is both a productive and subjected body.[93] As BeDuhn sums up:

---

88   These designations of mind, thought, insight, intellect, and reasoning come from the Coptic version of the Kephalaia found in Egypt. The Chinese calls the divine limbs air, wind, light, water, and fire, but the corresponding evil limbs added by the forces of darkness are dark mind, dark thought, dark insight, dark intellect, and dark reasoning. This adaptation is not surprising given the influence of Buddhism on Chinese Manichaeism.

89   It is indeed the Mind of Light—again associating the divine with mind.

90   The Turkic text T II D 173c, 1 as cited in BeDuhn, *The Manichaean Body in Discipline and Ritual*, 155.

91   BeDuhn, *The Manichaean Body in Discipline and Ritual*, 164-165.

92   From an interview with Jason BeDuhn in Miguel Conner, *Voices of Gnosticism*, 120, my italics.

93   As previously mentioned, BeDuhn has recourse to the work of Foucault, here alluding to his work *Discipline and Punishment*, which he uses as a hermeneutic.

Manichaean embodiment, then, must be understood with reference to its utility...the Manichaean 'docile body' must be put to use... Discipline makes of the Manichaean body an 'efficient machine.' The 'machinery' of the Manichaean body was able to process the raw material that entered it and refine from that material the 'spiritual gold' of the Living Self.[94]

In an almost arresting way, BeDuhn himself draws the relationship between modern society and the Manichaean community when he comments:

Modern industrial society and ancient Manichaean community were both interested in 'increases of utility' by which the body would become not just docile but efficient in the production of desired materials.[95]

And this is precisely the point, for, according to John Paul II, this is the type of culture that results from the New Manichaeism. When the body is not viewed subjectively and personally, but rather in exclusively utilitarian terms, the result is "...a civilization of production and of use, a civilization of things and not persons, a civilization in which persons are used the same way as things are used."[96] In such a civilization, "the criterion of personal dignity—which demands respect, generosity and service—is replaced by the criterion of efficiency, functionality, and usefulness: others are considered not for what they 'are,' but for what they 'have, do and produce.'"[97]

MANICHAEAN SEXUAL ETHICS

John Paul states that, according to the Manichees, since "Adam and Eve were begotten by two demons," and "our species was born from a series of repugnant acts of cannibalism and sexuality...it always carries the signs of this diabolical origin, namely, the body...which pushes man to copulate and reproduce and thus to keep the luminous soul always in prison."[98] He adds, "...since in

---

94 BeDuhn, *The Manichaean Body in Discipline and Ritual*, 258.
95 Ibid., 218.   96 John Paul II, *Letter to Families*, no. 13.
97 John Paul II, *The Gospel of Life*, no. 23.
98 John Paul II, *Man and Woman He Created Them: A Theology of the Body*, 44:5, footnote. (Cf. Julien Ries, "La doctrine de l'âme du monde et des trois sceaux

man bodiliness manifests itself above all through [one's] sex, the condemnation [against all things bodily] was extended to marriage and conjugal life...."99 These Manichaean attitudes towards sexuality are elaborated in the treatment of the first human couple in the Manichaean cosmogonic myth.

Eve, being more subject to the powers of Darkness in the myth, became their instrument against Adam. The demons stirred up concupiscence within her and she attempted to seduce Adam to carnal lust, and, through it, to reproduction in order to perpetuate the mixture of the Light with the Darkness, the Living Soul with matter. With his new knowledge of his true nature and the plight of the imprisoned light in all matter, Adam initially resisted her advances. So Eve had intercourse with the son of Darkness (Ashaqlan, her father) and conceived and bore Cain. Then Cain had incestuous relations with Eve, and she conceived multiple times and bore Abel and two daughters ("The Wise of Ages" and the "Daughter of Corruption"). So, the human race develops from acts of incest between a devil with his human daughter and human son with his mother.

Adam, in turn, eventually succumbed to Eve's seductive advances, and she conceived and bore Seth, who in fact is the first in a series of "saviors" or "prophets" in the pattern of Jesus the Splendor. As "bearers of *gnosis*-power,"100 these "saviors" are dispatched to humankind to extend the redemptive mission, for the "long and slow process of liberation is blocked by the sins of mankind."101 Included among them are Seth, Enoch, Noah, Shem, Abraham, Zoroaster, Buddha, and the historical Jesus.102

---

dans la controverse de Mani avec les Elchasaites," *Codex Manichaicus Coloniensis* [Consenza: Marra editore, 1986], 174, as cited in Jason David BeDuhn, *The Manichaean Body in Discipline and Ritual*, 121; H. C. Puech, *Le Manichéisme: son fondateur-sa doctrine*, 81).

99   Ibid., 44:5, my brackets.

100   Stoyanov, *The Other God: Dualist Religions from Antiquity to the Cathar Heresy*, 110.

101   H. C. Puech, *Le Manichéisme: son fondateur-sa doctrine*, 83–84. "Mais ce lent processus physique de libération est entravé et retarde par les péchés de l'humanité..."

102   Stoyanov, *The Other God: Dualist Religions from Antiquity to the Cathar Heresy*, 110. In the case of the historical Jesus, Manichaeism follows the gnostic tradition holding a Docetist view of Jesus: he is solely a divine being who only appeared to assume a material body, suffer, die, and rise from the dead, because he would never be identified with evil matter.

In Manichaean ethics, the Seal of the Breast (also referred to as the Heart or Womb) commanded absolute continence and abstinence from "demonic" procreation which perpetuates the imprisoning of the Light in matter, especially in human beings in which the largest amount of Light is trapped. While the Elect were not permitted to harm the least part of nature, they were nevertheless prohibited from doing anything that encouraged, directly or indirectly, the reproduction of plants or animals, for this would similarly retard the liberation of the Light.[103] All contact which might inspire pleasure was also strictly forbidden. The Third Commandment, called "Behavior in Accordance with Religion," corresponds precisely with the absolute rejection of sexual relations and sensual pleasure associated with the Seal of the Breast. Any sexual desire was considered concupiscence since it was a consequence of the "diabolical beginning" of the human race and was ordered to procreation. Any sensual pleasure was considered sinful, and all things bodily were rejected.

However, Auditors were not bound by the same strict moral code. While Manichaean ethics in general might be summed up in the word "abstain," due to its disdain for all things material and bodily, and while this was the ideal imposed upon the Elect, there was an attitude of toleration regarding the sexual practices of the Auditors. It is a common historical characterization of the Auditors that "their life is in every respect the opposite of that of the Elect—an existence of total indulgence, sanctioned merely by their benefactions to the [Elect]."[104] While it seems that John Paul II accepted this narrative about the Auditors, particularly since he claimed that our contemporary "neo-Manichaean culture" is one in which sexuality becomes "an area for manipulation and exploitation,"[105] current scholarship has roundly dismissed it.[106] As it was, there did exist a standard of morality for the Auditors that corresponded, though in a relaxed way, to that of the Elect.[107] This said, Auditors were

---

103   Tardieu, *Manichaeism*, 65.
104   BeDuhn, *The Manichaean Body in Discipline and Ritual*, 53.
105   John Paul II, *Letter to Families*, no. 19.
106   BeDuhn, *The Manichaean Body in Discipline and Ritual*, 61. Current textual research of primary and secondary sources has changed much of the way Manichaean belief and practice is now understood. See Tardieu, *Manichaeism*, x.
107   Ibid., 38–39.

permitted to marry[108] or engage in non-marital sexual liaisons,[109] even with prostitutes,[110] so long as they avoided "demonic" procreation.[111] They observed weekly and annual fasts,[112] which included sexual abstinence, but they did not practice the daily asceticism of the Elect. The Elect encouraged sexual abstinence or at least birth control, but accepted the sexual practices of the Auditors, though this cannot be construed as permission for sexual license.[113]

THE NEW MANICHAEISM'S TENDENCY TOWARDS RELATIVISM, UTILITARIANISM, AND "SEXUALITY BECOMING . . . AN AREA FOR MANIPULATION AND EXPLOITATION" AND MANICHAEAN SEXUAL ETHICS

While Manichaean ethics in general might be summed up in the word "abstain," due to its disdain for all things material and bodily, and be expressed by a rigorous asceticism, this is not where John Paul draws a relationship between the New Manichaeism and Manichaean ethical practice. Rather, it is in his understanding of Manichaean attitudes towards sexuality, even if contestable given current scholarship on Manichaeism, that one finds a connection between the New Manichaeism's tendency towards relativism and utilitarianism which leads to "sexuality becoming . . . an area for manipulation and exploitation"[114] and Manichaean ethical attitudes and practices.

---

108 Michel Tardieu indicates that those Auditors who married were exhorted to remain faithful to their spouses (Tardieu, *Manichaeism*, 68).

109 BeDuhn, *The Manichaean Body in Discipline and Ritual*, 61. While BeDuhn points out that sexual license was never encouraged, it is questionable to what degree it was discouraged for the Auditors.

110 In his *Answer to Secundinus, a Manichean*, 21, Augustine accused the Manichees of preferring prostitutes to marriage because they "spare God" by taking steps to avoid child-bearing. See *The Works of Saint Augustine: The Manichean Debate*, 384–385. This text is Augustine, a former Manichee replying to Secundinus, a pious Manichee.

111 Stoyanov, *The Other God: Dualist Religions from Antiquity to the Cathar Heresy*, 112.

112 The annual fast was thirty days, at the end of which there was a confession of sins and the celebration of the Bema festival at which they commemorated the "passion" of Mani (i.e., his imprisonment and execution by the Zoroastrian leadership). The festival was patterned after Christian celebrations like the Easter Vigil.

113 BeDuhn, *The Manichaean Body in Discipline and Ritual*, 61.

114 John Paul II, *Letter to Families*, no. 19.

The Manichees clearly held a negative view of human sexuality, and especially of procreation. Any sensual pleasure or sexual desire was considered sinful, and all things bodily were rejected. The Third Commandment, "Behavior in Accordance with Religion," corresponds precisely with the Seal of the Breast in the doctrine of the Three Seals, which commanded absolute continence and avoidance of procreation which perpetuates the imprisoning of the Light elements in matter congenitally. One could say that the Manichees outright denied procreation as a natural "end" of sexual union. In this one finds a relationship with the New Manichaeism, which is strongly associated with Cartesian Rationalism's rejection of "a truth of creation which must be acknowledged," i.e., that things have a given nature from the Creator, a substantial form and a final cause. If Manichaeism regarded procreation as an end at all, it could only be an evil end, for life/created being is not a "good" as an *ens participatum*, but rather an "evil" that perpetuates the Light's entrapment.

Manichaean Auditors were permitted to marry or engage in a variety of non-marital sexual practices so long as procreation was avoided. In his *Against Secundinus*, Augustine of Hippo—a former Manichaean Auditor turned Catholic apologist—accused the Manichees of preferring prostitutes to marriage because they "spare God" by taking steps to avoid child-bearing.[115] It is clear that while sexual liaisons were not encouraged by the Elect, they were indeed tolerated.

Additionally, marriage had no real value for the Manichees. In fact, it seems that sex between spouses was no more or less licit than any other sexual practice, for all such acts were rooted in the body and the libido, the stigmata of the genesis of the human race born by acts cannibalism and sexuality. Marriage was generally condemned as an institution (though permitted for Auditors), because it normalized sexual behavior and threatened the perpetuation of the Light's entrapment in matter due to its inclination to family life. Thus, it does not seem that marriage, as a rule, was encouraged over non-marital sexual relations; the ideal was to renounce both. The only real rule was that procreation be avoided. For John Paul the abjuration of marriage and procreation

---

115   Augustine, *Answer to Secundinus, a Manichean*, 21, in *The Works of Saint Augustine: The Manichean Debate*, 384-385.

while tolerating sexual liaisons would have effectively constituted a tolerance of acts performed exclusively to indulge the sexual urge.

John Paul had seen Cartesian Rationalism's rejection of "a truth of creation which must be acknowledged" as leading to relativism and utilitarianism. Regarding Manichaeism, John Paul would view the Manichaean Auditors as imposing their own ends on sexual practice, as using the body for the purpose of attaining sexual pleasure, and as manipulating the body in order to prevent procreation and isolate the pleasurable aspects of sex. For him, this is tantamount to persons reciprocally using one another for sexual pleasure and would betray a utilitarian view of the body, and thus of the person. In fact, according to John Paul, the very use of contraception, i.e., the intentional elimination of the possibility of children from the conjugal act, transforms the act into one of mutual use whereby the persons involved reduce themselves to being mere "partners in an erotic experience."[116] It is precisely in this attitude towards procreation that John Paul seems to draw another connection between the New Manichaeism and ancient Manichaeism. According to John Paul, contemporary culture, which he describes as "neo-Manichaean" in his *Letter to Families*, is marked by a pervasive "contraceptive mentality":[117] an attitude whereby procreation is regarded "as an obstacle to personal fulfillment,"[118] and the child, the fruit of conjugal union, is viewed "not as a blessing, but as a danger from which to defend oneself"[119] and as "an enemy to be avoided at all costs."[120] In ancient Manichaeism, procreation was an obstacle to the fulfillment of Manichaean existence, namely, the liberation of the Light elements or Living Soul from the shackles of matter, and thus the child an enemy to be avoided at all costs. Though the motives for avoiding procreation were different for the ancient Manichees than for men and women in our "neo-Manichaean culture," John Paul identifies a relationship between these views and attitudes.

The New Manichaeism, while not regarding the body, sex, and procreation as intrinsically evil as ancient Manichaeism did,

---

116   Wojtyła, *Love and Responsibility*, 234; John Paul II, *Man and Woman He Created Them: A Theology of the Body*, 47:1–48:5.
117   John Paul II, *The Gospel of Life*, no. 13.   118   Ibid.
119   John Paul II, *The Role of the Christian Family in the Modern World*, no. 6.
120   John Paul II, *The Gospel of Life*, no. 13.

does regard the body as an object or instrument to be used to accomplish the end willed by the person using it—an end which is relativistic and dependent on the will of the person imposing it. The Pope holds that this end is often the maximization of pleasure or enjoyment, which, though in contrast with the life-style recommended in ancient Manichaeism and practiced by the Elect, in his view would be expressed in the accepted practices of Manichaean Auditors.

CONCLUSION

By examining contemporary scholarship on the Manichaean views of creation, anthropology, and sexual ethics, since these most closely correspond to John Paul II's diagnosis of a New Manichaeism plaguing contemporary culture, the analogy between the "religion of Mani" and Cartesian Rationalism was established and John Paul's diagnosis supported. While the Pope is not asserting that the New Manichaeism is a form of religious syncretism that holds the eternal co-existence of two opposing principles or "gods," involves the performance of liturgical rites, is marked by the strict ascet-icism, or is in any way historically related to Manicheaism, when one considers both the traditional interpretation of Manichaeism culminating in the work of H. C. Puech and Julien Ries and more recent views expressed by Jason BeDuhn, one finds similarities between Manichaeism and those aspects of Cartesian Rationalism John Paul is identifying with the New Manichaeism.

First, ancient Manichaeism could be said to reject the philos-ophy of being and its corresponding "notion of creation" since it would not acknowledge the intrinsic goodness of creation as *ens participatum* or of the Creator as *Ens subsistens*, or hold that "being" and "the good" are convertible. For the Manichees, all matter is intrinsically evil; at best, the physical world has a utilitarian value. Manichaeism divided the cosmos into two substances, drawing a radical opposition between matter and spirit. While the New Manichaeism may not have held the existence of two opposing "gods," it did divide the cosmos into *res extensa* and *res cogitans*, and set a radical opposition between them. Furthermore, while the New Manichaeism does not consider matter to be intrinsically evil like ancient Manichaeism did, it does regard matter as "raw material" that is essentially value-free.

Second, ancient Manichaeism rejects the hylomorphic view of the human being. The Manichees denied the human being as a composite substance in which "the soul is the form of the body" and failed to view the body subjectively and personally. Also, one finds the "radical opposition" between spirit and matter that characterizes the entire cosmos in human beings in a dramatic fashion—a radical opposition analogous to the one made by Cartesian Rationalism and identified with the New Manichaeism by John Paul. The Manichees rejected the body as having positive intrinsic value; they viewed it as part of the material cosmos, which was regarded negatively. Like the material cosmos as a whole, any value the human body has would be exclusively an instrumental and utilitarian one. The New Manichaeism may not consider the body, as pure extension, to be intrinsically evil like ancient Manichaeism did, yet in its consideration of the body as "raw material," it views the body in primarily a utilitarian and instrumental way, whereby the body of human beings are used the same way things are used.

Lastly, in John Paul's understanding of Manichaean attitudes towards sexuality, particularly their renunciation of procreation and toleration of the sexual practices of the Auditors, the Manichees could be seen as exhibiting a tendency towards relativism, utilitarianism, and to "sexuality becoming . . . an area for manipulation and exploitation."[121] The Manichees outright denied procreation as "good" or as a natural "end" of sexual union. In this one finds a relationship with the New Manichaeism, which is strongly associated with Cartesian Rationalism's rejection of "a truth of creation which must be acknowledged," i.e., that things have a given nature from the Creator, a substantial form and a final cause. In John Paul's view, the practices of the Manichaean Auditors were such that they imposed their own subjective ends on sexual practice, using the body for the purpose of attaining sexual pleasure and manipulating it in order to prevent procreation and isolate the pleasurable aspects of sex, and that this would be tantamount to persons reciprocally using one another for sexual pleasure and would display a utilitarian view of the body, and thus of the person. In fact, in our contemporary "neo-Manichaean" culture marked by a pervasive "contraceptive mentality," the sexual act is reduced to an act of mutual use and the child is viewed as "an obstacle

---

121   John Paul II, *Letter to Families*, no. 19.

to personal fulfillment" and "an enemy to be avoided at all costs." John Paul seems to find a resemblance between this attitude and that of the ancient Manichees for whom procreation was to be avoided at all costs and was seen an obstacle to the fulfillment of Manichaean existence, i.e., to the liberation of the Light elements or Living Soul from the shackles of matter.

Since the Manichaean label has its own characteristic use in Christian tradition, a comparison of this use with John Paul's use of the label in *Letter to Families*, no. 19 could offer insight as to why John Paul chose to diagnose a New Manichaeism over other possible diagnoses. It also may serve to identify what is novel in the Pope's application of the Manichaean label in the letter, revealing the distinctive features of this spiritual disease.

CHAPTER 4

The Relationship of the New Manichaeism to Other Diagnoses of Manichaeism in Christian Tradition

INTRODUCTION

In order to appreciate fully John Paul's diagnosis of a New Manichaeism in the *Letter to Families*, one needs to understand the distinction between it and similar spiritual diseases that have plagued the Church in her history. This will necessitate a comparison between the way the Manichaean label typically has been used in Christian tradition with the way John Paul II employs it in the letter. Such a comparison will require looking to contemporary scholarship on medieval heterodox communities in order to show how orthodox theologians utilized the label during that period to describe certain sects that held heterodox positions. In turning to these heterodox positions and how they were associated with the ancient Manichees, however, it is neither the intent of the chapter to delve into all the complexities of this period in Christian history nor to gauge the historical accuracy of or place a value judgment on the merits or demerits of the label's use in that history. Such topics are beyond its scope. It is enough to say that the label's history is quite complex.[1]

---

1   The label "Manichaean" was often brusquely applied, and, because of the label's historical power, would immediately evoke a sense of horror and swift response from church and state (Malcolm Lambert, *The Cathars* [Oxford, UK: Blackwell Publishers, 1998], 5; Steven Runciman, *The Medieval Manichee: A Study of the Christian Dualist Heresy* [Cambridge, UK: Cambridge University Press, 1947], 17–18; Yuri Stoyanov, *The Other God: Dualist Religions from Antiquity to the Cathar Heresy* [New Haven, CT: Yale University Press, 2000], 293). It is widely attested that sects thus labeled were often subject to vilification,

THE GENERAL USE OF THE MANICHAEAN LABEL IN CHRISTIAN TRADITION

As is broadly known, the utilization of the Manichaean label by Christian apologists is not original to Pope John Paul II. During the Middle Ages—the period spanning roughly from the fifth century and the fall of the western Roman Empire to the fifteenth century and the early Modern period—there were a number of sects holding divergent views from orthodox Christianity which were described as "Manichaean" or "neo-Manichaean" by their opponents, be they political or religious ones. It was a common label assigned to those communities which were alleged to embrace beliefs and practices in common with ancient Manichaeism, whether or not those communities had any historical connection to Mani himself.[2]

According to the renowned historian Sir Steven Runciman:

> When an educated orthodox theologian spoke of sects
> or doctrines being 'Manichaean,' he had no intention
> of evoking all the complicated tenets that were Mani's.
> He merely wished to imply Dualism and Dualism in the
> strictest form.[3]

Dmitri Obolensky, author of the definitive work on the Bogomils, in reference to the use of the "Manichaean" label by one heresiologist,[4] states that he uses the term in a "general sense" and:

> ...conforms to the common habit of Orthodox writers of
> using this epithet to designate a number of sects whose
> teaching was based to a greater or lesser degree on the
> dualism associated with the doctrines of Mani...[5]

---

distortion, suppression, persecution, and even crusade (Malcolm Barber, *The Cathars: Dualist Heretics in Languedoc in the High Middle Ages* [Harlow, England: Pearson Education Limited, 2000], 11).

2   Some historians—among them Dmitri Obolensky, Steven Runciman, and Hans Soderberg and, more recently and tentatively, Yuri Stoyanov—have been prepared to accept the essential continuity of dualism, tracing it from Gnosticism and Manichaeism to the Paulicians and thence to the Bogomils and the Cathars. Others, like Malcom Barber and Malcolm Lambert, deny such a continuity.

3   Runciman, *The Medieval Manichee: A Study of the Christian Dualist Heresy*, 25.

4   John of Exarch (c. 860–930)

5   Dmitri Obolensky, *The Bogomils: A Study in Balkan Neo-Manichaeism* (Cambridge, UK: Cambridge University Press, 1948), 95.

In utilizing the Manichaean label, the Christian apologists of the Middle Ages generally did not intend to associate the intricacies of ancient Manichaean doctrine or practice with the heterodox communities with which they came into contact.[6] The label had come to be used as "a synonym for Dualist, to describe people with views like Mani's rather than followers of Mani."[7] Thus, it seems that one can posit two ways in which the term "Manichaean" (or "neo-Manichaean") was applied: 1) as a synonym for Dualism, and 2) as a term describing people with views, to a greater or lesser degree, like those of Mani.

It is important to note that the medieval heterodox communities to which the Manichaean label was applied did not see themselves as "dualists" or even as heretical sects, but simply as pure or good Christians.[8] The term "dualism" is a later development, "a theological and scholarly construct for discussing certain religious and philosophical ideas,"[9] first employed by Thomas Hyde (1636-1703) as a descriptive term for religions that hold to a belief in the existence of two coeternal principles,[10] and later by Christian Wolff (1679-1754) to define philosophical systems like Descartes's which were believed to posit mind and matter as two distinct substances. This latter use, while different than one referencing two coeternal principles, is not unrelated to it given that the belief in two coeternal principles in almost every case set spirit and matter into radical opposition, particularly the human soul and body.

It could be argued that "the most rigid and classical form of dualism in historical times is to be found in Manichaeism."[11] This

---

6 Runciman, *The Medieval Manichee: A Study of the Christian Dualist Heresy*, 18.
7 Ibid., 49; Stoyanov, *The Other God: Dualist Religions from Antiquity to the Cathar Heresy*, 1-2, 238.
8 In fact, the Bogomil and Cathar "Elect" or "Perfect" were called "Good Christians" by their followers. See Barber, *The Cathars: Dualist Heretics in Languedoc in the High Middle Ages*, 12, 101; Lambert, *The Cathars*, 30.
9 Stoyanov, *The Other God: Dualist Religions from Antiquity to the Cathar Heresy*, 228.
10 Ibid., 2. Even within this designation, the term dualism was used variously. Ugo Bianchi's typology of dualism defines three important lines of distinction: absolute dualism from moderate (also known as mitigated or "monarchian") dualism, dialectic dualism from eschatological dualism, and cosmic dualism from anti-cosmic dualism. It was anti-cosmic dualism that was strongly anti-somatic and drew a radical opposition between spirit and matter (see Stoyanov, *The Other God: Dualist Religions from Antiquity to the Cathar Heresy*, 4).
11 Obolensky, *The Bogomils: A Study in Balkan Neo-Manichaeism*, 5.

is partly why Malcolm Barber, an authority on crusading orders,[12] states, "it is entirely understandable that medieval churchmen should see contemporary dualists as Manichaeans."[13] And after considering the similarities between these medieval sects and the ancient Manichees in belief and practice, and even mythology, a leading scholar of medieval heterodox communities, Malcolm Lambert, admits that these likenesses "not wholly inappropriately, earned them the label Manichee."[14]

If the term "Manichaean" (or "neo-Manichaean") was applied generally in Christian tradition as a "synonym for Dualism" and as a term describing people "with views, to a greater or lesser degree, like those of Mani," then, based on the preceding chapter's analysis of the relationship between the New Manichaeism and the beliefs and practice of the ancient Manichees, one could say that John Paul II's use of the Manichaean label in the *Letter to Families* coincides with the label's general use in Christian tradition. John Paul's

12 Marcia L. Colish, "The Cathars/The Cathars," Review of Malcolm Barber's *The Cathars: Dualist Heretics in Languedoc in the High Middle Ages* (Harlow, England: Pearson Education Limited, 2000), and Malcolm Lambert's *The Cathars* (Oxford, UK: Blackwell Publishers, 1998), *Church History*, Vol. 71, Issue 1(March 2002): 181.

13 Barber, *The Cathars: Dualist Heretics in Languedoc in the High Middle Ages*, 12. That Barber makes this statement is quite significant given 1) He emphasizes the fact that Manichaeism itself had disappeared from the Byzantine Empire by approximately the mid-sixth century and rejects the historical derivation of the medieval "neo-Manichaeans" from ancient Manichaeism, and 2) He is intensely skeptical of the use of the term, citing its religious and political propaganda value and the intention to vilify, distort, and suppress those so labeled (11). See also Lambert, *The Cathars*, 12; Stoyanov, *The Other God: Dualist Religions from Antiquity to the Cathar Heresy*, 293.

14 Lambert, *The Cathars*, 11–12. When referring to certain Cathar leaders Runciman writes, "all to some extent deserve the epithet of Manichaean hurled at them" (*The Medieval Manichee: A Study of the Christian Dualist Heresy*, 121). It is important to note that one main reason why the opponents of these sects referred to them as "Manichaean" is because Manichaeism was well-known as an ominous adversary of the early Church that none less than Augustine of Hippo, a once Manichaean auditor turned Catholic apologist, had prolifically opposed (see Runciman, *The Medieval Manichee: A Study of the Christian Dualist Heresy*, 17–18). Some scholars even allege that heresiologists supplemented their gaps in knowledge about the doctrine of these sects or associated them with salacious behavior based on the works of Augustine and not on facts or experience (see Lambert, *The Cathars*, 6; Barber, *The Cathars: Dualist Heretics in Languedoc in the High Middle Ages*, 11).

identification of the New Manichaeism with the rejection of the hylomorphic view of the human being, with the rejection of the philosophy of being and its corresponding "notion of creation" (and thus of the intrinsic goodness of creation as *ens participatum* or of the Creator as *Ens subsistens*), with the tendency towards relativism, utilitarianism, and to "sexuality becoming... an area for manipulation and exploitation," and with the culturally pervasive "contraceptive mentality" could all be said to be views that are "dualistic" and "to a greater or lesser degree" resemble those of the ancient Manichees.

THE SPECIFIC APPLICATION OF THE MANICHAEAN LABEL TO THE PAULICIANS, BOGOMILS, AND CATHARS

A brief survey of the beliefs of the three most prominent sects that "earned the label Manichee" will serve to demonstrate how the label was applied in Christian tradition and provide the data necessary for making comparison with John Paul's application in *Letter to Families*, no. 19. The first of these medieval "Manichees," the Paulicians, can be safely placed in the middle of the seventh century[15] and were considered by Peter of Sicily and the Byzantine historians and theologians that followed him[16] to be direct descendants of the ancient Manichees.[17] The Paulicians believed

---

15   Runciman, *The Medieval Manichee: A Study of the Christian Dualist Heresy*, 46.
16   Obolensky, *The Bogomils: A Study in Balkan Neo-Manichaeism*, 31. In fact, for them "Manichaeism and Paulicianism are for them the same heresy..." (31–32); Stoyanov, *The Other God: Dualist Religions from Antiquity to the Cathar Heresy*, 127. Obolensky gives credence to this stating: "The Armenian historian Samuel of Ani describes the arrival in Armenia in 588 of heretics from Syria, 'men with words like honey,' equipped with a library of 'false books' which they translated into Armenian to benefit the local inhabitants. The list of these heterodox works includes the famous Living Gospel of Mani and two apocryphal scriptures, the *Liber Paenitentiae Adam* and the *Liber de infantia Salvatoris*, both known to have been used by the Manichaeans. The importance of this source lies in the proof it provides of the presence of Manichaeism at the close of the sixth century in the same country which, only some fifty years later, became the centre of the newly appeared neo-Manichaean sect of the Paulicians" (17–18).
17   According to Peter of Sicily, the Paulicians were named after a certain Paul of Samasota. Paul and his brother John were the sons of a Manichaean woman named Callinice, who formed them in Manichaean beliefs and practices. They engaged in the proselytization of the surrounding regions and their numbers grew. According to Dmitri Obolensky, Peter of Sicily must be regarded as "the fundamental, almost exclusive, source for all our knowledge of the Paulicians of Tephrice" (Obolensky, *The Bogomils: A Study*

in two coeternal principles: the "Heavenly Being," the "Three in One," who is the God of the spiritual world, and the Creator, the Demiurge who made the material world and rules it. As a result, they rejected the Old Testament and the God of the Old Testament. They followed a Docetic Christology, holding that Christ was not really born of Mary but "passed through her as through a pipe," and that he only "seemed to die" on the cross, to which they attached no value. Thus, the Incarnation and Resurrection were summarily excluded. The Paulicians did not ascribe to a strict asceticism and did not bind their leaders to abstain from sexual intercourse or wine as the ancient Manichees did.[18] They rejected the Sacraments and forsook Marriage, though they permitted extra-marital sexual liaisons. Additionally, the Paulicians were rather unruly and bellicose; they led an active life, which could even include war. Whether there existed a division between Elect and Auditor is unclear.

The Paulicians seem to have contributed to the rise of Bogomilism in Bulgaria,[19] which is a second group of so-called medieval

---

in *Balkan Neo-Manichaeism*, 31), and he, along with Steven Runciman, is a strong supporter of Peter's reliability (Obolensky, *The Bogomils: A Study in Balkan Neo-Manichaeism*, 43; Runciman, *The Medieval Manichee: A Study of the Christian Dualist Heresy*, 46–47).

18   Obolensky, *The Bogomils: A Study in Balkan Neo-Manichaeism*, 44; Stoyanov, *The Other God: Dualist Religions from Antiquity to the Cathar Heresy*, 127–128.

19   Ibid., 38. "Heresy ... developed in Bulgaria as a result of two factors: on the one hand, a basis of Eastern dualistic doctrines, Paulician and Massalian, which penetrated to Bulgaria as a result of the colonizing policy of the Byzantine emperors, and on the other, pre-existing and contemporary conditions in Bulgaria exceptionally favorable to the spread of anti-ecclesiastical teaching" (Obolensky, *The Bogomils: A Study in Balkan Neo-Manichaeism*, 107), e.g., the worldliness of the monks. Another key factor was the general religious toleration and syncretism that was characteristic of Bulgaria (Stoyanov, *The Other God: Dualist Religions from Antiquity to the Cathar Heresy*, 144). In order to defend the Empire in the east and in the north, several Byzantine emperors adopted the policy of transplanting Armenian heretical groups to Thrace, and the Paulicians seem to have been relocated there in 757 (Stoyanov, *The Other God: Dualist Religions from Antiquity to the Cathar Heresy*, 150). Yet, from the eighth through the tenth centuries the borderland between Byzantium and Bulgaria was continually changing rule, and it is possible that prisoners taken from Thrace by the Bulgarians may have included Paulicians. Eventually, they were able to proselytize in this new land. Then, in the middle of the ninth century, two great cities of Thrace were annexed by Bulgaria. According to Obolensky, "it is possible to state with certainty that the Paulician heresy was a strong and dangerous

"Manichees." The Bogomils are alleged to have been founded by Bogomil the Priest[20] during the reign of Peter the Tsar in the tenth century, and were characterized by Theophlact, the Patriarch of Constantinople, around the year 950, as both "ancient" and "Manichaen."[21] The Bogomils were Dualists who believed that the Devil created the world.[22] Their cosmogonic myth shared many similarities with that of the ancient Manichees: all matter, including the human body, had a diabolical origin and the human soul alone was associated with the Father, sex and procreation were linked to lustful desires and to Satan's work, and the goal of life was the final liberation of the soul from its imprisonment in matter and the eventual destruction of the material cosmos.[23] Thus, the Bogomils

---

force in Bulgaria in the third quarter of the ninth century…" (Obolensky, *The Bogomils: A Study in Balkan Neo-Manichaeism*, 82). By the middle of the tenth century, "the teachings of the Paulicians and Massalians had coalesced" and a new sect arose which "assumed a Slavonic character" (Obolensky, *The Bogomils: A Study in Balkan Neo-Manichaeism*, 111).

20   Everything that is known about Bogomil the priest comes from Cosmas's *Sermon against the Heretics*: "In the days of the Orthodox Tsar Peter there lived in the land of Bulgaria a priest called Bogomil (loved of God) who in reality was not loved of God (Bogu ne mil), who was the first to sow heresy in the land of Bulgaria" (as cited in Runciman, *The Medieval Manichee: A Study of the Christian Dualist Heresy*, 67).

21   Obolensky, *The Bogomils: A Study in Balkan Neo-Manichaeism*, 112; Runciman, *The Medieval Manichee: A Study of the Christian Dualist Heresy*, 67. Theophlact actually called the Bogomils "Paulicianism mixed with Manichaeism."

22   Barber, *The Cathars: Dualist Heretics in Languedoc in the High Middle Ages*, 24. According to Cosmas, a medieval Bulgarian priest and writer. He wrote an anti-Bogomil treatise called *Sermon against the Heretics*. Cosmas seems to have known of the heresy first-hand, and was "almost a contemporary with Bogomil" (Runciman, *The Medieval Manichee: A Study of the Christian Dualist Heresy*, 73.) Though there is some question as to whether the Bogomils were Monarchian or Absolute dualists, Cosmas associates them with the latter and Runciman states that this was likely Bogomil the Priest's own view (Runciman, *The Medieval Manichee: A Study of the Christian Dualist Heresy*, 79).

23   Satan created earth and a "second heaven" which he could rule. He created the material part of human beings, but their souls come from the Father and are of his substance. Satan, in the form of a serpent, seduced Eve, had intercourse with her with his tail, and in this way a son, Cain, and a daughter, Calomena, were created. This caused Adam to become jealous, and so he had intercourse with Eve, and in this way Abel, and later Seth, were created. The Father, desiring to save what was his in man, sent Christ to earth. Christ entered the Virgin through her ear and emerged the same

too rejected the Old Testament and the God of the Old Testament, and held a Docetic Christology, interpreting the miracles of Christ figuratively since he would not touch matter, "the principle of evil and corruption."[24] The Sacraments were spurned. A life of renunciation was demanded, one that avoided contact with the world of the flesh: they did not eat meat or drink wine, and they discouraged marriage and procreation.[25] They held that the human procreation was a law of the demon, and enforced sexual abstinence on their "Elect."[26] In fact, "the Bogomils were in the habit of turning away as from a bad smell, spitting and holding their noses whenever they met children of baptismal age."[27] While through the fourteenth century the Bogomils were never accused of sexual licentiousness, after that time, a merge between the Bogomils and Massalians (a group infamous for debauchery) occurred and even the Bogomils lost their reputation for puritanism.[28] The Bogomils of the eleventh and twelfth centuries had the classic Manichaean divisions: the "believers" who were not bound to rigorous asceticism and the 'perfect' who were. It is probable that this division may have existed in the tenth century as well.[29]

A third group of medieval "Manichees," the Cathars, likely emerged in the early twelfth century and can be considered "the greatest heretical challenge faced by the Catholic Church in the twelfth and thirteenth centuries."[30] It is probably the example of medieval "Manichaeism" most widely known (though by the name "Albigensians"[31]), and it attracted notable opponents like

---

way. In the end, the power of Satan would be overcome, the spiritual part of man belonging to the Father would be reclaimed, and the world and all flesh would be consumed.

24 Obolensky, *The Bogomils: A Study in Balkan Neo-Manichaeism*, 182.
25 Barber, *The Cathars: Dualist Heretics in Languedoc in the High Middle Ages*, 24; Obolensky, *The Bogomils: A Study in Balkan Neo-Manichaeism*, 127.
26 Obolensky, *The Bogomils: A Study in Balkan Neo-Manichaeism*, 115.
27 Ibid.
28 Obolensky, *The Bogomils: A Study in Balkan Neo-Manichaeism*, 251.
29 Ibid., 129.
30 Barber, *The Cathars: Dualist Heretics in Languedoc in the High Middle Ages*, 1.
31 It is interesting to note that the names of the dualist communities often came from the town or region in which their church was established. For example, the earliest bishopric in southern France was at Albi, and thus the heretics from there were called Albigensians, although this name became popularly associated with the heretical movement as a whole.

Bernard of Clairvaux and Dominic de Guzman, the latter of which established the Order of Preachers to oppose Cathar doctrines and to defend orthodoxy. Our knowledge of Cathar beliefs and practices is quite robust due to the chronicles of the Inquisitors who questioned vast numbers of heretics and meticulously recorded their replies.[32] Scholars generally hold that, whatever their intentions, the Inquisitors' records give us a "fair idea of what Cathars believed."[33] What is found is that "there is a remarkable similarity between Bogomil and Cathar doctrines and habits."[34] In fact, according to Malcolm Lambert, "that there was substantial transmission of ritual and ideas from Bogomilism to Catharism is beyond reasonable doubt."[35] The Cathars believed in the existence of two co-eternal and conflicting principles, the Father or Good Principle identified with all things spiritual and Satan or the Evil Principle with all things material. Thus, Cathars held a radical opposition between spirit and matter in the cosmos and within human beings. They ascribed to a sweeping anthropological dualism, and rejected the Old Testament and its Creator-God,

---

32   See Emmanuel Le Roy Ladurie, *Montaillou: The Promised Land of Error* (New York: George Braziller, Inc., 1978) for an analysis of these records in terms of the sociology of religion.

33   Runciman, *The Medieval Manichee: A Study of the Christian Dualist Heresy*, 147.

34   Ibid., 163.

35   Lambert, *The Cathars*, 33. According to Malcolm Barber, "The origins of Catharism remain controversial. Most historians accept that the dualist Bogomil Church, established in parts of Macedonia and Bulgaria from at least the 930s, played a role in the formation of western Catharism, although tracing possible links with earlier dualistic religions such as Paulicianism, and beyond that to the Manichaeans and the Gnostics, remains a virtually impossible task... there is, though, little agreement on the extent and importance of Bogomil influence, and still less on the chronology of its spread" (*The Cathars: Dualist Heretics in Languedoc in the High Middle Ages*, 2). Although, Malcolm Lambert cautions that the Bogomils and the Cathars were "far from being identical" (33) and that "The evidence is that, though Catharism was intimately linked with and owed much to the Bogomils and their teachings, it none the less emerged as an independent movement with characteristics of its own and, by the time it had been detected by Church authorities, had been thoroughly westernized... Powerful as it is, all our evidence of a link between Bogomilism and Catharism before 1143 is inferential based on likeness between ritual, diet, religious practice and doctrines. That Byzantium and the West came into more intimate contact from the eleventh century onwards is undeniable" (*The Cathars*, 34).

seeing physical creation as intrinsically evil. They thus repudiated the Sacraments and held a Docetic Christology. The Cathars seemed to share the cosmogonic myths of the Bogomils with some variations: "the movements shared a common aversion to matter and a set of vivid, even gross metaphors, allegories and narratives explaining creation."[36] One particular variation bears a striking resemblance to the ancient Manichaean myth and reveals a characteristic "Manichaean pessimism" about the world, for in it angels fell from heaven having been aroused to lust by the form of a beautiful woman and became entrapped in human bodies as the "souls" of men and women,[37] and the beasts and birds were made from the corpses of miscarried human fetuses. Such myths explain the Cathar contempt for all things bodily, a contempt that was manifested in a life of strict asceticism. However, while "the code of abstinence formed the backbone of Cathar morality,"[38] this life of denial was lived out differently depending on one's place in the Cathar hierarchy, similar to ancient Manichaeism. A rank of adepts, known as the *perfecti* (Perfect) were held to the ideal of abstinence and strict asceticism, and a rank of lay supporters, known as *credentes* (Believers),[39] were responsible for tending to

36   According to Lambert, "Beasts and birds, it was said, were of human flesh—the fetuses of pregnant women which fell from heaven on to earth after they had miscarried during battle between the forces of God and Satan. The prohibition of eating their flesh thus amounted to a prohibition of cannibalism" (*Medieval Heresy: Popular Movements from the Gregorian Reform to the Reformation* (New York: Barnes and Noble Books, 1998), 122). Then Satan "made man in his own image with a body of clay, and commanded the angel of the third heaven to enter the body of Adam and the angel of the second heaven that of Eve. Satan next created Paradise, in which he planted a reed, which was 'the tree of the knowledge of good and evil' referred to in the Book of Genesis. In this reed Satan hid himself, emerged in the form of a serpent and seduced Eve. Then he taught his angel who lived in Adam's body to commit sexual intercourse with her. A product of this intercourse, man, as a compound of a mortal body created by Satan and a soul originating from a fallen angel, was intended to perpetuate the rule of the Devil in the world until its consummation" (Obolensky, *The Bogomils: A Study in Balkan Neo-Manichaeism*, 227-228).

37   Lambert, *Medieval Heresy: Popular Movements from the Gregorian Reform to the Reformation*, 120, 124.

38   Ibid., 109.

39   There is evidence of three possible ranks: Listeners, Believers, and Perfect (Stoyanov, *The Other God: Dualist Religions from Antiquity to the Cathar*

the needs of the Perfect but were not bound by the same morality that they were.[40] The Cathars rejected the flesh and the world, abstained from meat, wine, marriage, and sexual intercourse, and condemned procreation for its perpetuation of evil flesh. For all their disdain for marriage, sex, and procreation, the Cathar Perfect generally tolerated the immoral sexual practices of the Believers as long as it did not result in procreation, though current scholarship on medieval heterodoxy disavows the popular narrative that the Cathars were characterized by sexual indulgence that included unnatural sexual acts and orgiastic behavior.[41] Children were considered as demons. Occasional sexual liaisons were preferred to marriage,[42] since marriage institutionalized sexual behavior and lent itself to family life.[43] The goal of life according to the Cathars was to release the soul from its imprisonment in matter, and thus they believed in metempsychosis or the transmigration of souls.[44] Some of the Perfect even seem to have practiced

---

Heresy, 188) and an "inner circle" of elite among the Perfect who pursued higher learning and were privy to certain "secret doctrine" (Stoyanov, *The Other God: Dualist Religions from Antiquity to the Cathar Heresy*, 261; Lambert, *Medieval Heresy: Popular Movements from the Gregorian Reform to the Reformation*, 58).

40   Lambert, *The Cathars*, 210-22.

41   Though Runciman states that, due to the regularity of such accusations, "the accounts of Dualist orgies cannot be all entirely fictitious" (Runciman, *The Medieval Manichee: A Study of the Christian Dualist Heresy*, 176), contemporary scholars, in light of improved textual criticism, see the inconsistencies among such accusations and the fact that they originate from those who opposed these sects as major blows to their credibility (see Carol Lansing, *Power and Purity: Cathar Heresy in Medieval Italy* [New York: Oxford University Press, 1998], 149-150; R. I. Moore, *The War on Heresy: Faith and Power in Medieval Europe* [London: Profile Books, 2014], 6-7). Yuri Stoyanov, for example, calls such accusations "high medieval anti-heretical stereotypes" (*The Other God: Dualist Religions from Antiquity to the Cathar Heresy*, 238).

42   Runciman, *The Medieval Manichee: A Study of the Christian Dualist Heresy*, 176.

43   Runciman holds that there was definitely an "easy-going attitude" about sexual morality (*The Medieval Manichee: A Study of the Christian Dualist Heresy*, 177), and that the Cathars "frankly admitted that they preferred casual debauchery to marriage, because marriage was a more serious affair, an official regularization of a wicked thing": casual debauchery involved isolated sins, while marriage was a "state of sin" (Runciman, *The Medieval Manichee: A Study of the Christian Dualist Heresy*, 176).

44   The Cathar goal was to have one's soul "escape the chain of being, reach the body of a man or woman who would receive the *Consolamentum* (a sort

suicide by starvation known as the *Endura*, or participated in non-voluntary euthanasia.[45]

By looking at the beliefs of these three sects in light of how the Manichaean label was traditionally applied, one can understand why they were called Manichaean. Placing to the side the potential historical connection to ancient Manichaeism as well as any political or propagandist reason for the label's use, one can discern that these sects were indeed Dualist and held views, to a greater or lesser degree, like those of Mani. The Paulicians, Bogomils, and Cathars all believed in the existence of two co-eternal principles, a good one associated with all things spiritual, and an evil one associated with all things material or bodily. They all viewed the created world, with its diabolical origin, as evil and the source of corruption. While the Paulicians did not demand a strict asceticism from their members, for the Bogomils and Cathars a code of strict abstention was the ideal, which included refraining from meat (only taking as much nourishment as was necessary to sustain life), wine, and sex. The cosmogonic myths of the Bogomils and Cathars bore striking resemblance to the ancient Manichaean myths, with human beings created through a series of repugnant acts of cannibalism and sexuality. Thus, all things having to do with sexuality and especially

---

of spiritual baptism brought about by the laying on of hands after making vows to the ascetic rigors of The Perfect) and so pass to heaven, discarding the material envelope in which the soul had been enclosed" (Lambert, *The Cathars*, 161). "The standard inquisitor's question about belief in a bodily resurrection was designed to tease out the heretical belief in the evil nature of the body" (161). An "un-*Consoled*" and evil life merited the soul's return as a lower creature in the chain of being, whereas one who inhabited the body of a human being who had received and preserved the *Consolamentum* would return to heaven. While Cathars seem generally to have been indifferent to sins committed before the *Consolamentum* (Barber, *The Cathars: Dualist Heretics in Languedoc in the High Middle Ages*, 94), the commission of sins afterward would annul it. Thus, there was a common practice of delaying the *Consolamentum* until close to death.

45 Runciman, *The Medieval Manichee: A Study of the Christian Dualist Heresy*, 158-159. The *Endura* was accompanied by a ritual and the deathbed was a scene of rejoicing, with the dying man or woman being regarded with deep reverential admiration. How far such an aggressive means to ending life was used to preserve the *Consolamentum* is not known—and this does seem to be the main reason for such measures—but the *Endura* was neither a marginal nor decadent phenomenon (see also Barber, *The Cathars: Dualist Heretics in Languedoc in the High Middle Ages*, 103-104 and Lambert, *The Cathars*, 241-244).

with procreation (which is the perpetuation of the evil and demonic in the world) were to be shunned. All three sects forsook marriage. However, the Paulicians did not demand sexual abstinence from their leaders, and though the Cathar "Perfect" did not sanction the immoral sexual practices of the "Believers," they tolerated them so long as "demonic procreation" was avoided. Occasional liaisons were preferred to marriage, which institutionalized sexual behavior and tended towards family life. While it is possible that the Paulicians held the traditional Manichaean divisions among members, it is clear that the Bogomils and Cathars were divided into the Perfect and the Believers, with the life of strict asceticism solely applying to the Perfect. All three sects held a Docetic Christology, repudiated the Sacraments, rejected the Old Testament and its Creator-God, believed in metempsychosis or the transmigration of souls, and viewed the goal of earthly existence as the liberation of the soul from its imprisonment in matter.

COMPARING JOHN PAUL II'S DIAGNOSIS OF A NEW MANICHAEISM WITH PREVIOUS DIAGNOSES OF MANICHAEISM IN CHRISTIAN TRADITION

This brief survey of the beliefs of the three most prominent sects of so-called medieval "Manichees," in light of the general introductory comments about the use of the Manichaean label in Christian tradition, has permitted us to see how the diagnoses of Manichaeism was made. When one compares these diagnoses to John Paul's in the *Letter to Families,* one discovers why John Paul chose to identify the spiritual disease infecting the human family as a New Manichaeism. Generally, John Paul's use of the Manichaean label coincides with certain ways the label was utilized by orthodox theologians to characterize medieval heterodox communities. However, there are instances in which the Pope's use of the label in the *Letter to Families* is quite novel and distinctive.

There are three main ways in which John Paul II's diagnosis of a New Manichaeism resembles like diagnoses during the Middle Ages. First, John Paul II associates the New Manichaeism with the rejection of the philosophy of being and its corresponding "notion of creation," as well as with its subsequent rejection a truth of creation which must be acknowledged and of the God of Creation who is *Ens subsistens.* It is clear that the Manichaean label was applied to the medieval heterodox communities in a similar way. The Paulicians, Bogomils, and Cathars all believed that Satan, the evil demiurge, was the creator and ruler of the material world. In all three cases, the Old Testament and the Creator-God of the Old Testament was rejected. Matter was considered the "principle of evil and corruption."[46] Like the New Manichaeism, medieval "Manichaeism" would reject the intrinsic goodness of creation as *ens participatum*, a Creator as *Ens subsistens*, or that "being" and "the good" are convertible. Thus, it would reject the notion that all finite, created being has a positive value, is "good," by virtue of its existence as a participated likeness or similitude of the divine *esse*.

Second, John Paul II associates the New Manichaeism with the failure to view the human body as having positive intrinsic value. The Manichaean label was applied to all three medieval sects for similar reasons. For the medieval "Manichees," the body was not identified personally or subjectively, but merely as a "material envelope"[47] which was to be discarded once the soul of the Perfect left it upon death. Additionally, John Paul uses the Manichaean label to identify a "radical opposition" placed between all that is spiritual and bodily in man and the rejection of hylomorphism. The medieval "Manichees" were labelled as such for similar beliefs: they clearly rejected hylomorphism and held the "conviction of the utter incompatibility of the body and soul."[48] For these medieval sects, the soul was associated with intrinsic goodness, either as a fallen angel entrapped in the bodily prison or as the creation of the Father who gave life to human beings at the request of Satan. In short, whatever is "spiritual" in man is substantially distinct from whatever is "bodily" in man. And while it seems that these medieval sects did not even regarded the body for its utilitarian value, as the ancient Manichees had (e.g., as the "salvation machine"), a utilitarian view of the body may be divined in the passive attitude of these medieval heterodox sects to the sexual

---

46 Obolensky, *The Bogomils: A Study in Balkan Neo-Manichaeism*, 182.

47 Lambert, *The Cathars*, 161.

48 Lambert, *Medieval Heresy: Popular Movements from the Gregorian Reform to the Reformation*, 121. " ... at the heart of the Cathar experience lay a profound conviction of the incompatibility of flesh and spirit, the fundamental Gnostic view of the jewel in the mud, the spirit imprisoned ... the conviction of the evil character of the flesh and all material creation" (Lambert, *The Cathars*, 198).

practices of the ordinary believer which allowed for the using of the body for sexual pleasure so long as procreation was avoided.

Third, John Paul identifies a culture in which sexuality becomes "more an area for manipulation and exploitation" than an expression of married love as "neo-Manichaean." A similar diagnosis was made by Catholic apologists in the Middle Ages. Especially for the Bogomils and Cathars, "the utter denial of the value of carnal affection and family life"[49] was foundational and "the rejection of marriage is a recurrent theme."[50] Marriage was viewed as a sinful state[51] not only because it institutionalized the indulgence of the flesh, but because it was ordered to the propagation of the species, which was seen as the perpetuation of evil and corrupt matter. The Paulicians forsook marriage but did not demand sexual abstinence from their adherents. For all their hostility to sexuality, the Bogomils eventually lost their reputation for puritanism,[52] and the Cathar Perfect tolerated the occasional immoral sexual practices of Believers so long as procreation was excluded. The Bogomils were so averse to procreation that they "were in the habit of turning away as from a bad smell" when they encountered babies.[53] For the Cathars, pregnancy was believed to be from Satan himself, and the fruit of the womb a "demon" from which a pregnant woman should pray to be liberated. For John Paul, all of these allegations, would indicate a certain acceptance of manipulation in the sexual sphere and a tolerance of acts performed exclusively to indulge the sexual urge. As with the ancient Manichees before them, though the toleration of sexual liaisons among the "laity" cannot be construed as permission for sexual license, the most pressing concern was that procreation be avoided. Herein lies another parallel between John Paul's diagnosis of a New Manichaeism and similar diagnoses in Christian tradition. Though the motives for avoiding procreation were different for the so-called medieval "Manichees" than for men and women in our "neo-Manichaean culture," as previously discussed, the "neo-Manichaean culture" that John Paul observes

---

49   Lambert, *Medieval Heresy: Popular Movements from the Gregorian Reform to the Reformation,* 114.   50   Lambert, *The Cathars,* 12.
51   Runciman, *The Medieval Manichee: A Study of the Christian Dualist Heresy,* 176.
52   Obolensky, *The Bogomils: A Study in Balkan Neo-Manichaeism,* 251.
53   Barber, *The Cathars: Dualist Heretics in Languedoc in the High Middle Ages,* 24; Obolensky, *The Bogomils: A Study in Balkan Neo-Manichaeism,* 127.

is marked by a pervasive "contraceptive mentality,"[54] whereby persons reciprocally use one another for sexual pleasure, procreation is regarded "as an obstacle to personal fulfillment,"[55] and the child is viewed "not as a blessing, but as a danger from which to defend oneself"[56] and as "an enemy to be avoided at all costs."[57]

Clearly, however, there are differences between how the Manichaean label was used with respect to the Paulicians, Bogomils, and Cathars and how John Paul II is employing it in the *Letter to Families*, which display the novelty of the Pope's use. First, John Paul does not identify the New Manichaeism with the belief in the existence of opposing co-eternal principles, a Good principle associated with all things spiritual and an Evil principle associated with all things material including the creation of the physical cosmos. This was a prime belief of the medieval sects. Additionally, and related, John Paul is not associating the New Manichaeism with the belief in the intrinsic evil of the material world. Consequently, he does not indicate that contemporary men and women undergoing the experience of the New Manichaeism participate in any of the rigorous ascetical practices in which these medieval heterodox communities participated and that would naturally accompany the rejection of matter.[58] This said, John Paul would hold that the New Manichaeism does include the belief in a type of cosmological dualism in which the universe is divided into two substances, mind and matter, with mind being the "self" or "thinking thing" and matter being "pure extension" and "raw material" that is intrinsically value-free. Moreover, John Paul does not claim that the New Manichaeism necessarily includes a docetic view of Christ. However, he would say that Cartesian Rationalism's rejection of God as *Ens subsistens* and *absolute uncreated Mystery* leads to a "vague deism" in which God is evicted from the world and thus to the central doctrines of Christianity, the Incarnation and the Pascal Mystery, becoming untenable. Finally, John Paul does not state that the New Manichaeism is a "religion" *per se* that involves elaborate

---

54 John Paul II, *The Gospel of Life*, no. 13.   55   Ibid.
56 John Paul II, *The Role of the Christian Family in the Modern World*, no. 6.
57 John Paul II, *The Gospel of Life*, no. 13.
58 If anything, contemporary "neo-Manichaeans" are "thoroughgoing materialists" (BeDuhn), and their rigorist practices apply mainly to a "cult of health" in which "frequenting the gym" and "obsessing about diet" are the new "religious" rituals.

creeds flowing from cosmogonic myths or joining in liturgical rites and rituals associated with deity worship, all of which were central to the belief and practice of the medieval "Manichees."

In conclusion, this comparison has discerned an identifiable similarity between the diagnoses of Manichaeism as applied to the Paulicians, Bogomils, and Cathars, and John Paul II's diagnosis of a New Manichaeism in *Letter to Families*, no. 19, thus providing support for his diagnosis. Even while admitting that the Manichaean label, when used by medieval heresiologists, could be seen as more fitting given that the medieval "Manichees" were indeed religious Dualists, held a Docetic Christology, saw the material world including the human body as intrinsically evil, ascribed to ascetical practices in varying degrees, and participated in worship rites and rituals, one can admit that John Paul is using the label "to describe people with views, to a greater or lesser degree, like those of Mani." It seems that medieval orthodox apologists attempted to apply the label more directly, whereas John Paul applies it more analogously. Yet, given that John Paul is not seeking to draw the direct relationship between Manichaeism and the New Manichaeism that the medieval apologists sought to establish with the Paulicians, Bogomils, or Cathars, it is reasonable to question why he would identify the current spiritual disease as "Manichaeism" at all. Why not use another label, perhaps of a more philosophical nature and thus more directly applicable, like "new Cartesianism" or "new Dualism" or "Scientism"?

WHY THE MANICHAEAN LABEL AND NOT SOME OTHER?

It seems the answer to this question can be found in three aspects of the New Manichaeism, which can be gleaned from the text of *Letter to Families*, no. 19. The first is that the term "Manichaeism" designates a religion or religious belief. The second is the term "experience," for, as was elucidated in Chapter 1, a more literal translation of the text states that the New Manichaeism is an "experience," which the human family is "forced to undergo." The third is that John Paul refers to the culture (specifically, to Western culture) as "neo-Manichaean." Thus, the New Manichaeism is something that characterizes culture and is thus part of what marks the distinctive way of life of Western societies—a way of life transmitted through social learning to those who live and grow up in these societies. A brief examination of how the New Manichaeism relates to these aspects—religion, experience, and culture—will help to establish a possible explanation of why Pope John Paul II chose the label of "New Manichaeism" over other possible labels for the spiritual disease he diagnoses.[59]

As has just been stated, Pope John Paul II does not claim that the New Manichaeism is a religion *per se* that involves elaborate creeds flowing from cosmogenic myths or participation in worship rituals. That said, it seems that John Paul may have held that the New Manichaeism was more akin to a religion than to a philosophy. A philosophy may or may not impact one's existence; it can be an intellectual exercise and remain in the realm of ideas. A religion is a "worldview," a set of beliefs (about God, human beings, and the human being's place in the world) and of corresponding values that orients one's life and behavior. A religion engages the whole person and orders one's existence—and this is how it seems John Paul thought the specific aspects of Cartesian Rationalism which he associates with the New Manichaeism have impacted contemporary men and women. In his comments in the *Letter to Families*, John Paul states that Rationalism "provides a radically different way of looking at creation and the meaning of human existence" than that of Christianity and the "great mystery" mentioned in the Letter to the Ephesians. Such a way of looking at creation and the meaning of human existence (anthropological dualism, a mechanistic view of nature, the rejection of the philosophy of being and its corresponding "notion of creation," including the rejection of formal and final causes), comes along with corresponding "values" (efficiency and production), and leads people to orient their lives and behavior accordingly (relativism and utilitarianism in ethics).

According to John Paul, the New Manichaeism is also an "experience." An experience is something lived through, and by nature indicates a certain participation of the experiencer with the thing experienced. While there are different types of experience, generally "experience" refers to something practical and not

---

59 It should be noted that a detailed study of the nature of religion, experience, or culture is beyond its scope and intention of this examination. A more general and vernacular understanding of these three terms will be sufficient to make the relevant points.

exclusively intellectual. According to John Paul, not only is the New Manichaeism an "experience," but one that the human family is "forced to undergo." Thus, one can reasonably conclude that this experience is something to which human beings are subjected that is neither sought nor willed by them. Rather, it is something received. Additionally, this experience is a "collective" experience—it is an experience of the "human family." It seems, therefore, that John Paul is referring to something "outside" any single individual person that pervades the consciousness of all persons.

Why is the human family having this "experience" of a New Manichaeism? Because the culture itself is neo-Manichaean. "Culture" indicates a way of living and being that is "received" as a heritage; the aggregate of values, beliefs, attitudes, traditions, etc. by which a member of society is formed. These cultural values and attitudes are taught and "caught," they are part of the very air breathed by those living in a particular culture. In this sense, the New Manichaeism, as a spiritual disease, is "airborne." If the culture is neo-Manichaean, it is because the philosophical ideas stemming from Cartesian Rationalism pervade it and characterize it, and are passed to those who grow up in it.

It appears that, to John Paul, the label "New Manichaeism" was better suited than other possibilities like "new Cartesianism," "new Dualism," or "Scientism." By indicating that the New Manichaeism operates like a "religion," is an "experience" which the human family is "forced to undergo," and characterizes the "culture," John Paul reveals how he believes these particular features of Cartesian Rationalism to have impacted contemporary men and women. The anthropological perspective of Cartesian Rationalism has amounted to a worldview that has been thrust upon and absorbed by the members of Western culture. It is experienced every day, and is transmitted through social learning to those who live and grow up in contemporary society. And it has formed (and continues to form) the very beliefs, attitudes, and behaviors of people today without their knowledge or volition.[60]

---

60   There are many scholarly studies on the consequences of the Cartesian tradition for contemporary men and women's understanding of themselves, the world, and God, even if they view this impact in varying ways and degrees. William Barrett's *Death of Soul: From Descartes to the Computer* (New York: Doubleday, 1986), Charles Taylor's *Sources of the Self: The Making of the*

It is a disease infecting the way contemporary men and women perceive themselves, the world, the body, and sex, but they do not even know they are thus infected.

In his introduction to the *Theology of the Body*, Michael Waldstein seems to lend support to what has just been proposed as the reason John Paul chose the Manichaean label over other possible labels. Reflecting on a passage from *Love and Responsibility* in which the then Cardinal Wojtyła implicated the Cartesian paradigm as the reason it is so difficult for contemporary men and women to understand the principles on which Catholic sexual teaching is based,[61] Waldstein comments:

> Wojtyła identifies a way of thinking and seeing that is deeply hammered into the minds of children in school and reinforced daily in adults by the cultural establishment— the way of thinking and seeing defined by a mechanist form of natural science, comfortably settled in the position of the self-evident.[62]

CONCLUSION

This chapter has examined how John Paul II's diagnosis of a New Manichaeism is related to the way the Christian tradition made similar diagnoses of Manichaeism throughout its history. It has been shown that while John Paul's use of the Manichaean label coincides with certain ways it was utilized by orthodox theologians to characterize medieval heterodox communities, there are a number of ways in which the Pope's use of the label in the *Letter to Families* is novel. Though John Paul applies the label more analogously than the medieval heresiologists, this chapter's examination offered an explanation as to why John Paul still opted to

---

Modern Identity (Cambridge: Harvard University Press, 1989) and *A Secular Age* (Cambridge: Belknap Press, 2007), and Carl Trueman's *The Rise and Triumph of the Modern Self: Cultural Amnesia, Expressive Individualism, and the Road to Sexual Revolution* (Wheaton: Crossway, 2020) are a few examples. Additionally, the most robust contemporary studies on the religious beliefs of youth in the United States reveal how deeply entrenched this "neo-Manichaean" worldview is (see Christian Smith with Melissa Lundquist Denton, *Soul Searching: The Religious and Spiritual Lives of American Teenagers* [New York: Oxford University Press, 2005]).

61   Wojtyła, *Love and Responsibility*, 56–57.
62   Waldstein, "Introduction," 98.

associate the Manichaean label with those features of Cartesian Rationalism he believed to provide "a radically different way of looking at creation and the meaning of human existence."

In summary, one can divine three ways in which John Paul II diagnosis of Manichaeism in *Letter to Families* is related to similar diagnoses in the Middle Ages. First, John Paul associates the New Manichaeism with the rejection of the intrinsic goodness creation and of the God of creation. Second, John Paul II associates the New Manichaeism with the failure to view the body subjectively and personally (and thus with the rejection of hylomorphism) or as having positive intrinsic value. Third, John Paul associates the New Manichaeism with a certain acceptance of manipulation in the sexual sphere and a tolerance of acts performed exclusively to indulge the sexual urge, as well as with an attitude towards procreation in which the child is viewed as an "enemy" and an obstacle to personal fulfillment rather than as a blessing. However, John Paul's diagnosis is novel in that he does not identify the New Manichaeism with the belief in the existence of opposing co-eternal principles (though he would claim that the New Manichaeism sees the universe as divided into two distinct substances, mind and matter) or in the intrinsic evil of the material world (though he would hold that the New Manichaeism sees the material world as value-free). John Paul also would not associate the New Manichaeism with participation in rigorous ascetical practices or holding to a Docetic view of Christ (though he would see Cartesian Rationalism as leading to a "vague deism" in which God is evicted from the world, and resulting in the central doctrines of Christianity, the Incarnation and the Pascal Mystery, being considered untenable). Finally, John Paul does not state that the New Manichaeism is a "religion" that involves elaborate creeds flowing from cosmogonic myths or joining in liturgical rites and rituals associated with deity worship, though his recourse to the label seems to imply that the New Manichaeism bears similarities to a religion.

By reflecting upon how the New Manichaeism is more akin to a religion than to a philosophy, is an "experience" which the human family is "forced to undergo," and characterizes contemporary "culture," it was shown why John Paul II saw the diagnosis of Manichaeism as more fitting, even though applied analogously, than other possible labels. For John Paul, the anthropological perspective of Cartesian Rationalism has amounted to a worldview that has infected men and women living in contemporary western culture, is experienced every day, and is transmitted through social learning to those who live and grow up in contemporary society, forming the very beliefs, attitudes, and behaviors of people today without their knowledge or volition. One could say that the spiritual disease of the New Manichaeism is "airborne" and inhaled every day in a variety of ways. Part of the reason it is so dangerous, is because it is a silent killer.

Having firmly established the nature of the New Manichaeism, and offered substantial support for John Paul II's cultural diagnosis, this work now investigates whether John Paul II prescribed a remedy for the spiritual disease he diagnosed, and, if so, what it is. This constitutes the subject matter of the next and final chapter. Such an investigation will also give credence to the claim of some commentators that John Paul II's anthropology represents an "antidote" to the Cartesian tradition and to "Manichaean" views and attitudes.

CHAPTER 5

John Paul II's
Theology of the Body:
A REMEDY FOR THE
NEW MANICHAEISM

INTRODUCTION

Any investigation into what John Paul II may have prescribed as a remedy for the New Manichaeism should examine the nature and structure of such a remedy, and demonstrate how the remedy itself effectively cures and inoculates people from the spiritual disease. As to the nature and structure of his remedy, this chapter will look to John Paul's method, showing that the maladies of Cartesian Rationalism he identified with the New Manichaeism, and the goal to root them out, informed the very construction of his approach to anthropology. As to how John Paul's anthropology effectively cures or inoculates people from the New Manichaeism, the chapter will look at the content of John Paul II's anthropological reflections, showing how his anthropology addresses the aforementioned maladies of Cartesian Rationalism. To accomplish the former, we will turn to contemporary scholarship on John Paul's anthropology to demonstrate how viewing it through the lens of the New Manichaeism substantiates the claims that his anthropology was "built in opposition to the Cartesian method."[1] To accomplish the latter, we will consider one work widely regarded as a superlative articulation of the Pope's anthropology and show how it effectively neutralizes those aspects of Cartesian Rationalism that John Paul associates with the New Manichaeism. Such a work should put forth what the Pope considers to be *"the teaching about God and man* which was brought to fulfillment by Christ,"[2] away from which he believed Western thought and a contemporary neo-Manichaean culture to have moved

---

1 Kupczak, *Gift and Communion: John Paul II's Theology of the Body*, 1.
2 John Paul II, *Letter to Families*, no. 19.

due to the errors of Cartesian Rationalism. Also, this particular articulation of the Pope's anthropology ought to include a reflection on sexuality since, according to John Paul, a prime consequence of Cartesian Rationalism's mechanistic understanding of nature and utilitarian view of the body is a "neo-Manichaean culture" in which sexuality becomes "an area for manipulation and exploitation."[3] And it should seek to restore "the basis for that *primordial wonder* which led Adam on the morning of creation to exclaim before Eve: 'This at last is bone of my bones and flesh of my flesh' (*Gen* 2:23) and "is echoed in the words of the *Song of Solomon*: 'You have ravished my heart, my sister, my bride, you have ravished my heart with a glance of your eyes' (*Song* 4:9)."[4] John Paul II's *Man and Woman He Created Them: A Theology of the Body* provides just such an expression of his anthropology. Michael Waldstein calls the *Theology of the Body* "John Paul's masterwork, in which the many strands of his philosophical and theological reflection come together in a rigorous and profound argument."[5] Also, as discussed in the General Introduction, it is a work specifically named by commentators as providing an "antidote" to the Cartesian tradition and to Manichaean views and attitudes, and as attempting to recover a sense of primordial wonder at the beauty of the human body and rediscover human sexuality as a treasure proper to the person.

JOHN PAUL II'S METHOD: GETTING BEYOND THE "CARTESIAN WATERSHED"

In his work *Memory and Identity: Conversations at the Dawn of a New Millennium*, after offering his interpretation of the philosophical underpinnings of contemporary errors in sexuality and bioethics (e.g., legalized same-sex unions and abortion), John Paul suggests a way to move beyond these faulty philosophical foundations in order to "speak rationally about good and evil."[6] As has been previously discussed, John Paul II holds that these ethical errors are "profoundly rooted" in "the revolution brought about by the philosophical thought of Descartes,"[7] in which the philosophy of Thomas Aquinas, particularly the philosophy of being (*esse*), was decisively abandoned,[8] and "the direction of philosophizing" was changed so that "doubt" and "thought" (*cogito/cognosco*) are placed as

---

3   Ibid.   4   Ibid.   5   Waldstein, "Introduction," 4.
6   John Paul II, *Memory and Identity*, 12.   7   Ibid., 7–8.   8   Ibid.

the starting point of philosophy instead of the reality of being and the principles of being.[9] The particular form of the "turn to the subject" that John Paul believes Descartes to have initiated led to an "incarceration in the subject" in which given metaphysical realities which ground reflection on the *cogito/cognosco* have been replaced by "products of thought freely formed and freely changeable according to circumstances."[10] This has resulted in the rejection of God as Creator and the one who determines good and evil, as well as in the rejection of human nature as a given reality.[11] Consequently, for John Paul, a fundamental concern is how we might get "beyond the Cartesian watershed"[12] in order to initiate an authentic "turn to the subject." To his mind, the only way to do so is "to return to St. Thomas Aquinas, that is, to the philosophy of being" so as to ground reflections on personal subjectivity in "realist presuppositions."[13] According to John Paul, a philosophy that takes into account human consciousness and lived experience, like phenomenology,[14] is helpful and can enrich our knowledge, but these analyses are predicated on a realist worldview—they "implicitly presuppose the reality of Absolute Being and also the reality of being human, that is, of being a creature," i.e., God as *Ens subsistens* and "the necessary ground for every *ens non subsistens, ens participatum*, that is, of all created beings, including man."[15] For the Pope, this is the only way for an authentic "turn to the subject" that safeguards against subjectivism.[16] As he states:

> With the phenomenological method, for example, we can
> study experiences of morality, religion, or simply what it is
> to be human, and draw from them a significant enrichment

---

9   Philosophies which accept the reality of being and the principles of being as "givens" are called "realist" philosophies and their adherents are said to ascribe to "metaphysical realism."

10   John Paul II, *Memory and Identity*, 12.

11   Ibid.   12   Ibid.   13   Ibid.

14   "Phenomenology is the study of human experience and of the ways things present themselves to us in and through such experience" (Robert Sokolowski, *Introduction to Phenomenology* [Cambridge: Cambridge University Press, 2000], 2).   15   Ibid.

16   Karol Wojtyła, "Subjectivity and the Irreducible in the Human Being," *Person and Community: Selected Essays* (New York: Peter Lang, 2008), 210. Cf. Karol Wojtyła, *The Acting Person, Analecta Husserliana*, ed. Anna-Teresa Tymieniecka, trans. Andrzej Potocki (Boston: D. Reidel Publishing Company, 1979), 58–59.

of our knowledge. Yet we must not forget that all these analyses implicitly presuppose the reality of Absolute Being and also the reality of being human, that is, being a creature. If we do not set out from such "realist" presuppositions, we end up in a vacuum." [17]

Since John Paul asserts that this is the way beyond the Cartesian watershed, if we were to find that this was the method he employed, it could be surmised that John Paul II developed his method to help lead us beyond the alleged errors of Descartes and to oppose the Cartesian paradigm while addressing the modern concern of subjectivity and the philosophy of consciousness. This claim would be reinforced if it could be shown that his method relates to those specific aspects of Cartesian Rationalism he associates with the New Manichaeism and have been elucidated in this book.

In order to examine the question of whether John Paul's method can be seen as a response to Descartes and to those specific aspects of Cartesian Rationalism he associates with the New Manichaeism, reference to works prior to his election and published as Karol Wojtyła is necessary. While the works of John Paul II, the Pope and visible head of the Catholic Church, must be distinguished from the works of Karol Wojtyła, the priest and philosopher, for each are subject to their own mode of interpretation, there exists a continuity between the two, especially regards his method and anthropology. [18] Since the aim of this chapter is to analyze this method and anthropology in order to determine how far they represent a remedy to Descartes and to Manichaeism, it accepts this continuity and thus sees references to the works of Wojtyła as of particular relevance and importance. [19]

---

17 John Paul II, *Memory and Identity*, 12.

18 For an example of how understanding the method and anthropology of Karol Wojtyła is important for gaining a fuller sense of John Paul II's teachings, see Deborah Savage, "The Centrality of Lived Experience in Wojtyła's account of the Person," *Roczniki Filozoficze*, LXI, 4, 2013.

19 As previously mentioned, throughout the text of the book, the "voices" of Karol Wojtyła and Pope John Paul II are maintained as distinct by referencing them accordingly. At times, the book attempts to maintain this distinctiveness while acknowledging the continuity of his method and anthropology by the use of a virgule, especially when discussing the common themes from the works of both. In these cases, the virgule does not mean

In his article "The Person: Subject and Community," Karol Wojtyła identifies the main philosophical challenge to which his anthropology is responding and in light of which his method is to be interpreted:

> The problem of the subjectivity of the human person is a problem of paramount philosophical importance today. Divergent tendencies contend with one another over it; their cognitive [epistemological] assumptions and orientations often give it a diametrically opposed form and meaning. The philosophy of consciousness would have us believe that it first discovered the human subject. The philosophy of being is prepared to demonstrate that quite the opposite is true, that in fact an analysis of pure consciousness leads inevitably to an annihilation of the subject. The need arises to find the actual point at which the phenomenological analyses based on the assumptions of the philosophy of consciousness begin to work in favor of an enrichment of the realistic image of the person. The need also arises to authenticate the foundations of such a philosophy of the person.[20]

Wojyła recognized that the "present age" is a time of "great crisis and confrontation" about "the meaning of human existence, and thus about the nature and significance of the human being."[21] Yet, he also recognized that "it has become clear that at the center of this debate is not cosmology or the philosophy of nature but philosophical anthropology and ethics."[22] And so, Wojtyła seeks to "turn toward the human person as a subject" in order to discover the person through his actions.[23] In accepting that "operation/action follows being" (*operare sequitur esse*), Wojtyła not only stresses the primacy of being (since something must exist in order to act), but also his conviction that it is in the sphere

---

"either/or" but rather indicates that the reflections that follow will be taken from the works of both or represent a shared method and anthropology. Even in these cases, the distinct "voices" are clearly distinguished in the text when referencing and discussing particular works.

20   Karol Wojtyła, "The Person: Subject and Community," *Person and Community: Selected Essays* (New York: Peter Lang, 2008), 219–220.

21   Ibid., 220.   22   Ibid.

23   Wojtyła, *The Acting Person, Analecta Husserliana*, xiv.

of human acts that is revealed "the image of the acting subject in what properly constitutes his being."[24]

In his attempt to find the actual point at which the phenomenological analyses work in favor of an enrichment of the realistic image of the person, he himself states that he "owes everything to the systems of metaphysics, of anthropology, and of Aristotelian-Thomistic ethics on the one hand, and to phenomenology, above all in Scheler's interpretation ... on the other hand."[25] It has been suggested that "Wojtyła's entire project reflects his interest in addressing the modern problem introduced by the so-called turn to the subject without relinquishing the possibility of knowledge of an objective moral order" by synthesizing "a Thomistic framework (in the existential tradition of Gilson) with the insights of modern phenomenological method."[26] For Wojtyła, if "the fundamental categories of Thomistic metaphysics can be regained on the basis of a phenomenological reflection upon the moral experience of the person," then "one would regain the anthropological and Christian position, by freeing it from all those elements which placed it in opposition to modern science," while at the same time assimilating "what is most authentic and legitimate in the will of modern thought to 'start from man.'"[27]

Wojtyła understands that the phenomenological method is not able to replace metaphysical reflection on the question of

24   Karol Wojtyła, "The Anthropological Vision of *Humanae Vitae*," trans. William May,
http://www.christendom-awake.org/pages/may/anthrop-visionjpII.htm.
25   Wojtyła, *The Acting Person*, *Analecta Husserliana*, xiv. Scheler is Max Scheler, the student of Edmund Husserl whose work was the topic of Karol Wojtyla's habilitation thesis.
26   Deborah Savage, "The Centrality of Lived Experience in Wojtyla's account of the Person," 25. As for John Paul II following the tradition of existential Thomism associated with Gilson, this is well attested by John Knasas (see his "*Fides et Ratio* and the twentieth Century Thomistic Revival"), Rocco Buttiglione (see *Karol Wojtyła: The Thought of the Man who became Pope John Paul II* [Grand Rapids: William B. Eerdmans Publishing Co., 1997], 75-76), and Jaroslaw Kupczak (see *Destined for Liberty: The Human Person in the Philosophy of Karol Wojtyla/John Paul II* [Washington, D. C.: The Catholic University of America Press, 2000, 52 78]). Existential Thomism was the approach preferred by the Catholic University of Lublin at which Wojtyła was a Professor of Ethics, especially by Stefan Swieżawski, a friend and colleague.
27   Buttiglione, *Karol Wojtyła: The Thought of the Man who became Pope John Paul II*, 74.

being.[28] The phenomenological method, concerned exclusively as it is with human experience, cannot penetrate the essence of moral values, determine why one act is good as opposed to another, or explain why the acting person becomes good or bad through the performance of such acts. Yet, though phenomenology can only describe the acting person's experience of moral values and of being the efficient cause of his or her acts, Wojtyła argues that "it may provide a route into the realm of ontology from a starting place of the phenomenology of the human person."[29] So, Wojtyła accepts the "fundamental postulate of modern thought" that "the starting point is man" and human experience, when understood as "starting from the concrete reality of the person," i.e., the reality of a conscious being who is not constituted by consciousness but instead constitutes it.[30] As will be seen in the following brief summary of his method:

> Without a doubt, Wojtyła's formulation of the good, and of the human person and his capacity to know, is based in Thomistic metaphysics and reflects the ontic structures grasped by Thomism. What differentiates Wojtyła's account from this tradition is his way of reaching them, the way we come to understand and know them. Wojtyła is a realist in the Thomistic sense of that term. The good and the true have an independent existence. These realities are accessible to human consciousness and cognition. But he will argue that they are grasped, not only through metaphysical

---

28   It is incorrect, as some claim, to say that John Paul II was a phenomenologist. Rather, his thought was deeply Thomistic. In his own habilitation thesis on Max Scheler (*An Evaluation of the Possibility of Constructing a Christian Ethic on the Principles of the System of Max Scheler*) he concludes that, though there are aspects of Scheler's ethics that could enrich Christian ethics, Scheler's ethics cannot form a solid basis for Christian ethics because it is not sufficiently rooted in realist presuppositions and objective good and evil due to its strict reliance on phenomenology. As has previously been stated, John Paul believed that employing the principles of phenomenology independent of metaphysical realism would result in one ending up in a vacuum.

29   Savage, "The Centrality of Lived Experience in Wojtyła's account of the Person," 25; Buttiglione, *Karol Wojtyła: The Thought of the Man who became Pope John Paul II*, 61.

30   Wojtyła, "The Person: Subject and Community," 226.

reflection, but first and fundamentally, through the lived experience of the acting person.[31]

Wojtyła holds that "it is only through a realist ontology that the whole content of human experience can be properly understood,"[32] for "only metaphysics is able to provide some notions and categories that can adequately interpret the content of human experience."[33] Thus, there is an organic movement[34] in Wojtyła's method between phenomenological reflection on the lived experience of the personal subject and metaphysical analysis that presupposes the realism of Aristotelian-Thomistic ontology, anthropology, and ethics while allowing the former to enrich and supplement the latter.[35]

It seems clear that, in the development of his philosophical method, Wojtyła seeks to address the modern concern about human subjectivity and the philosophy of consciousness but "to return to St. Thomas Aquinas, that is, to the philosophy of being" so as to ground reflections on personal subjectivity in "realist presuppositions."[36] Thus, it can be posited that he fashioned his method, at least in part, to get beyond the "Cartesian watershed" and as a response to the Cartesian method.

A "BROADENED DISCOVERY OF THE PERSON"[37] THROUGH A SYNTHESIS OF PHENOMENOLOGICAL DESCRIPTION AND THOMISTIC METAPHYSICS: A BRIEF SUMMARY AND ANALYSIS IN LIGHT OF THE NEW MANICHAEISM

It is not necessary, for the purposes of this book, to provide a detailed exposition of Karol Wojtyła/John Paul II's approach

---

31   Savage, "The Centrality of Lived Experience in Wojtyła's account of the Person," 26-27.

32   Kupczak, *Destined for Liberty*, 62.   33   Ibid., 81.

34   "Wojtyła does not clearly separate these two methodological steps" (Kupczak, *Destined for Liberty*, 63, footnote 46).

35   Wojtyła clearly held that Thomistic anthropology "lacks consideration of human consciousness, so crucial for modernity" (Kupczak, *Destined for Liberty*, 57). Cf. George F. McLean, "Karol Wojtyla's Mutual Enrichment of the Philosophies of Being and Consciousness," *Karol Wojtyla's Philosophical Legacy*, Cultural Heritage and Contemporary Change Series I, Culture and Value, Volume 35, ed. Nancy Mardas Billias, Agnes B. Curry, and George F. McLean, http://www.crvp.org/publications/Series-I/I-35.pdf.

36   Kupczak, *Destined for Liberty*, 57.

37   Wojtyła, *The Acting Person*, xiv.

to anthropology as it is constructed through the synthesis discussed above. It is sufficient to approach key aspects in order to demonstrate how they can be shown to remediate those features of Cartesian Rationalism he associates with the New Manichaeism. The following analysis seeks to provide such a demonstration and is organized in light of these features of Cartesian Rationalism, namely, anthropological dualism, the mechanistic view of nature, the rejection of the philosophy of being, and the tendency to relativism and utilitarianism in ethics.

KAROL WOJTYŁA'S METHOD AS A REMEDY FOR ANTHROPOLOGICAL DUALISM

Wojtyła's approach to anthropology clearly offers a remedy for the first aspect of the New Manichaeism: the Cartesian rejection of hylomorphism. Wojtyła accepts unequivocally both Aristotle's definition that the human being is a "rational animal" and Boethius's definition (accepted by Aquinas) that the person is an "individual substance of a rational nature." These definitions provide a necessary ground, metaphysical frame, and essential reference point for his analysis of human subjectivity and lived experience. They are a key component of the *compositum humanum*, of an "integral vision of man." Another key component of this *compositum humanum* is the human body. For Wojtyła, any anthropology that leaves out the body as a constitutive component only presents the human person in a partial way, as in Descartes's view. In his article "Thomistic Personalism," Wojtyła states that Descartes's "splitting of the human being into an extended substance (the body) and a thinking substance (the soul), which are related to one another in a parallel way and do not form an undivided whole, one substantial *compositum humanum* . . . lacks a sufficient basis for including the body, the organism, within the structural whole of the person's life and activity . . ."[38] It lacks this, in his opinion, because it does not regard the Aristotelian-Thomistic hylomorphic notion of the soul being the form of the body. Wojtyła seeks to reveal the person as a composite substance through his discussion of "integration." He holds that all manifestations of human life that are not bodily or material reveal some somatic conditioning. The goal of integration is to match the reactive subjectivity of

38 Wojtyła, "Thomistic Personalism," 169.

the body with the efficacious and transcendental subjectivity of the person. Somatic reactivity is the ability of the body to react to external stimuli; emotivity refers to the internal reactions to external stimuli that result in feelings and transcend mere bodily reactions. Because of this complex interdependence and cooperation between the "soma" and the "psyche," they should not be considered as totally separate entities, and the human person's experience of his own body shows this. According to Wojtyła, it is through feelings that man experiences his own body—an experience he terms "self-feeling"—and this does not point to a separate subjectivity of the body but to an intrinsic cohesiveness of the personal ego and the somatic ego.

Understanding the New Manichaeism thus helps to clarify the aims of Wojtyła's method. His acceptance of the traditional definitions of the human person and hylomorphism, though expanded and enriched with the help of phenomenology, reveals that his anthropology is constructed to give adequate attention to personal subjectivity as constitutive of the *compositum humanum* (which he believed had not been accomplished by the Aristotelian-Thomistic approach and was the prime concern of modern thought) while maintaining the body likewise as a constitutive part of that *compositum humanum*. For him, any discussion of human subjectivity must begin from "the reality of being human," of "human nature as a given reality," i.e., of the person as a composite substance wherein the soul is the form of the body. Thus, he seeks to correct the error of the Cartesian approach which rejects hylomorphism and advances mechanism.

KAROL WOJTYŁA'S METHOD AS A REMEDY FOR THE MECHANISTIC VIEW OF NATURE

Wojtyła's method can also be seen as a remedy for the mechanistic view of nature advanced by Descartes, which is the second aspect of the New Manichaeism. As was stated previously, according to Wojtyła, the Aristotelian and Boethian definitions of the person, as necessary as they are, are insufficient in and of themselves for they exclude discussion of the person in his or her unique subjectivity and consciousness, as one who freely acts in a self-expressing and self-determining way. For example, one of the difficulties with Aristotle's definition of the person as a "rational animal" is that, while satisfying Aristotle's own criterion of classifying creatures by genus and specific difference, it begins with the person's likeness to other creatures, albeit with reason as a distinguishing characteristic. For Wojtyła, personal being is radically different than non-personal being, and a great gulf exists between these two modes of existence. So, in order to reflect upon human subjectivity, Wojtyła proposes what he calls "pausing at the irreducible": to analyze the person as a self-experiencing subject while preserving the objective nature of the person and his place in the created order. In fact, subjectivity is proof of and a synonym for the irreducibility of the person to the natural world.

How does Wojtyła delve into the inner life of the human person? By beginning with human action. Accepting that "operation/action follows being" (*operare sequitur esse*), Wojtyła holds that it is in the sphere of human acts that is revealed "the image of the acting subject in what properly constitutes his being."[39] It is conscious human activity that has the "most basic and essential significance for grasping the subjectivity of the human being," because it is in it that "the freedom proper to the human person is simultaneously expressed and concretized."[40] Such activity is his path into human subjectivity because "consciousness interiorizes all that the human being cognizes, including everything that the individual cognizes from within acts of self-knowledge, and makes it all a content of the subject's lived experience."[41] This conscious human activity includes the consciousness and experience of one's own body.

Thus, Wojtyła will discuss what for him are two fundamental categories of human activity: 1) "man-acts," in which the human being is "the conscious cause of his own causation" and in which "I act" means that I am the efficient cause of my action, and 2) "something happens in man," in which the human being "is not aware of his efficacy and does not experience it."[42] Wojtyła also distinguishes between "conscious acting," which refers exclusively to the voluntariness of acting (i.e., acting with knowledge and will)

---

39 Wojtyła, "The Anthropological Vision of *Humanae Vitae*"; cf. Wojtyła, "The Person: Subject and Community," 223-225, footnote 6.

40 Wojtyła, "The Person: Subject and Community," 224.

41 Ibid., 227.

42 Wojtyła, *The Acting Person*, 65. "Man-acts" is associated with the traditional *actus humanus* and "something happens in man" with *actus hominis*.

and "the consciousness of acting," which refers to the *experience* of a person who "has the consciousness that he is acting and even that he is acting consciously."[43] It is "the consciousness of acting" that particularly interests Wojtyła, because it reveals the subjectivity and dynamism of the person.

In Wojtyła's view, the person experiences himself as existing as the subject and the efficient cause of his own action. Through self-possession and self-governance, he experiences that he is his own master (*sui iuris*) as well as the non-transferable nature of his acts. These acts, when voluntary (*actus personae*), are self-determining—through them the person gives him or herself a moral identity as good or bad. There is a double orientation of the human will: towards the intended object and towards the subject's own ego. The person experiences his own unique subjectivity in every self-determining act. And so, "in deciding about the object of his acts, man also decides about himself and is the most immanent object of his actions."[44]

It is clear that Karol Wojtyła rejects the notion that the human person or any part of the person can be simply reduced to the natural world. Yet, at first glance this may not seem so different than Descartes's splitting reality into thinking substances and extended substances. In Descartes's view, human beings, as "thinking things," would be completely unlike the rest of creation too. However, it is the mechanistic view of the body and its separation from the *compositum humanum* that is the issue. As was mentioned above, for Wojtyła, conscious human activity includes the consciousness and experience of one's own body. The body is integrated into the whole person and thus the person's experiences of subjectivity in and through free human action involve the human body. There is a complex interdependence and cooperation between the "soma" and the "psyche," an intrinsic cohesiveness of the personal ego and the somatic ego, and they should not be considered as totally separate entities. Thus, for Wojtyła, the person's irreducibility includes his body, which is part of his essence, part of the *compositum humanum*, and this is not so for Descartes and his rationalist tradition. And so, this aspect of Karol Wojtyła's approach to anthropology would

---

43   Ibid., 28–29.
44   Savage, "The Centrality of Lived Experience in Wojtyła's account of the Person," 43.

be in opposition to the mechanistic view of the human body that is held by Cartesian Rationalism, the second feature of the New Manichaeism. According to Wojtyła, for Descartes, "Consciousness is an object of inner experience, of introspection, whereas body, like all other bodies in the natural world, is accessible to observation and external experience."[45] By reducing the body to the natural world, the person him or herself is thus reduced. This is an untenable position for Wojtyła, and his method seeks to remediate it.

KAROL WOJTYŁA'S METHOD AS A REMEDY FOR THE REJECTION OF THE PHILOSOPHY OF BEING

As has been discussed, it was imperative for Karol Wojtyła/John Paul II that one begins from "realist presuppositions" in constructing an anthropological method. For him, this meant accepting Thomas Aquinas's philosophy of being—the rejection of which, according to John Paul II, characterizes Cartesian Rationalism and is the third aspect of the New Manichaeism. This aspect of Wojtyła's method has already been treated, particularly in consideration of Wojtyła's synthesis of Thomas's realism with phenomenological reflection. Nonetheless, there are a few additional observations that can be made.

In his epistemology, Wojtyła takes a realist position in the tradition of Aristotle and Thomas Aquinas[46]—he presupposes the existence of objective extra-mental reality, an *esse*, that can be experienced and cognized, i.e., that "something exists with an existence that is real and objectively independent of the cognizing subject and the subject's cognitive act, while at the same time existing as the object of that act."[47] Yet, one's experience is not only of some "thing" (*res*) in its sensible qualities, but also includes "the particular structure and essential content of that perception."[48] While Wojtyła's understanding of essence will be treated in short order, in his epistemology, "every experience already includes some kind of understanding," for "the sensory

---

45 Wojtyła, "Thomistic Personalism," 169.
46 Kupczak, *Destined for Liberty*, 147.
47 Karol Wojtyła, "The Problem of Experience in Ethics," *Person and Community: Selected Essays* (New York: Peter Lang, 2008), 115.
48 Savage, "The Centrality of Lived Experience in Wojtyła's account of the Person," 36.

and intellectual cognition constantly penetrate and supplement each other."[49] Wojtyła identifies a process of *induction* by which the person comprehends the essential "sameness" among data given in experience (i.e., the *stabilization of the object*). This process of induction "transforms the experience into a problem and a subject for theoretical reflection."[50] And so, for Wojtyła, the process of induction is followed by the process of reduction, which "seeks to retrieve what is irreducibly given in experience, to explain and interpret experience by revealing the most fundamental principle of an experienced object."[51]

Wojtyła's theory of consciousness is also "realistic" in the Thomistic sense. The fundamental function of consciousness is to "mirror" to the personal subject "what happens in him as well as his acting,"[52] i.e., to reflect what has already been cognized. This includes "all the things that the subject meets externally through his activities, whether cognitive or otherwise."[53] Since "cognition conditions consciousness," consciousness is thus determined by "the extent and degree to which objective reality is constituted and comprehended by the human person."[54] In addition to its mirroring function, however, consciousness has a "reflexive" function. The reflexive function, which is determined by the mirroring function, serves to form the experience of the human subject and its relation to his subjectiveness, that is, to experience one's own action and oneself as the subject and efficient cause of his actions. As Wojtyła states: "It is one thing to *be* the subject, another to be *cognized* (that is, objectivized) as the subject, and still a different thing to *experience* one's self as the subject of one's own acts and experiences. (The last distinction we owe to the reflexive function of consciousness.)"[55]

Additionally, in Wojtyła's consistent quoting of the Scholastic maxim *operare sequitur esse*, he is emphasizing the primacy of being, for something must exist in order to act. Since no being in the created world, including human beings, can be said to necessarily exist or to give themselves existence, there must be

---

49 Kupczak, *Destined for Liberty*, 70.   50 Ibid.   51 Ibid.
52 Savage, "The Centrality of Lived Experience in Wojtyła's Account of the Person," 33.   53 Ibid.
54 Savage, "The Centrality of Lived Experience in Wojtyła's account of the Person," 33–34.   55 Wojtyła, *The Acting Person*, 44.

an *Ipsum Esse Subsistens*, an Absolute and Necessary Being, from which they receive this existence. Thus, they are contingent beings. The Absolute Being is Pure Act (*Actus Purus*)—there is nothing potential in him. Contingent beings are not fully actualized in respect to their essence. Contingent being involves the constant actualization of a being's really existing inherent potentialities. So, Wojtyła accepts the Aristotelian-Thomistic notions of Potency and Act, and of Becoming (*fieri*), which is the movement from potency to act. Though this "becoming" exists on multiple levels—bodily, emotional, intellectual—it is the moral level that most interested Wojtyła. He chooses to highlight the "ethical aspect of man's contingency":[56] a person can only become "fully actualized" through his freely chosen self-determining acts, which make him either a morally good or morally bad person.

Also, in his emphasis on the primacy of a person's existence over his action (*operare sequitur esse*), Wojtyła indicates that the person is a "substance," a "real existence." Thus, as we have seen, Wojtyła accepts the Boethian definition of the person that Aquinas likewise accepted that "man is an individual substance of a rational nature." As a substance, parts are subordinated to the whole being in both the ontological and epistemological orders. While in the study of anthropology human cognition may necessitate the isolation of particular aspects or parts of the person, Wojtyła consistently reminds that he is treating a whole, really existing human being. He resists and warns against the absolutizing of any "partial aspect" of the human person, like the absolutizing of human consciousness.

Wojtyła also follows Aquinas in holding that "substantial existence though real and constitutive for every being as being, never exists without substantial essence, i.e., without some substantial content."[57] This content is what makes any being that particular being. Though being (existence) is the first thing cognized, more can be said about essence because it is grasped by names and thus by definitions and descriptions.[58] As for Aquinas, for Wojtyła, names and their respective meanings refer to actual beings existing in extra-mental reality and grasp the essences of these beings (thus,

56 Malgorzata Jalocho-Palicka, "Thomas Aquinas' Philosophy of Being as the Basis for Wojtyła's Concept and Cognition of the Human Person," *Studia Gilsoniana* 3, 2014, 132.　　57 Ibid., 137.　　58 Ibid., 142.

Wojtyła takes a realist position over and against Nominalism[59] and Idealism[60]). Wojtyła also accepts Aquinas's position that both the form and the matter constitute the essence of worldly, contingent beings. In persons, this essence includes both the substantial spiritual soul and the material body. To arrive at this essence of the person, Wojtyła looks again to the maxim *operare sequitur esse*—to a human being's acting in *all his aspects*—his consciousness, self-cognition, free will, emotions, and body—for he sees the essence of the person as revealed best through his action (not simply through consciousness). Thus, particular sciences, while aiding our understanding of the person under some aspect, can never reach the person's "integrum"—only philosophy can do that, and in particular Thomas Aquinas's philosophy of being.[61]

Additionally for Wojtyła, in agreement with Thomistic epistemology, all other concepts of the intellect are formed in addition to being. All beings are "real existences" with "real essences," and the dynamism of any being (involving potency, act, becoming) is conditioned on its existence and specific essence. His epistemology and theory of consciousness presuppose the existence of extramental reality and the fundamental reliability of the senses to provide the matter of intellectual knowledge to be formally judged in light of first principles. According to the Thomists, Descartes and his tradition erroneously held that the intellect could know itself before it knows being (i.e., the being of sensible things) and could move to *ergo sum* from *cogito,* without supposing *objectum intellectus est ens* or accepting the Principle of Non-contradiction

---

59   In dealing with the question of how our mental concepts correspond to things existing outside our mind, Nominalism states, generally speaking, that universal concepts are mere terms or "names" that signify individual things or stand for them in propositions, but that do not have any existence in extra-mental reality. Thus, Nominalism is anti-realist. (Frederick Copleston, *A History of Philosophy, Volume 3: Late Medieval and Renaissance Philosophy* [London: Bloomsbury Continuum, 2003], 56–57.)

60   Broadly understood, Idealism is an epistemological position that states we ascribe reality to our ideas. It is ideas that we perceive directly and not things; a material thing is what we perceive it to be. This, however, exists as an idea in the mind and to say that such a thing exists is unknowable. Thus, Idealism is also anti-realist. (Frederick Copleston, *A History of Philosophy, Volume 4: The Rationalists, Descartes to Leibniz* [London: Bloomsbury Continuum, 2003], 27.)

61   Cf. John Paul II, *Fides et Ratio,* nos. 4, 97.

upon which his *Cogito* argument depends.[62] Descartes's method of doubt entertains the hypothesis that there can be a sensation without real objects of the senses. On the contrary, Wojtyła's epistemology and theory of consciousness accept human beings' "capacity to recognize and cognize both the essential nature of created things and the fact of their existence."[63]

Due to the fact that Karol Wojtyła's method can be said to be thoroughly realistic in its epistemology and its theory of consciousness, accepting the reality of being and the principles of being, the reliability of the senses and the existence of extra-mental reality, and a created order in which each created being receives its essence from its unique participation in Supreme Being, it can be seen as constituting a remedy for the Cartesian method, which systematically rejected such realist presuppositions. Such a rejection is one of the symptoms of the New Manichaeism as diagnosed by Pope John Paul II. Thus, viewing Karol Wojtyła's anthropological method through the lens of the New Manichaeism lends credence to the claim that his anthropology was developed in response to the Cartesian paradigm.

KAROL WOJTYŁA'S METHOD AS A REMEDY FOR THE TENDENCY TO RELATIVISM AND UTILITARIANISM IN ETHICS

Karol Wojtyła's anthropological method also can be seen as a remedy for the tendency to relativism and utilitarianism in ethics, which is another aspect of Cartesian Rationalism that John Paul associates with the New Manichaeism. With respect to relativism/subjectivism in ethics, Wojtyła affirms the Thomistic view

---

62   See Reginald Garrigou-Lagrange's "The Thomistic Critique of the Cartesian Cogito," which was published in French in 1937 and in Spanish in 1950 (a new English translation has been published in Reginald Garrigou-Lagrange, *Philosophizing in Faith: Essays on the Beginning and End of Wisdom*, trans. Matthew K. Minerd, [Providence: Cluny Media, 2019], 261–272). In between these years, Karol Wojtyła studied with Garrigou-Lagrange at the Angelicum in Rome. In fact, Garrigou-Lagrange was the director of Wojtyła's doctoral thesis. It would seem unlikely that this Thomistic critique of Descartes's philosophy, which states that the "Cogito" argument is impossible without presupposing being and the principles of being, would not have been discussed by the two and have influenced Wojtyła's own critique of Descartes.

63   Savage, "Metaphysical Realism as the Foundation of Environmental Stewardship and Economic Development," 237.

that the human person is naturally ordered to the true and the good through the cooperation of the intellect and will. He also accepts Thomas's notions that God is the first exemplar cause of all things and that "being and the good convert" (*ens et bonum convertuntur*). For Thomas, the divine ideas are exemplar forms, i.e., are as archetypal patterns existing in the divine mind, and things are real or true or good or have being (since these are convertible according to Thomas) to the degree that they match those patterns. The "special way in which the divine perfection is imitated that constitutes the special essence of a thing."[64] For this reason, for Wojtyła, the philosophy of being can be qualified as a philosophy of the good.[65] Yet, Wojtyła "is most interested in grasping the dynamism of these realities inherent in human experience."[66] The good, constituted by essence and existence, is not only known through metaphysical reflection, but primarily through human experience. As Rocco Buttiglione observes:

> To begin from the phenomenology of moral experience and to graft metaphysical reflection and the problems which phenomenology emphasizes (but because of its own internal dynamics must leave unresolved), permits one to arrive at the question of being from the question of man, through the question of the good.[67]

For Wojtyła, all human cognition is experiential in some way, and this presupposes the objective nature of reality. Cognition must go beyond itself—it is realized not through the truth of its own act but through the truth of a transcendent object. Morality is cognized in a like manner. Morality is a form of reality given in experience but that transcends cognition. The reality of morality manifests itself through our feelings—very deep emotional experiences often accompany human acts precisely in terms of their moral value. We often recognize our feelings as indicators of the

---

64 Pieper, "The Negative Element in the Philosophy of St. Thomas," 66.
65 Thus, "it would be impossible to understand and to participate in Thomas' ethics if one does not grasp and accept his fundamental ontology" (Buttiglione, *Karol Wojtyła: The Thought of the Man who became Pope John Paul II*, 72).
66 Savage, "The Centrality of Lived Experience in Wojtyła's account of the Person," 29.
67 Buttiglione, *Karol Wojtyła: The Thought of the Man who became Pope John Paul II*, 74.

moral content of our acts: feelings of joy and contentment accompany good acts and feelings of despair and sorrow accompany bad acts.[68] However, for Wojtyła, we apprehend the specific moral good or evil contained in acts through understanding, for the specific aspect of morality could not be felt unless it was understood.[69] Thus, morality transcends the subject and is not identified simply with feelings. Moral values are "displayed" through feelings, but are apprehended through intellectual insight, through an act of judgment by which the subject comes to the realization of the truth about the good. In the act of judgment, there is a "moment of truth" in which one recognizes the truth or goodness of the external object and experiences him or herself as the subject who is cognizing this fact. The decision of the will presupposes a judgment of values, a recognition of the truth about the good, and it is only in such a judgment that the person can exercise self-governance and self-determination.

It is clear from the method of Karol Wojtyła that, while the experience of morality is a deeply subjective experience, moral values themselves are objective and transcend human cognition and feelings. The specific moral good or evil in acts is something that must be apprehended through intellectual insight and reflection on experience. Again, this reflection, for Wojtyła, is endeavored by setting out from the realist presuppositions previously discussed: accepting that the specific moral good or evil is something that can be cognized and exists in extra-mental reality and accepting the Aristotelian-Thomistic notion of causality, i.e., the relationship between the moral species of an act and formal and final causes.[70] That said, the *experience* of good and evil is something deeply subjective and personal. As Wojtyła indicates, "Moral experience always resides within the experience of a human being, and in some sense even *is* this experience . . . the essence of morality and humanity are inseparably linked."[71] So, Wojtyła's method avoids slipping into

68 Karol Wojtyła, "The Problem of Experience in Ethics," *Person and Community: Selected Essays* (New York: Peter Lang, 2008), 123–124.
69 Ibid., 125.
70 For example, when reflecting on the sexual urge in his article "Catholic Sexual Ethics" in *Person and Community: Selected Essays* (New York: Peter Lang, 2008), Wojtyła states that "the sexual urge possesses its own nature and a purpose connected with this nature" (287–288).
71 Wojtyła, "The Problem of Experience in Ethics," 120–121.

the relativism and subjectivism of Cartesian Rationalism, which is characteristic of the New Manichaeism, while providing a robust philosophy of subjectivity, consciousness, and lived experience. Thus, Wojtyła's anthropological method is a remedy for this aspect of the Cartesian paradigm and the New Manichaeism.

Wojtyła's method can also be said to oppose the tendency towards utilitarianism in ethics, particularly in his formulation of what he terms the "Personalistic Norm." Due to his nature as a self-possessing, self-governing, self-determining subject—as a *somebody* with a unique and incommunicable inner life, and not a *something*—the person can never be used as a mere means to another's end.[72] He or she can never become an object of use. The only adequate and proper response to the person is love: to affirm the good of the person by willing his or her integral fulfillment and specific, concrete goods. According to Wojtyła, the principle of utility, which is the principle of the maximization of pleasure, will always stand in the way of love and reduces the person to an object of appropriation.[73]

All in all, by reflecting upon Karol Wojtyła's method in light of the maladies of Cartesian Rationalism which he associates with the New Manichaeism as Pope, one could conclude that, assuming a continuity between the method and anthropology of John Paul II as Pope and prior to his election, the claim that John Paul's method is constructed to remediate the Cartesian method (and thus the New Manichaeism) proves true.

APPROACHING THE *THEOLOGY OF THE BODY* IN LIGHT OF THE NEW MANICHAEISM

In her reflection on the centrality of lived experience in Karol Wojtyła's account of the person, Deborah Savage suggests that his approach of "accounting for the subjectivity and dynamism of the person," while remaining grounded in Thomistic metaphysical and ontological categories "provides a key hermeneutical device for understanding the enormous importance of the work of Pope John Paul II."[74] At the conclusion of her reflections, she offers an example of how such an interpretation of John Paul's work

---

72 Wojtyła, *Love and Responsibility*, 27.   73 Ibid., 40.
74 Savage, "The Centrality of Lived Experience in Wojtyla's account of the Person," 21.

can be endeavored by looking at the encyclical *Veritatis Splendor*. This present work would like to affirm and advance this insight by Savage by showing how the maladies of Cartesian Rationalism that John Paul associates with the New Manichaeism can serve in a complementary way as a "hermeneutical device" when seeking a fuller understanding of John Paul II's anthropology as a prescribed remedy to those very maladies. Thus, this present work will turn to what many consider a superlative expression of John Paul's anthropology, the *Theology of the Body*, and will examine how it provides an antidote to these maladies and to the New Manichaeism of which they are symptoms.

At the beginning of the *Theology of the Body*, which could be considered an extended reflection on the opening chapters of Genesis, John Paul's method is already clearly present. He states that the first creation account has a "powerful metaphysical content" wherein man is defined primarily in "the dimensions of being and existing (*'esse'*),"[75] while the second creation account gives us the "oldest record of man's self-understanding" and the "first witness of human consciousness," and thus the "creation of man especially in the aspect of his subjectivity."[76] He states that lived experience "is a legitimate means for theological interpretation" and provides "an indispensable reference point" for interpreting Genesis, since "bodily man is perceived by us above all in experience."[77] These two creation accounts—one that approaches the creation of the world and human beings from "metaphysical realism" and another that approaches creation from "lived experience"—are related. John Paul makes clear that "when we compare the two accounts, we reach the conviction that this subjectivity corresponds to the objective reality of man created 'in the image of God.'"[78] So lived experience is a way to metaphysical realities, and metaphysics provides a lens through which one can interpret experience. When one looks throughout the *Theology of the Body*, however, one can see that those aspects of Cartesian Rationalism that John Paul associates with the

---

75 John Paul II, *Man and Woman He Created Them: A Theology of the Body*, 2:5.
76 John Paul indicates that in Genesis 2 we "find '*in nucleo*' almost all the elements of the analysis of man to which modern, and above all contemporary, philosophical anthropology is sensitive."
77 John Paul II, *Man and Woman He Created Them: A Theology of the Body*, 4:4.
78 Ibid., 3:2.

New Manichaeism are so clearly identifiable that it could be said that the *Theology of the Body* represents a remedy for the Cartesian paradigm. And since the *Theology of the Body* is considered a superlative articulation of John Paul's anthropology, it can be extrapolated that his anthropology itself can likewise be seen as such a remedy.

THE *THEOLOGY OF THE BODY* AS A REMEDY FOR ANTHROPOLOGICAL DUALISM

John Paul associates the New Manichaeism with Descartes's anthropological dualism and with the "radical contrast in man between spirit and body, between body and spirit,"[79] which he makes. Descartes posited that man is comprised of two separate and distinct substances, mind (the "thinking thing") and matter (pure extension). For him, the person is identified with his or her mind, as "a thing that thinks," and the human body is pure extension or "mere matter." In the *Theology of the Body*, John Paul strenuously advances the hylomorphic view of the person that he believes Descartes to have rejected.

When reflecting on Adam's experience of "original solitude" in Genesis 2, John Paul indicates that the first man becomes aware of being alone through the experience of the meaning of his own body. The man is a "body among bodies" in the visible world. While this could have easily led to Adam concluding that he was "substantially similar to other living beings," he instead reached the conviction that he was "alone."[80] It is through his experience of his own body that Adam "separates himself" from the rest of creation because, he intuitively grasps that it is through his body that he is a person.[81] It is here that John Paul believes one touches upon "a central problem in anthropology."[82] He states, "Consciousness of the body seems to be identical in this case with the discovery of the complexity of one's own structure, which in the end, based on philosophical anthropology, consists in the relation between soul and body. The Yahwist account expresses this complexity with its own language (that is, with its own terminology) by saying, 'The Lord God formed man with dust of the ground and blew into his nostrils the breath of life and man

---

79 John Paul II, *Letter to Families*, no. 19.
80 John Paul II, *Man and Woman He Created Them: A Theology of the Body*, 6:3.
81 Ibid.   82 Ibid., 7:1.

became a living being' (Gen 2:7)."[83] Also, man is the only creature that can "cultivate" and "subdue" creation, and this work certainly gives rise to an awareness of the meaning of his own bodiliness.

Yet this "original description of human consciousness" in Genesis 2, which shows "the discovery of one's own bodiliness" and "the perception of the meaning of one's own body," does not do so "on the basis of some primordial metaphysical analysis, but on the basis of man's sufficiently clear concrete subjectivity."[84] As the Pope states, "Man is a subject not only by his self-consciousness and by self-determination, but also based on his own body."[85] It is the body that permits the person to be "the author of genuinely human activity," in which "the body expresses the person."[86] Due to the structure of his consciousness and self-determination, the body can make clear "who man is."[87] John Paul mentions that while there is no clear distinction between body and soul in the Old Testament (the Scriptures more distinguish body and life), "the body is an expression of man's personhood and, though it does not completely exhaust this concept, one should understand it in biblical language as 'pars pro toto' [the part standing for the whole]."[88] This is why the human person does not just *have* a body, but *is* a body.[89]

Additionally, John Paul reflects upon the creation of the human person as "male and female." John Paul states that "Masculinity and femininity... are, as it were, two different 'incarnations,' that is, two ways in which the same human being, created 'in the image of God' (Gen 1:27), 'is a body.'"[90] The woman being created from "the rib" of the man, according to John Paul, indicates the homogeneity of the whole being of both. This homogeneity, first of all, regards the somatic structure of the person, that is, his or her body—it is upon seeing the woman's body that the man exclaims, "This time she is flesh from my flesh and bone from my bones" (Gen 2:23). To John Paul, this exclamation is the equivalent to stating "*Look, a body that expresses the 'person'!*"[91] and reveals the depth

---

83 Ibid.   84 Ibid., 7:2.   85 Ibid.   86 Ibid.
87 Ibid.   88 Ibid., 9:4, footnote 18.   89 Ibid., 8:1, 10:4.
90 Ibid., 8:1. Deborah Savage's work on understanding "sex" (i.e., being male or female) as a "proper accident" is important. See "The Nature of Woman in Relation to Man: Genesis 1 and 2 through the Lens of the Metaphysical Anthropology of Aquinas," *Logos: A Journal of Catholic Thought and Culture* 18 (1):71–93 (2015).   91 Ibid., 14:4.

of the man's joy at the creation of a "help similar to himself." (It is also in the naming of the animals and the lack of finding such a "help" among them that also indicates the unique meaning of the human body as a "body among bodies.") John Paul states that, "Despite the diversity in constitution tied to the sexual difference, somatic homogeneity is so evident that the man, on waking up from genetic sleep, [he] expresses it immediately..."[92] The man and the woman share the same humanity, which includes the human body as the visible manifestation of the unique subjectivity of the person. From "original solitude," man now "emerges in the dimension of reciprocal gift, the expression of which—by that very fact the expression of his existence as a person—is the human body in all the original truth of its masculinity and femininity."[93] For John Paul, sexual difference itself is an imprint in the structure of the human person that indicates reciprocal gift as a fundamental characteristic of personal existence. Masculinity and femininity "is the original sign of a creative donation"[94] and while this, according to the Pope, reveals the generative meaning of the body, it also manifests the "spousal" meaning, that is, the body's *"power to express the kind of love in which the human person becomes a gift,"* and thus "fulfills the very meaning of his being and existence" as a person.[95] According to John Paul, the person created in the image of God is created for love and communion, and so the body, as part of the personal structure, is ordered to love and communion. This is indicated by the biblical phrase, "This is why a man leaves his father and mother and cleaves to his wife and the two become one flesh" (Gen 2:25). The sexual union of spouses is a sign of the total reciprocal gift of their persons. Marriage, as a "primordial sacrament" is *"a sign that* efficaciously *transmits in the visible world the invisible mystery hidden in God from eternity,"*[96] the mystery of a God who is "love" and a "communion of persons" as Trinity. According to the Pope, it is the body, in its masculinity and femininity, which makes this possible.

The author of Genesis identifies that the first man and woman were "naked and not ashamed," and this, according to John Paul, is one more manifestation of the hylomorphic structure of the human person. "Nakedness" indicates a certain "purity of vision"

---

92 Ibid., 8:4. 93 Ibid., 14:4. 94 Ibid.
95 Ibid., 15:1. 96 Ibid., 19:4.

in which the person is seen as manifested in his or her body. The dignity of the person shines forth through the body and its sex. There is no reduction of the person to his or her body or to an "object of appropriation." The person is perceived integrally, in his or her unified totality: the body manifests the person created in the image of God with all the dignity that implies. "In the state of original innocence...nakedness did not express a lack, but represented the full acceptance of the body in its whole human and thus personal truth... Thus, in the mystery of creation, the human body carried within itself an unquestionable sign of the 'image of God' and also constituted a specific source of certainty about this image, present in the whole human being."[97]

All of this reflection indicates that "the original revelation of the body as expressed in particular by Genesis 2:25, does not contain an inner break and antithesis between what is spiritual and what is sensible, just as it does not contain a break and antithesis between what constitutes the person as human and what is determined by sex in man, that is, what is male and female."[98] According to John Paul, sin creates a certain rupture within the nature of the human person and radically changes his experience of himself and the meaning of his body. Due to sin there is no longer the full acceptance of the body in its whole human and thus personal truth: the spousal and generative meanings of the body are in some sense suffocated by self-interest,[99] and man looks "lustfully," reducing the other to an object of appropriation,[100] to a means of egotistical enjoyment,[101] to "just" a body (instead of a person manifested in his or her body). Yet, John Paul states that the grace of Redemption in Christ and Life in the Spirit renews and reorders what sin has disfigured. This process of sanctification (or re-integration) finds its fulfillment in the Resurrection, which "is a revelation of man's destiny in all the fullness of his psychosomatic nature and of his personal subjectivity" and "means restoration to the true life of human bodiliness."[102] Taken altogether, this represents a clear response to and remedy for the anthropological dualism and rejection of hylomorphism that John Paul identifies with Cartesian Rationalism and associates with the New Manichaeism in *Letter to Families*, no. 19.

---

97   Ibid., 27:3.   98   Ibid., 13:1.   99   Ibid., 39:5.
100 Ibid., 33:1.   101 Ibid., 33:4.   102 Ibid., 66:5.

THE *THEOLOGY OF THE BODY* AS A REMEDY
FOR THE MECHANISTIC VIEW OF NATURE

John Paul associates the New Manichaeism with Descartes's mechanistic view of nature. According to Descartes, bodies are like machines composed of parts, "raw material" whose nature lies exclusively in extension. Since Descartes does not view man as a single substance which is comprised of matter and form, but rather as two separate substances, mind and matter, he considers the human body in terms of extension alone and consigns it exclusively to the realm of the mechanical cosmos. John Paul saw "the separation of spirit and body in man" as leading to the "tendency to consider the human body, not in accordance with the categories of its specific likeness to God, but rather on the basis of its similarity to all the other bodies present in the world of nature, bodies which man uses as raw material in his efforts to produce goods for consumption."[103] In the *Theology of the Body*, John Paul noticeably seeks to correct this very tendency.

Reflecting on what he calls "original solitude," John Paul II emphasizes the irreducibility of the person to the natural world. Man experiences himself as "alone"—as substantially distinct from the rest of creation, that "he cannot be identify himself essentially with the visible world of other living beings (*animalia*)."[104] While the human being is created together with the visible world, he is placed above the world through the Creator's command to "subdue" and to "cultivate," and "the biblical narrative does not speak of his likeness with the rest of creatures, but only with God."[105] The human being's relationship with God ("in the image of God he created him") includes "an affirmation of the absolute impossibility of reducing man to the 'world'"—the person "can neither be understood nor explained in his full depth with categories taken from the 'world,' that is, from the visible totality of bodies."[106]

---

103 Ibid.   104 Ibid., 6:3.
105 "In the cycle of the seven days of creation, a precise step-by-step progression is evident; man, by contrast, is not created according to a natural succession, but the Creator seems to halt before calling him to existence, as if he entered back into himself to make a decision, 'Let us make man in our image, in our likeness' (Gen 1:27)" (John Paul II, *Man and Woman He Created Them: A Theology of the Body*, 2:3).
106 John Paul II, *Man and Woman He Created Them: A Theology of the Body*, 2:4.

According to John Paul, from the beginning, the man stands before God in search of his own identity, and his observations of the natural world act as a *via negativa* in this search—they indicate what the man "is not." While the human being is a "body among bodies," no other body means what his does; no other body expresses a personal subject; none "offers man the basic conditions that *make it possible to exist in a relation of reciprocal gift.*"[107] This is seen very concretely in the man's naming of the animals and none proving to be a "help similar to himself." Thus, the body makes him aware of his being "alone." In order to give oneself as a gift—which John Paul states is "the existential content inscribed in the truth of the 'image of God'" and is "a particular characteristic of personal existence, or even the very essence of the person"—one must possess oneself and be able to choose to give oneself, that is, be one's "own master" (*sui iuris*), a self-possessing, self-determining subject.[108] Only the human person possesses the requisite freedom and self-mastery which at one and the same time distinguishes him from the rest of creation and makes him "the image of God."[109]

So, for John Paul "The meaning of man's original solitude: being called to subdue and rule the earth, being given the conditions of the first covenant, being given the task of naming the animals—all... point to man's superiority and subjectivity."[110] However, the irreducibility of the person, and his body, to the natural world is also seen in John Paul's reflections on the nature of the sexual urge in human beings. When discussing the relationship between the sexual instinct in human beings and "the instinct that stimulates fruitfulness and procreation in the whole world of living beings," John Paul states that the words of Genesis "sufficiently connect the perspective of procreation with the fundamental characteristic of human existence in the personal sense."[111] Thus, while there is an analogy between the human body and of sex in relation to the world of animals, in human beings this "is raised in some way to the level of 'image of God' and to the level of the person and communion among persons."[112] The term "knowledge" used in Genesis 4:1-2 and often in the Bible, also "raises the conjugal relation of man

---

107 Ibid., 14:1.   108 Ibid., 14:2.   109 Ibid., 15:2.
110 Ibid., 5:4.   111 Ibid., 14:5.   112 Ibid., 20:3.

and woman ... and brings it into the specific dimension of the persons."[113] Genesis 4 rejects a "one-sidedly 'naturalistic' mentality" and does not indicate "a passive acceptance of one's own determination on the part of the body and of [its] sex, precisely because it is a question of 'knowledge'!"[114] According to John Paul, "...'knowledge' in the biblical sense signifies that man's 'biological' determination, on the part of his body and his sex, is no longer something passive but reaches a level and content specific to self-conscious and self-determining persons; therefore, it brings with it a particular consciousness of the meaning of the human body bound to fatherhood and motherhood."[115]

Reflecting on the contemporary situation at the conclusion of his reflections in both Chapters 1 and 2, John Paul raises concerns that due to the development of various disciplines, an "integral vision of man can easily be rejected and replaced by many partial conceptions that dwell on one or another aspect of the *compositum humanum* but do not reach man's *integrum*."[116] One such discipline is contemporary science, which tends to view the human being exclusively in terms of bio-physiology, and therefore in a partial and not comprehensive way.[117] Because "various cultural tendencies" based on these partial truths influence human beings so powerfully, contemporary men and women no longer identify themselves readily with their bodies. Rather, the body is seen as an object of manipulations and of technology, and therefore is identified with the purely mechanistic and material cosmos. This is the very malady that John Paul identifies with Cartesian Rationalism and the New Manichaeism, and which he is trying to remediate through his anthropology as found in the *Theology of the Body*.

---

113   Ibid., 14:5.   114   Ibid., 21:1.
115   Ibid., 21:4. This is why the Church's phrase "responsible parenthood" (which Janet Smith translates as "conscious parenthood" in her translation of Pope Paul VI's *Humanae Vitae*) refers to the personal character of the conjugal act and the couple's willful orientation toward its procreative end. "Responsible" here means "the ability to respond" or "conscious assent" and not "having only a responsible number of children." In fact, it must not be understood as the latter, though it is often used this was even by theologians, popular authors, and ecclesiastical authorities.
116   Ibid., 22:3.   117   Ibid., 59:3.

THE *THEOLOGY OF THE BODY* AS A REMEDY FOR
THE REJECTION OF THE PHILOSOPHY OF BEING

John Paul II connects the New Manichaeism with the rejection of Thomas Aquinas's philosophy of being and its corresponding "notion of creation." Along with rejecting the philosophy of being comes the rejection of formal and final causes and a truth of creation which must be acknowledged, as well as of the God of Creation who is *Ens subsistens.* Ultimately, Thomas's philosophy of being underlies a realist metaphysics—a metaphysics which Descartes abandons. In the *Theology of the Body,* it is clear that John Paul is returning to the philosophy of being, which for him, as has been noted, is the way beyond the Cartesian watershed.

Using Jesus's words to the Pharisees about the "beginning" in response to their question about marriage as his point of departure, John Paul states that these words must have caused the Pharisees " ... to reflect about the way in which, in the mystery of creation, man was formed precisely as 'male and female.'" [118] Right from the first audience, John Paul demonstrates his realist presupposition about the "mystery of creation" (i.e., the "mystery of being"). In fact, the word "mystery" is used 373 times in the *Theology of the Body* and the phrase "mystery of creation" is used 88 of those times. As was demonstrated in Chapter 1 of this book, the terms "mystery" and "mystery of creation" (being) corresponds to Thomas Aquinas's philosophy of being (*esse*). In his meditation on Genesis 1, which he states has a "powerful metaphysical content," he relates Thomas Aquinas's philosophy of being to the Scripture text. It is such a poignant example of John Paul's attempt to return to the philosophy of being that, though lengthy, it bears being quoted in full.

> One should not forget that precisely this text of Genesis has become the source of the deepest inspirations for the thinkers who have sought to understand "being" and "existing" (perhaps only Exodus 3 can be compared with this text). Despite some detailed and plastic expressions in this passage, man is defined in it primarily in the dimensions of being and existing ("*esse*"). He is defined in a more metaphysical than physical way. To the mystery of his creation ("in the image of God he created him") corresponds the perspective of procreation ("be fruitful and multiply"), of

118   Ibid., 1:4.

coming to be in the world and in time, of "*fieri*," which is necessarily tied to the metaphysical situation of creation: of contingent being ("*contingens*"). Precisely in this metaphysical content of the description of Genesis 1, one must understand the entity of the good, that is, the aspect of value. In fact, this aspect returns in the rhythm of almost all the days of creation and reaches its high point after the creation of man, "God saw everything that he had made, and indeed, it was very good" (Gen 1:31). This is why one can say with certainty that the first chapter of Genesis has formed an incontrovertible point of reference and solid basis of a metaphysics and also for an anthropology and an ethics according to which "*ens et bonum convertuntur*" [being and good are convertible]. Of course, all of this has its own significance for theology as well, and above all for the theology of the body."[119]

Here, a number of themes that appeared in the previous reflections on Karol Wojtyła's method are brought to bear on the Scripture text. Because "being and the good convert," things are "good" simply because they exist, and all created (contingent) being is a participation in Supreme Being by way of likeness. In his footnote to this section referencing Etienne Gilson, John Paul states that while the revelation of God's name as "I Am He Who Am" in Exodus 3 constitutes an object of reflection for many philosophers, it was St. Thomas who "bridged the gap" that separated "the being of essence" from "the being of existence" with his proofs of God's existence. Thus, it is clear that Aquinas's philosophy of being underlies John Paul's reflections, and he is attempting to draw out these fundamental "realist presuppositions."

According to John Paul, in Genesis God reveals himself above all as Creator, and Christ appeals to this fundamental revelation in his words to the Pharisees. Yet, God creates the world and human beings in the world "in love," and so creation itself represents a "fundamental and radical gift." God calls to existence from nothing and establishes the world in existence and man in the world, because he "is love" (1 Jn 4:8). While John Paul admits that the word love or phrase "God is love" is not found in the creation account, since the phrase "God saw everything that he had made, and indeed, it

119   Ibid., 2:5.

was good" is often repeated, one is able to acknowledge love as "the divine motive for creation, the source, as it were, from which it springs," for "only love, in fact, gives rise to the good and is well pleased with the good (see 1 Corinth 13)."[120] So, for John Paul, creation does not only mean "calling from nothing to existence and establishing the world's existence as well as man's existence in the world," but it also signifies a "fundamental and radical gift, that is, an act of giving in which the gift comes into being precisely from nothing."[121] And so, according to John Paul, the first chapters of Genesis introduce us into the mystery of creation, that is, to a cosmos created by the will of God, who is the First and Exemplar Cause, *Ipsum esse subsistens*, omnipotence and love. Every creature, every *ens contingens* or *ens participatum*, though limited and susceptible to nonexistence,[122] bears within itself the sign of the original and fundamental gift.[123] "He who is—he who lives and is Life—constitutes the inexhaustible fountain of existence and life, just as he revealed himself at the 'beginning' in Genesis."[124]

One can also see that John Paul invokes the Thomistic notion of final cause in the *Theology of the Body*. For John Paul, there is an "economy of Truth and Love, which has its source in God himself and was revealed already in the mystery of creation."[125] This is especially evident in his reflections on God's plan for human sexuality found in the early chapters of Genesis. For example, John Paul states that "Genesis 2:24 speaks about the ordering of man's masculinity and femininity to an end, in the life of spouses-parents" and "man enters 'into being' with the consciousness that his own masculinity-femininity, that is, his own sexuality, is ordered to an end," namely, to procreation.[126] John Paul states that the "sexual urge," as an "objective dimension of human nature," has a "procreative finality that is proper to it..."[127] When, as a consequence of original sin, both the man and the woman tend to view one another as objects for the satisfaction of sexual urge, "such a 'reduction' of the rich content of reciprocal and perennial attraction among human persons in their masculinity and femininity does not correspond to the 'nature' of the attraction in question. Such a 'reduction,' in fact, extinguishes the meaning

---

120 Ibid., 13:3.	121 Ibid.	122 Ibid., 7:3.
123 Ibid., 13:4.	124 Ibid., 65:5.	125 Ibid., 19:5.
126 Ibid., 14:5.	127 Ibid., 41:4.	

proper to man and woman, a meaning that is personal and 'of communion.'"[128] Even John Paul's discussions about the spousal and generative meanings of the body indicate a "purpose" or "end" of the body: the body is for love and life. When discussing the Catholic Church's traditional teaching opposing the use of artificial contraception, John Paul states that "the conjugal act 'signifies' not only love, but also potential fruitfulness" and that "it is not licit to separate artificially the unitive from the procreative meaning, because the one as well as the other belong to the innermost truth of the conjugal act."[129]

And so, from this analysis it is clear that for John Paul reflection on creation and the "mystery of being" is at the heart of the *Theology of the Body*, and that he accepts the "realist presuppositions" of Thomas Aquinas's philosophy of being throughout it, including final causality. As such, John Paul's anthropology as expressed in the *Theology of the Body* can be said to seek to get "beyond the Cartesian watershed" by returning to Aquinas's philosophy of being, and can be seen as a remedy for the Cartesian paradigm and the New Manichaeism which John Paul held to have rejected the philosophy of being and formal and final causes.

THE *THEOLOGY OF THE BODY* AS A REMEDY FOR THE TENDENCY TO RELATIVISM AND UTILITARIANISM IN ETHICS, ESPECIALLY IN SEXUAL ETHICS AND BIOETHICS

John Paul associates the New Manichaeism with the tendency to relativism and utilitarianism that results from Cartesian Rationalism. The placing of God outside of the world and denial of formal and final causality which leads to the rejection of a "truth of creation" and of human nature, underlies this tendency. From Descartes's goal to make man the master and possessor of nature with "the power to construct orders" (and, in effect, to determine the "truth" about creation) John Paul saw a "short jump" to "claiming autonomy in one's ethical views."[130] After all, for Descartes, man has the first word and the last word in the matter of determining what is and what is not to be accepted as truth. And when in *theory* one denies a "truth of creation" and only accepts as true that which can be empirically verified, in *practice* production and efficiency become

---

128   Ibid., 41:5.   129   Ibid., 123:6.
130   Wojtyła, *Love and Responsibility*, 57.

the standards. To John Paul II's mind, this inevitably leads to "a civilization of production and of use ... a civilization in which persons are used in the same way things are used," [131] to "the tendency to use the human body as raw material in the same way that the bodies of animals are used" [132] like in experimentation on embryos and fetuses, and "to human sexuality being regarded more as an area *for manipulation and exploitation.*" [133] While Descartes himself cannot be classified as proponent of utilitarianism, one can see how his goal to develop a practical philosophy that would facilitate "our enjoyment of the fruits of the earth and all the goods we find there," promotes the "general welfare" and "contentment" through the discernment of what is most useful and beneficial, and views the physical world (including the human body) mechanistically (i.e., as "raw material" without intrinsic ends and upon which human beings can impose their own ends) would set the stage for the utilitarian thinkers of the Enlightenment. And though one finds no expressed mention of sexuality or bioethics in Descartes's moral writings, his dualistic views, his mechanistic view of the body, his rejection of ends and purposes in nature, his paving the road for Deism (for a God who is remote from creation), and preparing the ground for modern unbelief as well as for relativism and utilitarianism in ethics, could all be said to have helped to set the foundations for the contemporary approaches to sexual ethics and bioethics.

In the *Theology of the Body*, John Paul II asserts that the person can never become a mere means to another's end, that he or she can never be used or become an object of use, and that the only adequate and proper response to the person is love: to affirm the good of the person by willing his or her integral fulfillment and specific, concrete goods. He also affirms that the human person is naturally ordered to the true and the good through the cooperation of the intellect and will, that "the good" means acting in accordance with the particular essence of a thing (i.e., with formal and final causes, with a "truth of creation" established by the Creator), and that, while the experience of morality is a deeply subjective experience and is apprehended through reflection on experience, moral values themselves are objective and transcend human cognition and feelings.

---

131   John Paul II, *Letter to Families*, no. 13.
132   Ibid., no. 19.   133   Ibid.

John Paul states that "Those who seek the fulfilment of their own human and Christian vocation in marriage are called first of all to make the 'theology of the body' ... the content of their lives and behavior" and "this all the more against the background of a civilization that remains under the pressure of a materialistic and utilitarian way of thinking and evaluating."[134] It seems evident that John Paul II is offering the *Theology of the Body* as an antidote to such materialism and utilitarianism. In fact, John Paul will contrast the "rightness of intention" in the "exchange of the gift," which consists of an "acceptance" or "welcoming" of the other as a gift and someone the Creator has willed "for his own sake" (which "signifies a moral participation in the eternal and permanent act of God's will") with "the contrary of such 'welcoming' and 'acceptance' of the other human being as a gift" which results in "a loss of the gift itself and thus a transmutation and even reduction of the other to an 'object for myself' (object of concupiscence, of 'undue appropriation,' etc.) ..." This latter utilitarian attitude, this reduction of the other to a mere "object for me," contradicts moral participation in the act of God's willing the other for his or her own sake, and is a form of "extortion."[135] According to the Pope's interpretation of the verse from Genesis, "The man and the woman, his wife, were both naked but were not ashamed" (Gen. 2:25), the reason there was no shame was because "the woman was not an 'object' for the man, nor he for her." Prior to sin and its effects, the first man and woman possessed the requisite "purity of heart" and "reciprocal *awareness of the spousal meaning of their bodies*" to exclude subjectively any reduction of the other to an object.[136] After sin, "*the relationship of the gift changes into a relationship of appropriation.*"[137] This manifests itself clearly and immediately in the area of sexual ethics, and in particular in the "lustful look" which Christ spoke of and John Paul reflects upon in Chapter 2 of the *Theology of the Body*. Instead of the value of sex being "part of the whole richness of values with which a feminine being appears to a man," the "whole personal richness of femininity" is reduced to this one value, that is, to sex as the fitting object of the satisfaction of one's own sexuality."[138] This same reasoning can apply for the woman to the man. This "lustful look" born of

---

134 John Paul II, *Man and Woman He Created Them: A Theology of the Body*, 23:5.
135 Ibid., 17:3.   136 Ibid., 19:1.   137 Ibid., 32:6.
138 Ibid., 40:3.

concupiscence "tramples on the ruins of the spousal meaning of the body" and "aims directly toward one and only one end as its precise object: *to satisfy only the body's sexual urge.*"[139] Thus, the sexual urge does not "serve the *building of the unity 'of communion'*" in the relationship between man and woman as it did in "the beginning" prior to sin when there was a shared consciousness of the spousal meaning of the body. In fact, John Paul sees in the words of Genesis 3:16 about "domination" an essential "change in the structure of communion in interpersonal relations...,"[140] for "from the moment in which man 'dominates' her, the communion of persons—which consists in the spiritual unity of the two subjects who gave themselves to each other—is replaced by a different mutual relationship, namely, by a relationship of possession of the other as an object of one's own desire."[141] This utilitarian attitude which reduces the other to an "object of enjoyment for the satisfaction of mere concupiscence," and to an "anonymous object of appropriation" or "object of abuse" is also highlighted by John Paul in his discussion of the body in art, and in particular of the problem of "pornovision" and "pornography."[142]

It is also clear that the *Theology of the Body*, while penetrating the interior of the person and his subjectivity, clearly rejects the tendency of Cartesian Rationalism to subjectivism and relativism. John Paul understands relativism as being, like utilitarianism, rooted in the "Fall" of human beings through the eating of the Tree of the Knowledge of Good and Evil. While the *Theology of the Body* does not state this as expressly as it does with utilitarian attitudes in its reflections on the contrast of the human person in the state original innocence and of original sin, this is in fact John Paul's view and must form the background of all his comments about the "Fall" in the text. While God has granted human beings an extremely far-reaching freedom—for they can "eat freely of every tree in the garden"—it is not unlimited, must "halt before the 'tree of the knowledge of good and evil,'" and "is called to accept the moral law given by God."[143] In eating from the tree of the knowledge of good and evil, human beings effectively attempt to "decide for themselves" what is good and what is

---

139   Ibid., 40:4.   140   Ibid., 30:6.   141   Ibid., 31:3.
142   Ibid., 61:3, 62:3, 5, 63:5.
143   John Paul II, *The Splendor of the Truth*, no. 35.

evil.[144] Here is where relativism is born—it is an exaltation of human freedom that assumes for itself a prerogative that rightly belongs to God; a human freedom that is "able to 'create values' and would enjoy a primacy over truth, to the point that truth itself would be considered a creation of freedom" and "would thus lay claim to a *moral autonomy* which would actually amount to an *absolute sovereignty.*"[145]

John Paul II, in response, demonstrates there to be no conflict between freedom and law. To his mind, God, "who alone is good" and "knows perfectly what is good for man," [146] in lovingly proposing this good to human beings in the commandments, offers them the means to love truly (which is "willing the good" for the person) and thus to fulfill themselves. The Pope's reflections in the *Theology of the Body* begin by meditating on Christ's answer to the Pharisees' question about marriage in which he refers twice to the "beginning," to the first divine order. John Paul states that Christ's answer is "decisive and clear" and that "*we must draw the normative conclusions from it,* which have an essential significance not only for ethics, but above all for the theology of man and the theology of the body, which, as a particular aspect of theological anthropology, is constituted on the foundation of the word of God who reveals himself."[147] Later on the Pope states that "[Christ's] answer [to the Pharisees in which he appeals to the "beginning"] recalled fundamental and elemental truths about the human being as man and woman."[148] And what are these fundamental and elemental truths that lead to Christ's teaching on the indissolubility of marriage? That human beings are created as persons in the image of God for love and communion, that the body manifests the person, and that it is through the body, in its spousal and generative meanings, that the person becomes a gift and by means of this gift fulfills the meaning of his being and existence. According to John Paul, the body is meant to express love and it

---

144 Ibid. John Paul states that God's command to "eat freely of every tree in the garden" but not of "the tree of the knowledge of good and evil" (Gen 2:16–17) indicates that "*the power to decide what is good and what is evil does not belong to man, but to God alone.*"

145 John Paul II, *The Splendor of the Truth*, no. 35.

146 Ibid.

147 John Paul II, *Man and Woman He Created Them: A Theology of the Body*, 3:4.

148 Ibid., 23:3, my brackets.

"speaks" a language. And since, "every language is an expression of knowledge ... the categories of truth and untruth (or falsity) are essential to it."[149] Thus, the "language of the body" is subject to "objective moral norms."[150] The "truth" here refers both to the ontological dimension, i.e., the "innermost structure" of the act, and the subjective dimension, i.e., the "meaning."[151] Therefore, as John Paul states, "If the human being *gives to* his *behavior a meaning in conformity with the fundamental truth of the language of the body*, then he too 'is in the truth.' In the opposite case, he commits lies and falsifies the language of the body."[152] And so, the mastery required to subordinate freedom to love, or rather to fulfill freedom in the self-determining choice to give oneself as a "disinterested gift," manifests itself in choosing the good for the other[153]—in the body "speaking the truth" and thus speaking the language of Goodness and Love. Since "man *is person precisely because he is master of himself and has dominion over himself*" and "inasmuch as he is master over himself he can 'give himself' to another," it is "the dimension of the freedom of the gift—that becomes essential and decisive for the 'language of the body,'" and this language "must be judged according to the criterion of truth."[154]

It is the rejection of such a criterion of truth (i.e., of an intrinsic meaning of the human body, which is both spousal and generative and of the sexual act, which is simultaneously unitive and procreative), and the distortion of human freedom which, in John Paul's mind, impacts sexual ethics and leads, for example, to the acceptance of contraception. John Paul states that contemporary men and women demonstrate the tendency to transfer the methods of "dominating the forces of nature" to the sphere of "self-mastery," and that this threatens the human person for whom "self-mastery" is fundamentally constitutive, because it "deprives him of the subjectivity proper to him" and instead "treats him as an object of manipulation."[155] Instead of understanding freedom as the necessary prerequisite for the giving of oneself in love, and thus as requiring the consideration of the rational and objective ends of specific actions, it is understood as the capacity to manipulate nature (including one's own body) in order to achieve one's own ends.

---

149 Ibid., 104:8. 150 Ibid., 123:4. 151 Ibid., 118:6.
152 Ibid. 106:3. 153 Ibid, 51:6, 53:2. 154 Ibid., 123:5.
155 Ibid., 123:1.

However, according to John Paul, when one does consider "the criterion of this truth," it is apparent that the conjugal act "'signifies' not only love, but also potential fruitfulness," and thus "it is not licit to separate artificially the unitive from the procreative meaning, because the one as well as the other belong to the innermost truth of the conjugal act."[156] John Paul will state that when the conjugal act is deprived of its innermost truth through an "artificial separation" of its two "significances" or "meanings," it cannot constitute an "act of love" because the "language of the body" ceases to "speak" the truth of "the reciprocal gift of self" or of "the reciprocal acceptance of oneself by the person."[157] This "violation of the inner order of conjugal communion, a communion that plunges its roots into the very order of the person, *constitutes the essential evil of the contraceptive act.*"[158]

As regards bioethics, while the *Theology of the Body* does not deal specifically with bioethics, one can highlight a few passages in which such a connection between utilitarianism, relativism, and bioethics is made and responded to by the Pope. For example, John Paul highlights Genesis 4:1, which treats *"the act that* originates being, or, *in union with the Creator, establishes a new human being in existence"* [159] when it describes the conjugal union as "knowledge" and Eve exclaims, "I have gotten a man with the help of the Lord" upon giving birth. John Paul states that since in the communion of persons expressed in conjugal union man and woman recognize themselves as the image of God, every time they enter into conjugal union "both man and woman take this image again, so to speak, from the mystery of creation and transmit it 'with the help of God-Yahweh.'"[160] Thus, "the words of Genesis that bear witness to the first birth of man on earth contain, at the same time, everything that one can and should say about the dignity of human generation."[161] In other words, the conjugal act is the privileged place of the transmission of the image of God from person to person.[162] In fact, "despite all the experiences of his own life, despite the sufferings, the disappointments in himself, his sinfulness, and, finally, despite the inevitable prospect of death, man always continues, however, to place 'knowledge' at the 'beginning' of 'generation'; in this way he seems to participate in that first 'vision'

---

156 Ibid., 123:6.   157 Ibid.   158 Ibid., 123:7.
159 Ibid., 21:7.   160 Ibid.   161 Ibid.
162 Cf. John Paul II, *The Role of the Christian Family in the Modern Word*, no. 28.

of God himself: God, the Creator, 'saw everything...and indeed, it was good.'"[163] This vision of the human being as "God's image" and ontologically "very good" in virtue of existence is threatened when, according to John Paul, due to the whole development of contemporary science the human person is reduced to a partial aspect, namely bio-physiology, and the human body is treated more or less systematically as an object of manipulations which deprives man of "the meaning and dignity that stem from the fact that this body is proper to the person."[164] It is not difficult to see, given John Paul's other references to such developments in contemporary science, a veiled reference to abortion, fetal experimentation, embryonic stem cell research, and other manipulations of the human person performed in the name of bio-medical research. In any event, the Pope views the root of these activities in the lack of an "adequate anthropology" which considers the human being in his or her integral totality.

CONCLUSION

It seems manifest that John Paul's anthropology was constructed as an antidote to the Cartesian paradigm and "Manichaean" views and attitudes about the body and sex. By reviewing contemporary scholarship on Karol Wojtyła's method and relevant passages in the *Theology of the Body* in light of the maladies of Cartesian Rationalism that John Paul associates with a New Manichaeism infecting the human family and his concerns about a "neo-Manichaean culture," one can conclude that his method and anthropology provide a remedy to the rejection of hylomorphism, the mechanistic view of nature and the reduction of the person (via his body) to the natural world, the rejection of "realist presuppositions" (including a truth of creation and a created order) associated with Thomas Aquinas's philosophy of being, and the tendency towards utilitarianism and relativism in ethics (particularly in sexual ethics and bioethics). By setting out from "realist presuppositions" and drawing on lived experience with the phenomenological method, thus aiding the development of a sound philosophy of subjectivity and human consciousness so important to the modern mind, John Paul II seeks to point the way beyond the Cartesian watershed and such "Manichaean" views and attitudes, and towards an "integral vision" of the human person.

---

163   John Paul II, *Man and Woman He Created Them: A Theology of the Body*, 22:7.
164   Ibid., 59:3.

GENERAL CONCLUSION

THIS BOOK HAS SOUGHT TO ELUCIDATE JOHN Paul II's diagnosis of the spiritual disease of a New Manichaeism infecting the human family, which he identifies with the maladies of Cartesian Rationalism. At the onset, it was acknowledged that contemporary research on John Paul II's anthropology proposes that his anthropology was developed as a response to the Cartesian paradigm and an antidote to "Manichaean" views and attitudes. Since Descartes's philosophy and Manichaeism are linked by John Paul II under the label "New Manichaeism" in *Letter to Families*, no. 19, this author suggested an examination of what John Paul II meant by the label "New Manichaeism" would elucidate his diagnosis of the ills of the present age, as well as the remedy he prescribed. I also suggested that such an examination would provide a useful interpretive tool for approaching his anthropology, for it would demonstrate precisely how his anthropology was a response to Descartes and an antidote to Manichaeism. In so doing, it would offer a novel contribution to studies of John Paul II's thought.

First, I offered a close textual analysis of *Letter to Families*, no. 19 to establish the structure of the New Manichaeism as it pertains to John Paul's critique of Cartesian Rationalism in that section, drawing out the specific maladies of Cartesian Rationalism that John Paul identifies as "Manichaean": 1) the rejection of hylomorphism, 2) a mechanistic view of nature, 3) the rejection of the philosophy of being and its corresponding "notion of creation," and 4) the tendency towards relativism and utilitarianism in ethics, especially exemplified in contemporary culture in the areas of sexual ethics and bioethics. Other works of John Paul in which he treats similar themes also were consulted in order to provide greater clarification of how the Pope understood these maladies of Cartesian Rationalism. Then, I examined these features in Cartesian tradition and their relationship to Manichaean tradition, as well as the relationship between the Pope's diagnosis of a New Manichaeism in the letter and similar diagnoses in Christian tradition for even further clarification. Then, with the New Manichaeism in mind, I turned to John Paul II's anthropology and showed how he attempted to provide an antidote for the ills of the Cartesian Rationalism and

"Manichaean" views and attitudes by it. What follows is a summary of the Pope's diagnosis and prescribed remedy.

AN INTEGRAL VISION OF MAN AS A REMEDY FOR THE REJECTION OF HYLOMORPHISM

The first problematic feature of Cartesian Rationalism constitutive of the New Manichaeism is Descartes's anthropological dualism and the "radical contrast in man between spirit and body, between body and spirit" which he makes. The second chapter's analysis of this aspect of Descartes's philosophy showed that this was the result of his attempt to describe mechanistically most of what was traditionally attributed to the soul. Descartes did not hold that the soul "informs" the body as in hylomorphism, but, at best, saw the person as an aggregate, never as a composite. The person is primarily identified with his or her mind, as a "thinking thing." The human body is like a machine, and simply a modification of a single extended substance which is somehow or another "related" to the soul. The body cannot accommodate or be penetrated by the soul. Thus, the human body is no longer viewed personally and subjectively, but rather in the same categories of other bodies in nature are viewed.

In this rejection of hylomorphism, a key component of the relationship forged between Cartesian Rationalism and Manichaeism by John Paul is discovered. Chapter 3 explained that, whether the Manichees believed that there existed a "self" which is identified with the Living Soul or no true "self" at all but mere portions of Light substance, they nonetheless denied the human being as a composite substance in which "the soul is the form of the body" and failed to view the body subjectively and personally. They rejected the body as having positive intrinsic value; they viewed it as part of the material cosmos, which was regarded negatively. Like the material cosmos as a whole, any value the human body has would be exclusively an instrumental and utilitarian one, derived from its potential function as a "salvation machine." This application of the Manichaean label by John Paul is similar to the way the label was employed in Christian tradition. Chapter 4 showed that the medieval "Manichees" did not identify the body personally or subjectively, but merely as a "material envelope" which was to be discarded once the soul of the Perfect left it upon death. They rejected hylomorphism and believed in the utter incompatibility of the body and soul, associating the soul with the "self" and as intrinsically good, either as a fallen angel entrapped in the bodily prison or as the creation of the Father who gave life to human beings at the request of Satan. Additionally, the tolerance of the sexual practices of the ordinary believer by the leaders of these medieval heterodox sects, in John Paul's view, would exhibit a utilitarian view of the body which allowed for the using of the body for sexual pleasure so long as procreation was avoided.

It seems clear that Karol Wojtyła's anthropology was developed as a remedy to this rejection of hylomorphism. He accepts unequivocally the hylomorphic notion of the soul being the form of the body. The body is a key component of the *compositum humanum*, of an "integral vision of man." In his philosophy, Wojtyła seeks to reveal the person as a composite substance through his discussion of "integration." He holds that all manifestations of human life that are not bodily or material reveal some somatic conditioning. Because of this complex interdependence and cooperation between the "soma" and the "psyche," they should not be considered as totally separate entities, and the human person's experience of his own body shows this. According to Wojtyła, there is an intrinsic cohesiveness of the personal ego and the somatic ego.

When one turns to the *Theology of the Body* as a mature expression of the Pope John Paul II's anthropology, one can see that the hylomorphic understanding of the human person is a fundamental theme. When reflecting on Adam's experience of "original solitude" in Genesis 2, John Paul indicates that the first man becomes aware of being alone through the experience of the meaning of his own body. The man is a "body among bodies" in the visible world and he intuitively grasps that it is through his body that he is a person.[1] For the Pope, the human being is a personal subject based on his body and not merely on his consciousness.[2] The persons acts through the body such that "the body expresses the person."[3] According to John Paul, though the person is not merely his body, in the Judeo-Christian tradition, the term "body" is used as "the part standing for the whole" such that the person does not just *have* a body, but *is* a body.[4]

---

1 John Paul II, *Man and Woman He Created Them: A Theology of the Body*, 6:3.
2 Ibid.   3 Ibid.
4 John Paul II, *Man and Woman He Created Them: A Theology of the Body*, 8:1, 10:4.

THE IRREDUCIBILITY OF THE HUMAN PERSON AS A
REMEDY FOR THE MECHANISTIC VIEW OF NATURE

The second problematic feature of Cartesian Rationalism that is constitutive of the New Manichaeism is Descartes's mechanistic view of nature. John Paul saw "the separation of spirit and body in man" as leading to the "tendency to consider the human body, not in accordance with the categories of its specific likeness to God, but rather on the basis of its similarity to all the other bodies present in the world of nature, bodies which man uses as raw material in his efforts to produce goods for consumption."[5] To the mind of the Pope, this leads to a utilitarian view of the human body in which the body's value is not intrinsic, but instrumental, and results in a "dreadful ethical defeat."[6] The second chapter's analysis of Descartes's mechanism showed that an important goal of Descartes's project was to replace the Aristotelian-Scholastic view of the physical world with his own mechanistic view. For Descartes, it is the principal attribute that makes a substance a being in its own right as opposed to a being in something else, i.e., a mode. He considered extension (i.e., having dimensions and occupying space) to be the principal attribute of matter and all properties of material things (which he termed "bodies") as fundamentally geometrical.[7] This is also how he saw the human body. According to Descartes, bodies, including the human body, are like machines composed of parts. The ultimate goal of Descartes's mechanistic worldview was to make man the master and possessor of nature.

In mechanism, another component of the relationship forged between Cartesian Rationalism and Manichaeism by John Paul can be discerned. As examined in Chapter 3, in Manichaeism a "radical opposition" between spirit and matter characterizes the entire cosmos, which is the battleground of the Light and the Darkness. In Manichaean cosmogony the material cosmos was created either by the Prince of Darkness or as a defensive and strategic response by the Father of Greatness to the onslaught of the Darkness. Thus, all material bodies including the human body are viewed negatively, and the same as and part of the material cosmos. However, since the cosmos was constructed in such a

---

5   John Paul II, *Letter to Families*, no. 19.   6   Ibid.
7   Descartes, *Principles of Philosophy*, II, 1; Garber, *Descartes' Metaphysical Physics*, 76; Cottingham, *Descartes*, 83.

way as to allow for the efficient release of the Light from its entrapment in matter, the physical world, including the human body, did possess a utilitarian or instrumental value. Chapter 4 showed that this application of the Manichaean label by John Paul is novel and distinct from the way the label was employed in Christian tradition, for the medieval "Manichees" did not seem to hold such a utilitarian view of the material cosmos, and particularly of the human body, as a means of redemption. However, as was previously noted, the tolerance of the sexual practices of the ordinary believer by the leaders of these medieval heterodox sects, in John Paul's view, would exhibit a utilitarian view of the body which allowed for the using of the body for sexual pleasure so long as procreation was avoided.

It seems clear that Karol Wojtyła's anthropology seeks to remediate this mechanistic view of nature in general, and the mechanistic view of the human body in particular. He accepts unequivocally Aristotle's definition that the human being is a "rational animal" and Boethius's definition (accepted by Aquinas) that the person is an "individual substance of a rational nature." For John Paul, these definitions provide a necessary ground, metaphysical frame, and essential reference point for his analysis of human subjectivity and lived experience. According to Wojtyła, personal being is radically different than non-personal being, and a great gulf exists between these two modes of existence. So, in order to reflect upon human subjectivity, Wojtyła proposes what he calls "pausing at the irreducible": to analyze the person as a self-experiencing subject while preserving the objective nature of the person and his place in the created order. In fact, subjectivity is proof of and a synonym for the irreducibility of the person to the natural world. Because for him, "action follows being" (*operare sequitur esse*), the person experiences himself as existing as the subject and the efficient cause of his own action. The person experiences his own unique subjectivity in every self-determining act. While Descartes also may have considered human beings as "thinking things" to be completely unlike the rest of creation, his mechanistic view of the body and its separation from the *compositum humanum* results practically in the person being reduced to the natural world. For Wojtyła/John Paul II, conscious human activity includes the consciousness and experience of one's own body. The body is integrated into the whole person and thus the person's experiences of subjectivity in and through free human action involve the human body. Thus the person's irreducibility includes his body, which is part of his essence, of the *compositum humanum.*

When one turns to the *Theology of the Body,* one finds manifest John Paul's efforts to emphasize the irreducibility of the person to the natural world. Reflecting on what he calls "original solitude," John Paul states that man experiences himself as "alone" — as substantially distinct from the rest of creation, that he cannot be identified with other living beings.[8] He highlights that the words of Genesis do not speak of man's likeness with the rest of creatures, but only with God,[9] affirming "the absolute impossibility of reducing man to the 'world'" or being fully understood or explained "categories taken from the 'world.'"[10] While the human being is a "body among bodies," no other body means what his does; no other body expresses a personal subject; none "offers man the basic conditions that *make it possible to exist in a relation of reciprocal gift.*"[11] Only the human person possesses the requisite freedom and self-mastery, which at one and the same time distinguishes him from the rest of creation and makes him "the image of God."[12] The irreducibility of the person and his body (since he *is* his body) to the natural world is also seen in John Paul's reflections on the nature of the sexual urge in human beings, for while there is an analogy between the human body and of sex in relation to the world of animals, in human beings this "is raised in some way to the level of 'image of God' and to the level of the person and communion among persons,"[13] as indicated by the term "knowledge."[14]

REALIST PRESUPPOSITIONS ABOUT CREATION AS A REMEDY
FOR THE REJECTION OF THE PHILOSOPHY OF BEING

The third problematic feature of Cartesian Rationalism that is constitutive of the New Manichaeism is Descartes's rejection of the philosophy of being. As was discussed, for Pope John Paul II, the rejection of mystery found in Cartesian Rationalism is related to its "decisive abandonment" of Thomas's philosophy of being and its "notion of creation," including the rejection a truth of creation

---

8   John Paul II, *Man and Woman He Created Them: A Theology of the Body,* 6:3.
9   Ibid., 2:3.   10   Ibid., 2:4.   11   Ibid., 14:1.
12   Ibid., 14:2, 15:2.   13   Ibid., 20:3.   14   Ibid., 14:5.

which must be acknowledged and of the God of Creation who is *Ens subsistens.* For Thomas, nothing exists that is not creature (*ens participatum*) except the Creator (*Ens subsistens*), and created things have an essential nature due to the special way in which the divine essence is imitated in them and are intelligible because they are creatively thought and fashioned by God. Thus, Thomas's philosophy of being underlies a realist metaphysics, one that "presupposes the reality of Absolute Being and also the reality of being human, that is, of being a creature." [15] The second chapter's analysis of this aspect of Cartesian tradition explained how Descartes changed the direction of philosophizing through his methodical doubt, moving from the mind to things instead of from things to the mind. Fixed on mathematical certitude, Descartes demonstrates an intolerance for mystery. He rejects the reality of being and the principles of being as the starting point of philosophy, [16] and denies that the senses put us in direct contact with external reality and enable us to cognize the being and essence of things. According to Descartes, the world God creates is not one of contingent beings participating in Supreme Being with their essences being specified by their unique modes of participation (such that "being" and "good" convert) or one of substantial forms with intrinsic ends (such that "operation follows being"), but rather one of pure extension void of intrinsic meaning in which God is remote and human beings are ignorant of his purposes. Though Descartes requires God to validate the existence of his "clear and distinct ideas," he is ultimately unsuccessful in proving God's existence from pure consciousness and the idea of God, which his system demands. Thus, "God is reduced to an element within human consciousness" and can no longer be considered the "ultimate explanation of the human sum." [17] At best, what remains is a "vague deism" in which God is evicted from the world.

In the rejection of the philosophy of being (and its corresponding "notion of creation") is discovered yet another correlation between Cartesian Rationalism and Manichaeism forged by John

---

15 John Paul II, *Memory and Identity*, 12.

16 Though, as Reginald Garrigou-Lagrange demonstrates, such principles, e.g., the Principle of Non-contradiction, are necessary even for Descartes's "Cogito" argument.

17 John Paul II, *Memory and Identity*, 10.

Paul in his diagnosis of a New Manichaeism. In Chapter 3, it was shown that Manichaeism certainly would reject the intrinsic goodness of creation as *ens participatum* or of the Creator as *Ens subsistens*. It would not hold that "being" and "the good" are convertible, and thus would reject the notion that all finite, created being has a positive value, is "good," by virtue of its existence as a participated likeness or similitude of the divine *esse*. Thus, the Manichees would deny any God ordained purposes in creation or the maxim "action follows being" (*operare sequitur esse*). As has been discussed, for the Manichees the cosmos was divided into two substances, with a radical opposition between matter and spirit, in which created being is intrinsically evil. Thus, they rejected the God of the Old Testament—"He Who Is"—for they identified him with physical creation. At best, matter may prove *useful* as a vehicle of liberation. This application of the Manichaean label by John Paul to the rejection of creation, a created order, and the God of creation finds similarity with the way the label was employed in Christian tradition. Chapter 4 illustrated how the Paulicians, Bogomils, and Cathars all believed that Satan, the evil demiurge, was the creator and ruler of the material world. In all three cases, the Old Testament and the Creator-God of the Old Testament was rejected. Matter was considered the "principle of evil and corruption."[18]

It seems clear that Karol Wojtyła's anthropology seeks to counteract this rejection of the philosophy of being and its corresponding "notion of creation" in its very method. Wojtyła takes a realist position in his epistemology in the tradition of Aristotle and St. Thomas Aquinas, presupposing the existence of objective extramental reality, an *esse*, that can be experienced and cognized. This is seen in the processes of induction and reduction. Wojtyła's theory of consciousness is also "realistic" in the Thomistic sense, since the fundamental function of consciousness is to "mirror" or reflect what has already been cognized. Additionally, in Wojtyła's reliance on the Scholastic maxim *operare sequitur esse* he is emphasizing the primacy of being: something must exist in order to act.[19] Also,

---

18 Obolensky, *The Bogomils: A Study in Balkan Neo-Manichaeism*, 182.
19 Malgorzata Jalocho-Palicka, "Thomas Aquinas's Philosophy of Being as the Basis for Wojtyła's Concept and Cognition of the Human Person," *Studia Gilsoniana* 3, 2014, 130.

since no being in the created world, including human beings, can be said to necessarily exist or to give themselves existence, there must be an *Ipsum Esse Subsistens*, an Absolute and Necessary Being, from which they receive this existence. Thus, they are contingent beings and, as such, involve the constant actualization of their *really existing* inherent potentialities. In his method, Wojtyła also follows Aquinas's philosophy of being in holding that "substantial existence" never exists without "substantial essence."[20] This essence is what makes any being that particular being. Though being (existence) is the first thing cognized, we can also cognize the essence of things,[21] and for Wojtyła the best way to penetrate the essence of the person the human being's acting in *all his aspects*—his consciousness, self-cognition, free will, emotions, and body.

When one turns to the *Theology of the Body*, one becomes aware that the entire work is an argument in favor creation in its goodness and intrinsic meaning. As such, it represents a clear attempt to return to the philosophy of being. Using Jesus's words to the Pharisees about the "beginning" in response to their question about marriage as his point of departure, John Paul states that these words must have caused the Pharisees " . . . to reflect about the way in which, in the mystery of creation, man was formed precisely as 'male and female.'"[22] Right from the first audience, John Paul demonstrates his realist presupposition about the "mystery of creation" (i.e., the "mystery of being"). In his meditation on Genesis 1—which he states has a "powerful metaphysical content" and forms "an incontrovertible point of reference and solid basis of a metaphysics and also for an anthropology and an ethics according to which '*ens et bonum convertuntur*' [being and good are convertible]"[23]—he relates Thomas Aquinas's philosophy of being (*esse*) to the Scripture text, showing how creation is intrinsically good by virtue of proceeding from God, how man is defined primarily "in the dimensions of being and existing ('*esse*')," and how procreation "is necessarily tied to the metaphysical situation of creation: of contingent being ('*contingens*')."[24] Since God sees creation as "good," John Paul holds that one is able to acknowledge love as "the divine motive for creation, the source, as it were, from which it springs,"[25] and thus all life as a "fundamental

---

20   Ibid., 137.   21   Ibid., 142.
22   John Paul II, *Man and Woman He Created Them: A Theology of the Body*, 1:4.
23   Ibid., 2:5.   24   Ibid.   25   Ibid., 13:3.

and radical gift."[26] So, according to John Paul, the first chapters of Genesis introduce us into the "mystery of creation": to a cosmos created by the will of God—who is the First and Exemplar Cause, *Ipsum esse subsistens*, omnipotence and love—in which every creature, every *ens contngens* or *ens participatum*, though limited and susceptible to nonexistence,[27] bears within itself the sign of the original and fundamental gift.[28] As John Paul states, "He who is—he who lives and is Life—constitutes the inexhaustible fountain of existence and life, just as he revealed himself at the "beginning" in Genesis."[29]

John Paul also returns to the philosophy of being in the *Theology of the Body* by introducing the Thomistic notions of formal and final causes. For John Paul, there is an "economy of Truth and Love, which has its source in God himself and was revealed already in the mystery of creation."[30] This is especially evident in his reflections on God's plan for human sexuality found in the early chapters of Genesis. For example, John Paul states that the human person enters into being with the consciousness that sexuality—masculinity and femininity—are ordered to an end fulfilled in the life of spouses-parents.[31] He asserts that the "sexual urge," as an "objective dimension of human nature," has a "procreative finality that is proper to it..."[32] When, as a consequence of original sin, both the man and the woman mutually exist as objects for the satisfaction of sexual urge, this "reduction" of the reciprocal attraction among human persons in their masculinity and femininity does not correspond to the "nature" of that attraction.[33] Even John Paul's discussions about the spousal and generative meanings of the body, the artificial separation of which would contradict "the innermost truth of the conjugal act," [34] indicate a "purpose" or "end" of the body and sex.

AN OBJECTIVE TRUTH OF CREATION AS A REMEDY FOR THE TENDENCY TO RELATIVISM AND UTILITARIANISM IN ETHICS, ESPECIALLY IN SEXUAL ETHICS AND BIOETHICS

The fourth problematic feature of Cartesian Rationalism that is constitutive of the New Manichaeism is its tendency to relativism and utilitarianism in ethics, which, in John Paul's opinion, is

26 Ibid.   27 Ibid., 7:3.   28 Ibid., 13:4.
29 Ibid., 65:5.   30 Ibid., 19:5.   31 Ibid., 14:5.
32 Ibid., 41:4.   33 Ibid., 41:5.   34 Ibid., 123:6.

especially manifest in the contemporary "neo-Manichaean" culture in the areas of sexual ethics and bioethics. According to John Paul, the placing of God outside of the world and the denial of formal and final causality, which leads to the rejection of a "truth of creation" and of human nature as a "given reality" (all part of Descartes' rejection of the philosophy of being) underlie this tendency. When the relationship between the tendency to relativism and utilitarianism in ethics and Descartes's philosophy was examined in Chapter 2, it was found that, though not establishing a "perfect moral science" or writing a treatise on moral philosophy, Descartes's writings indicate a subjectivist turn in moral decision making, even though he could not be considered strictly a relativist. For him, man has the first word and the last word in the matter of determining what is and what is not to be accepted as truth, describing the virtue that leads to "contentment" as "the firm and constant resolution to do everything *we judge to be best*."[35] According to Descartes, virtue does not lie in the objective "rightness" of the action itself or in acting in accordance with the nature in terms of formal or final cause (i.e., in consort with a being's characteristic function or its end), for he does not recognize these causes or that one can know God's purposes in creating things. In fact, Descartes is intentionally modest in his ethical claims, and ascribes to a form of moral agnosticism. There is no inherent "created order," or at least one cannot be known, so man has "the power to construct orders" (and, in effect, to determine the "truth" about creation) in light of what is judges as most beneficial. While Descartes himself cannot be classified formally as proponent of utilitarianism, one can see how a combination of his mechanism with his goal to develop a practical philosophy that seeks to promote the "general welfare" and "contentment" through the discernment of what is most useful and beneficial would set the stage for the utilitarian thinkers of the Enlightenment. To John Paul, all of this inevitably leads to "a civilization of production and of use ... a civilization in which persons are used in the same way things are used,"[36] to "the tendency to use the human body as raw material"[37] like in experimentation on embryos and fetuses, and "to human sexuality being regarded ... as an area for manipulation

---

35   Ariew, *Descartes and the First Cartesians*, 155, my italics.
36   John Paul II, *Letter to Families*, no. 13.   37   Ibid., no. 19.

and exploitation."[38] Though Descartes never advocated a permissive view of sexual ethics, his dualistic views, his mechanistic view of the body, his rejection of ends and purposes in nature, his paving the road for Deism (for a God who is remote from his creation), and preparing the ground for modern unbelief as well as for relativism and utilitarianism in ethics, could all be said to have helped to set the foundations for the contemporary approaches to sexual ethics and bioethics, with which John Paul had particular concern.

For John Paul II, the tendency to relativism and utilitarianism in ethics, and to "sexuality becoming an area for manipulation and exploitation" is another connection between Cartesian Rationalism and Manichaeism. Chapter 3 showed that the Manichees could be seen as denying procreation as a natural "end" of sexual union. To them, procreation was an obstacle to the fulfillment of Manichaean existence, namely, the liberation of the Light elements or Living Soul from the shackles of matter. Though the motives for avoiding procreation were different for the ancient Manichees than for men and women in our "neo-Manichaean culture," John Paul identifies a relationship between these views and attitudes, stating that our contemporary "neo-Manichaean" culture is marked by a pervasive "contraceptive mentality" in which the sexual act is reduced to an act of mutual use and the child is viewed as "an obstacle to personal fulfillment" and "an enemy to be avoided at all costs." While never officially sanctioned, in practice, the immoral sexual practices of Manichaean Auditors were tolerated so long as procreation was avoided. To John Paul, this is tantamount to denying a "truth of creation" and imposing subjective ends on sexual practice, using the body for the purpose of attaining sexual pleasure and manipulating it in order to prevent procreation and isolate the pleasurable aspects of sex. Since he would see this as persons reciprocally using one another for sexual pleasure, it would exhibit a utilitarian view of the body, and thus of the person. Human sexuality, therefore, is an area for manipulation and exploitation for both the Manichees and the contemporary neo-Manichaean culture in John Paul's view. This application of the Manichaean label by John Paul finds similarity with the way the label was employed in Christian tradition. One finds generally among the medieval "Manichees" the rejection of marriage and

---

38   Ibid.

family life as a recurrent theme. Though sexual abstinence was the ideal, the leaders accepted the sexual liaisons of the ordinary believers so long as procreation was excluded, for pregnancy was believed a great evil and the fruit of the womb a "demon" from which a pregnant woman should pray to be liberated.

It seems clear that Karol Wojtyła's anthropology can be seen as an antidote to the tendency to relativism and utilitarianism in ethics, especially as seen in sexual ethics and bioethics in contemporary culture. With respect to relativism in ethics, Wojtyła's method affirms the Thomistic view that the human person is naturally ordered to the true and the good. The good is not known only through metaphysical reflection, but through human experience. Yet, it is clear from the method of Karol Wojtyła that, while the experience of morality is a deeply subjective experience, moral values themselves are objective and transcend human cognition and feelings. The specific moral good or evil in acts in something that must be apprehended through intellectual insight and reflection on experience. Again, this reflection, for Wojtyła, is endeavored by setting out from the realist presuppositions previously discussed: accepting that the specific moral good or evil is something that can be cognized and exists in extra-mental reality and accepting the Aristotelian-Thomistic notion of causality, i.e., the relationship between the moral species of an act and formal and final causes. Against utilitarianism in ethics, Wojtyła's method formulates the "Personalistic Norm," which states that, due to his nature as a self-possessing, self-governing, self-determining subject, the person can never be used as a mere means to another's end. The only adequate and proper response to the person is love: to affirm the good of the person by willing his or her integral fulfillment and specific, concrete goods. According to Wojtyła, the principle of utility, which is the principle of the maximization of pleasure, will always stand in the way of love and reduces the person to an object of appropriation.

When one turns to the *Theology of the Body*, one finds John Paul II's rejection of relativism and utilitarianism in ethics clearly displayed. With regard to his rejection of relativism, one can turn to his meditation on Christ's answer to the Pharisees' question about marriage and to his reflections on the "language of the body." In his answer to the Pharisees question about marriage, John Paul highlights that in Christ referring twice to the "beginning," to the first divine order, he provides normative conclusions which have "an essential significance . . . for ethics."[39] The Pope states that Christ's answer points to "fundamental and elemental truths" about the human person,[40] one of which is that the body is meant to express love and "speaks" a language. This "language of the body," like all languages that as expressions of knowledge include the categories of truth and falsity,[41] is subject to "objective moral norms,"[42] and must be judged according to the criterion of truth.[43] The "truth" here refers both to the ontological dimension, i.e., the "innermost structure" of the act, and the subjective dimension, i.e., the "meaning."[44] It is the rejection of such a criterion of truth, i.e., of an intrinsic meaning of the human body which is both spousal and generative, and of the sexual act, which is simultaneously unitive and procreative, which, in John Paul's mind, impacts sexual ethics and leads to the acceptance of contraception.[45]

The *Theology of the Body* also manifests John Paul's opposition to a utilitarian mindset that reduces the person to an object or a mere means to another's end. John Paul contrasts the "acceptance" or "welcoming" of the other as a gift and someone the Creator has willed "for his own sake" with "the contrary of such 'welcoming' and 'acceptance' of the other human being as a gift," which results in the "reduction of the other to an 'object for myself' (object of concupiscence, of 'undue appropriation,' etc.) . . ."[46] This latter utilitarian attitude, this reduction of the other to a mere "object for me," contradicts moral participation in the act of God's willing the other for his or her own sake, and is a form of "extortion."[47] Prior to sin and its effects, the first man and woman possessed the requisite "purity of heart" and "reciprocal *awareness of the spousal meaning of their bodies*" to exclude subjectively any reduction of the other to an object.[48] After sin, "*the relationship of the gift changes into a relationship of appropriation.*"[49] This manifests itself clearly and immediately in the area of sexual ethics, and in particular in the "lustful look" which Christ spoke of and John Paul reflects upon in the *Theology of the Body*.[50] In fact, John Paul sees in the

---

39 John Paul II, *Man and Woman He Created Them: A Theology of the Body*, 3:4.
40 Ibid., 23:3, my brackets. 41 Ibid., 104:8.
42 Ibid., 123:4. 43 Ibid., 123:5. 44 Ibid., 118:6.
45 Ibid. 46 Ibid., 17:3. 47 Ibid.
48 Ibid., 19:1. 49 Ibid., 32:6. 50 Ibid., 40:4.

words of Genesis 3:16 about "domination" an essential "change the structure of communion in interpersonal relations..."[51] for "from the moment in which man 'dominates' her, the communion of persons—which consists in the spiritual unity of the two subjects who gave themselves to each other—is replaced by a different mutual relationship, namely, by a relationship of possession of the other as an object of one's own desire."[52] This utilitarian attitude which reduces the other to an "object of enjoyment for the satisfaction of mere concupiscence," and to an "anonymous object of appropriation" or "object of abuse" is also highlighted by John Paul in his discussion of the body in art, and in particular of the problem of "pornovision" and "pornography."[53]

While the *Theology of the Body* does not deal specifically with bioethics, one can highlight a few passages in which such a connection between utilitarianism, relativism, and bioethics is made and responded to by the Pope, mainly in the Pope's reflections on Genesis 4:1.[54] According to the Pope, "the words of Genesis that bear witness to the first birth of man on earth contain, at the same time, everything that one can and should say about the dignity of human generation."[55] Conjugal love being described as "knowledge" and associated as such with procreation, suggests, according to the Pope, that human beings "participate in that first 'vision' of God himself" which sees everything, all being, and especially the human being in God's image, as "very good." This vision of the human being as "God's image" and ontologically "very good" in virtue of existence is threatened when, according to John Paul, due to the whole development of contemporary science the human person is reduced to a partial aspect, namely bio-physiology, and the human body is treated more or less systematically as an object of manipulations, which deprives man of "the meaning and dignity that stem from the fact that this body is proper to the person."[56]

AN "ANTIDOTE" TO "MANICHAEAN" VIEWS AND ATTITUDES

In Christian tradition, the label "Manichaean" (or "neo-Manichaean") was applied generally in Christian tradition as a "synonym for Dualism" and as a term describing people "with

---

51 Ibid., 30:6.   52 Ibid., 31:3.   53 Ibid., 61:3, 62:3, 5, 63:5.
54 Ibid., 21:7.   55 Ibid.   56 Ibid., 59:3.

views, to a greater or lesser degree, like those of Mani." As has been demonstrated, John Paul's identification of the New Manichaeism with the rejection of the hylomorphism, a mechanistic view of nature, the rejection of the philosophy of being and its corresponding "notion of creation," the tendency towards relativism and utilitarianism in ethics, and to "sexuality becoming... an area for manipulation and exploitation" could all be said to be views that are "dualistic" and "to a greater or lesser degree" resemble those of the ancient Manichees. While John Paul is not associating the New Manichaeism with a form of cosmological dualism that holds the intrinsic evil of the material world or with the performance of corresponding ritualistic and ascetical practices—which is a prominent way the label was applied in Christian tradition—he would hold that the New Manichaeism does include the belief in a type of cosmological dualism in which the universe is divided into two substances, mind and matter, with mind being the "self" or "thinking thing" and matter being "pure extension" and "raw material" that is intrinsically value-free. In his uses of the Manichaean label apart from the *Letter to Families* John Paul seems to actually coincide more closely with the traditional use of the label, for in those he criticizes a "rigorist" or "puritanical" interpretation of the sexual urge which condemns sexual pleasure and enjoyment as evil and considers all that is "carnal" as "evil and unclean in itself,"[57] even if tolerated solely for the good of procreation. Yet, since John Paul states that such a view "lapses" into utilitarianism by seeing the very essence of marriage as using "a person for the objective end of procreation,"[58] a link can be made between his more "traditional" use of the label in his other works and his use of the label in the letter. Additionally, while John Paul does not claim that the New Manichaeism necessarily includes a docetic view of Christ, he would say that Cartesian Rationalism's rejection of God as *Ens subsistens* leads to a "vague deism" in which God is evicted from the world and thus to the central doctrines of Christianity, the Incarnation and the Pascal Mystery, becoming untenable.

Since John Paul's anthropology can be said to be constructed as a remedy to the rejection of the hylomorphism, to a mechanistic view of nature, to the rejection of the philosophy of being and its corresponding "notion of creation," to the tendency towards

57 Wojtyła, *Love and Responsibility*, 59.   58 Ibid.

relativism and utilitarianism in ethics, and to "sexuality becoming ... an area for manipulation and exploitation," all of which bear striking similarity with Manichaean beliefs and practices, one can conclude that his anthropology is likewise represents a response to "Manichaean" views and attitudes. While in proposing that the Pope's anthropology is an "antidote" to "Manichaean" views and attitudes, commentators on John Paul II's work seem to be most directly referencing the Pope as responding to an attitude, which condemns sexual pleasure and enjoyment as evil and considers all that is "carnal" as "evil and unclean in itself,"[59] this book has demonstrated that a utilitarian view of the body, which manifests itself in "sexuality becoming ... an area for manipulation and exploitation" was also a "Manichaean" attitude. This said, it is clear that John Paul's rigorous defense of hylomorphism and return to the philosophy of being which emphasizes the goodness of creation and of sexual love likewise responds to the very attitude that these commentators were more directly intending.

FINAL CONSIDERATIONS

It is this author's hope that this examination has shown why John Paul II diagnosed the heresy of our times as a New Manichaeism, and how his anthropology is the remedy which he prescribed for this spiritual disease. In so doing, a useful and novel interpretive tool for approaching John Paul II's anthropology has been offered, as well as support to those commentators that have proposed that his anthropology was constructed as a response to Descartes and an antidote to Manichaeism.

While it was not the intention of this study to demonstrate how far there actually is a New Manichaeism being experienced by the human family, but rather John Paul II's diagnosis of it and his prescribed remedy, further research could substantiate this. By surveying and growing existing research on the philosophical roots of contemporary culture,[60] on the beliefs and attitudes of

---

59   Weigel, *Witness to Hope*, 140, 342; West, *Theology of the Body Explained*, 230–233.
60   See Charles Taylor's *Sources of the Self: The Making of the Modern Identity* (Cambridge: Harvard University Press, 1989) and *A Secular Age* (Cambridge: Belknap Press, 2007), and Carl Trueman's *The Rise and Triumph of the Modern Self: Cultural Amnesia, Expressive Individualism, and the Road to Sexual Revolution* (Wheaton: Crossway, 2020) as examples.

contemporary men and women about themselves, the world, religion, and ethics,[61] and on the presence of body-spirit dualism in contemporary ethics,[62] and by analyzing this research in view of those aspects of Cartesian Rationalism which John Paul associates with the New Manichaeism, one may be able to show that John Paul's assessment of contemporary culture as "neo-Manichaean" can be supported.

It was also beyond the scope of this work to demonstrate how the New Manichaeism may be related to other spiritual diseases associated with the Enlightenment or how other strains of it may have developed and require their own precise remedies. For example, one might suggest a relationship between the errors of Cartesian Rationalism and Freemasonry, or between the heresy of a New Manichaeism and that synthesis of all heresies known as Modernism. One might demonstrate how Descartes's application of the methods of the "new science" to philosophy led quite naturally to Auguste Comte's Positivism, or how Descartes's "method of doubt" underlies the "hermeneutics of suspicion" associated with Freud, Nietzsche, and Marx. Perhaps this very author will investigate these relationships in a future study, but they were not the aim of this present one.

If the anthropological perspective of Cartesian Rationalism, as John Paul II proposed, has amounted to a worldview forming the very beliefs, attitudes, and behaviors of those who live and grow up in contemporary society, then understanding the New Manichaeism could prove exceedingly important for those involved in the work of evangelization and catechesis. Such an understanding would help to establish the context for their work and identify the presuppositions of those to whom they offer the Gospel and teach the Catholic Faith. In addition, if John Paul II's

---

61 See the research of Christian Smith in *Soul Searching: The Religious and Spiritual Lives of American Teenagers* (New York: Oxford University Press, 2005) and *What Is a Person?:Rethinking Humanity, Social Life, and the Moral Good from the Person Up* (Chicago: University Of Chicago Press, 2011) as examples. One of Smith's keen insights is that contemporary Christians themselves do not hold the precepts of traditional Christianity, but rather what he terms "Moralistic Therapeutic Deism." The similarity between Moralistic Therapeutic Deism and those of the New Manichaeism is a further area of study.

62 See Robert George and Patrick Lee's *Body-Self Dualism in Contemporary Ethics and Politics* (Cambridge: Cambridge University Press, 2008) as an example.

anthropology, especially the *Theology of the Body*,[63] is an "antidote" for Cartesian Rationalism and "Manichaean" views and attitudes (since it addresses the modern focus on personal subjectivity and the philosophy of consciousness while situating them within a realist metaphysics), then one may find in it a relevant and effective approach to evangelizing and catechizing men and women formed in a "neo-Manichaean" culture.

An interlocutor might argue that since the "turn to the subject" (and away from God as *Ipsum Esse Subsistens*) was the cause of the disease in the first place (as it was in Eden and even before that in the heavenly realm where "*Non serviam*" first rung out), then the employing of a "subjective" method such as a phenomenological one is doomed to perpetuate the very disease it seeks to heal. Such an interlocutor might propose that the only way to repair the "crisis of truth" stemming from a "crisis of concepts" is to, for example, return fully to a more "objective" method, such as the Scholastic one. This quite likely would have been the opinion of Karol Wojtyła's mentor, Reginald Garrigou-Lagrange, who did not approve of a departure from the Scholastic method supremely articulated in the work of Thomas Aquinas. If getting beyond the Cartesian watershed indeed requires a return to the philosophy of Thomas Aquinas, why stop at his metaphysical realism and not employ his method as well? Might not more of the "perennial philosophy," sidelined as it was after Vatican II, need to be retrieved? In this author's opinion, this view must be given its due respect, especially in light of the current crisis in the Church and in the West writ large. Once man takes his eyes off God and looks to himself, problems are bound to follow. Yet, what do you do with contemporary men and women, who are stuck staring at themselves as in a pool of water? John Paul II suggested going through the self to the One whose image it is, through our fundamental desires and longings to the One who alone can fulfill them, through subjective experience to objective truth. That is, to "arrive at the question of being from the question of man, through the question of the good."[64] Every inoculation

---

63   In this context it is interesting to note that the *Theology of the Body*, as a series of General Audiences, is a catechesis.
64   Buttiglione, *Karol Wojtyła: The Thought of the Man who became Pope John Paul II*, 74.

uses something of the disease to effect an immunity to it. It is arguable whether the "turn to the subject" was the disease, but perhaps with John Paul II's anthropology, particularly as expressed in the *Theology of the Body*, the "subject's" disorientation can be reoriented, enabling him "to become a gift, and by means of this gift, fulfill the meaning of his being and existence."[65] Perhaps John Paul II has provided a remedy for healing the family and the culture so the family can become the "communion of life and love"[66] God created it to be, and we can build a "culture of life" and "civilization of truth and love to the praise and glory of God, the Creator and lover of life."[67]

---

65 John Paul II, *Man and Woman He Created Them: A Theology of the Body*, 15:1.

66 John Paul II, *Letter to Families*, no. 7, 12; Cf. Vatican II, *Pastoral Constitution on the Church in the Modern World*, no. 48.

67 John Paul II, *The Gospel of Life*, no. 105.

BIBLIOGRAPHY

Anderson, Carl, and Jose Granados. *Called to Love: Approaching John Paul II's Theology of the Body*, New York: Doubleday, 2009.

Aquinas, Thomas. *On Being and Essence*, Translated by Armand Maurer. Toronto: Pontifical Institute of Mediaeval Studies, 1968.

——. *Thomas Aquinas: Selected Writings*, Translated by Ralph McInerny. London: Penguin Books, 1998.

——. *Summa Theologiae*. Translated by Fr. Laurence Shapcote. Green Bay: Aquinas Institute, 2012.

Ariew, Roger. *Descartes and His Contemporaries: Meditations, Objections, and Replies*. Edited with Marjorie Grene. Chicago: The University of Chicago Press, 1995.

——. *Descartes and the First Cartesians*. Oxford: Oxford University Press, 2014.

——. "Descartes and scholasticism: the intellectual background to Descartes' thought." *The Cambridge Companion to Descartes*. Edited by John Cottingham, 58–90. Cambridge: Cambridge University Press, 1992.

Augustine of Hippo. *Answer to Secundinus, a Manichean. The Works of Saint Augustine: The Manichean Debate.* Ed. Boniface Ramsey, 357–390. Hyde Park, NY: New City Press, 2006.

——. *Contra Faustum Manichaeum.* http://www.newadvent.org/fathers/1406.htm.

——. *The Catholic Way of Life and the Manichean Way of Life. The Works of Saint Augustine: The Manichean Debate.* Edited by Boniface Ramsey, 28–116. Hyde Park, NY: New City Press, 2006.

Bacon, Francis. *The New Organon and Related Writings.* Edited with an introduction by Fulton H. Anderson. Indianapolis: Bobbs-Merrill, 1960.

Barber, Malcolm. *The Cathars: Dualist Heretics in Languedoc in the High Middle Ages.* Harlow, England: Pearson Education Limited, 2000.

Barrett, William. *Death of Soul: From Descartes to the Computer.* New York: Doubleday, 1986.

BeDuhn, Jason David. *Augustine's Manichaean Dilemma.* Philadelphia: University of Pennsylvania Press, 2010.

——. *The Light and the Darkness: Studies in Manichaeism and Its World.* Edited with Paul Mirecki. Boston, MA: Brill Academic Publishers, 2001.

——. *The Manichaean Body in Discipline and Ritual.* Baltimore, MD: The Johns Hopkins University Press, 2000.

Beyssade, Jean-Marie. "The idea of God and the proofs of his existence." *The Cambridge Companion to Descartes.* Edited by John Cottingham, 174–199. Cambridge: Cambridge University Press, 1992.

Burkitt, Francis. *The Religion of the Manichees: Donnellan Lectures for 1924.* New York: Cambridge University Press, 2010.

Buttiglione, Rocco. *Karol Wojtyła: The Thought of the Man who Became Pope.* Cambridge, UK: Wm. B. Eerdmans Pub. Company, 1997.

Byrne, James M. *Religion and the Enlightenment: From Descartes to Kant.* Louisville: Westminster John Knox Press, 1996.

Chervin, Ronda and Eugene Kevane. *Love of Wisdom: An Introduction to Christian Philosophy.* San Francisco: Ignatius Press, 1988

Chesterton, G.K. *The Dumb Ox.* New York: Image Books, 1956.

Cholish, Marcia L. "The Cathars/The Cathars," Review of *The Cathars: Dualist Heretics in Languedoc in the High Middle Ages* by Malcolm Barber and *The Cathars* by Malcolm Lambert. *Church History*, Vol. 71, Issue 1. March 2002.

Clarke, Desmond. *Descartes' Philosophy of Mind.* Oxford: Oxford University Press, 2003.

——. "Descartes philosophy of science and the scientific revolution." *The Cambridge Companion to Descartes.* Edited by John Cottingham, 258-285. Cambridge: Cambridge University Press, 1992.

Conner, Miguel. *Voices of Gnosticism: Interviews with Elaine Pagels, Marvin Meyer, Bart Ehrman, Bruce Chilton and Other Leading Scholars.* Dublin: Bardic Press, 2011.

Copenhaver, Brian P. and Charles B. Schmitt. *Renaissance Philosophy.* Oxford: Oxford University Press, 2002.

Copleston, Frederick. *Aquinas.* New York: Penguin Books, 1955.

——. *A History of Philosophy Volume 3: Late Mediaeval and Renaissance Philosophy.* London: Bloomsbury Continuum, 2003.

——. *A History of Philosophy Volume 4: The Rationalists, Descartes to Leibniz.* London: Bloomsbury Continuum, 2003.

Cottingham, John. *A Descartes Dictionary.* Cambridge, MA: Blackwell Publishers, 1993.

——. "Cartesian dualism: theology, metaphysics, and science." In *The Cambridge Companion to Descartes.* Ed. John Cottingham, 236-257. Cambridge: Cambridge University Press, 1992.

——. *Cartesian Reflections: Essays on Descartes' Philosophy.* New York: Oxford University Press, 2008.

——. *Descartes.* Oxford: Blackwell Publishing, 1986.

de Araujo, Marcelo. *Scepticism, Freedom and Autonomy: A Study in the Moral Foundations of Descartes' Theory of Knowledge.* Berlin: Walter de Gruyter GmbH & Co., 2003.

Descartes, René. *Discourse on Method and Related Writings.* Translation with introduction by Desmond Clarke. London: Penguin Books, 2003.

——. *Meditations on First Philosophy: With Selections from the Objections and Replies.* Translation with introduction by John Cottingham. Cambridge: Cambridge University Press, 1996.

——. *Principles of Philosophy.* Radford, VA: Wilder Publications, 2008.

Dicker, Georges. *Descartes: An Analytic and Historical Introduction.* Oxford University Press, 2013.

Doolan, Gregory T. *Aquinas on the Divine Ideas as Exemplar Causes.* Washington, D.C.: Catholic University of America Press, 2008.

Garber, Daniel. *Descartes Embodied: Reading Cartesian Philosophy through Cartesian Science.* Cambridge: Cambridge University Press, 2001.

——. *Descartes' Metaphysical Physics.* Chicago: The University of Chicago Press, 1992.

——. "Descartes' physics." In *The Cambridge Companion to Descartes.* Edited by John Cottingham, 286–333. Cambridge: Cambridge University Press, 1992.

Garner, Iaian and Samuel N. C. Lieu. *Manichaean Texts from the Roman Empire.* Cambridge: Cambridge University Press, 2004.

Garrigou-Lagrange, Reginald. "*The Essence and Topicality of Thomism.*" Translated by Alan Aversa, 2013. Brescia: La Scuola editrice, 1946.

——. "La critica tomista del cogito cartesiano." *Frumentum.* 1950, 273–283.

——. *Reality: A Synthesis of Thomistic Thought.* Charleston: CreateSpace Independent Publishing Platform, 2012.

George, Robert P. *Body-Self Dualism in Contemporary Ethics and Politics.* Cambridge: Cambridge University Press, 2008. (with Patrick Lee)

——. *Embryo.* New York: Doubleday, 2008. (with Christopher Tollefson)

——. *What is Marriage? Man and Woman: A Defense.* New York: Encounter Books, 2012. (with Sherif Girgis and Ryan T. Anderson)

——. "What Marriage Is—And What It Isn't." *First Things,* August–September 2009.

Gilson, Etienne. *A History of Philosophy: Modern Philosophy, Descartes to Kant.* New York: Random House, 1963.

——. *From Aristotle to Darwin and Back Again: A Journey in Final Causality, Species, and Evolution.* San Francisco: Ignatius Press, 2009.

——. *History of Christian Philosophy in the Middle Ages.* London: Sheed and Ward, 1955.

——. *The Christian Philosophy of St. Thomas Aquinas.* Notre Dame: Notre Dame University Press, 1994.

——. *The Unity of Philosophical Experience.* San Francisco: Ignatius Press, 1999.

Hamlyn, D.W. *The Penguin History of Western Philosophy.* London: Penguin Books, 1989.

Israel, Jonathan I. *Radical Enlightenment: Philosophy and the Making of Modernity 1650–1750.* New York: Oxford University Press, 2001.

Jalocho-Palicka, Malgorzata. "Thomas Aquinas' Philosophy of Being as the Basis for Wojtyla's Concept and Cognition of the Human Person." *Studia Gilsoniana* 3, 2014.

John Paul II, Pope. *Crossing the Threshold of Hope.* New York: Alfred A. Knopf, 1994.

——. *Letter to Families*. 1994.

——. *Man and Woman He Created Them: A Theology of the Body*. Boston: Pauline Books and Media, 2006.

——. *Memory and Identity: Conversations at the Dawn of a Millennium*. New York: Rizzoli, 2005.

——. *On the Relationship between Faith and Reason* [Fides et Ratio]. 1998.

——. *On the Role of the Christian Family in the Modern World* [Familiaris Consortio]. 1981.

——. *The Gospel of Life* [Evangelium Vitae]. 1995.

——. *The Splendor of the Truth* [Veritatis Splendor]. 1993.

Jonas, Hans. *The Gnostic Religion*, 3rd Edition. Boston: Beacon Press, 2001.

——. *The Phenomenon of Life: Toward a Philosophical Biology*. Evanston, IL: Northwestern University Press, 2001.

Jones, Vivien. "Advice and Enlightenment: Mary Wollstonecraft and Sex Education." *Women, Gender, and Enlightenment*. Ed. Sarah Knott and Barbara Taylor. New York: Palgrave Macmillan, 2005.

Kupczak, Jaroslaw. *Destined for Liberty: The Human Person in the Philosophy of Karol Wojtyła/John Paul II*. Washington, D.C.: Catholic University of America Press, 2000.

——. *Gift and Communion: John Paul II's Theology of the Body*. Washington, D.C.: Catholic University of America Press, 2014.

Lambert, Malcolm. *Medieval Heresy: Popular Movements from the Gregorian Reform to the Reformation*. New York: Barnes and Noble Books, 1998.

——. *The Cathars*. Oxford, UK: Blackwell Publishers, 1998.

Lansing, Carol. *Power and Purity: Cathar Heresy in Medieval Italy*. New York: Oxford University Press, 1998.

Le Roy Ladurie, Emmanuel *Montaillou: The Promised Land of Error*. New York: George Braziller, Inc., 1978.

Markie, Peter. "Descartes's Concept of Substance." *Reason, Will, and Sensation: Studies in Descartes' Metaphysics*. Edited by John Cottingham. New York: Oxford University Press, 1994, 63–87.

Maritain, Jacques. *A Preface to Metaphysics: Seven Lectures on Being*. London: Sheed and Ward, 1939.

Marshall, John. *Descartes's Moral Theory*. Ithaca, NY: Cornell University Press, 1998.

McLean, O.M.I., George F. "Prologue: Cardinal Karol Wojtyła's Creative Response to His Philosophical Context." *Karol Wojtyła's Philosophical Legacy*. Cultural Heritage and Contemporary Change Series I, Culture and Value, Volume 35. Edited by Nancy Mardas Billias, Agnes B. Curry, and George F. McLean, http://www.crvp.org/publications/Series-I/I-35.pdf.

Mitchell, Margaret M. and Frances M. Young. Ed., *The Cambridge History of Christianity, Volume 1: Origins to Constantine*. Cambridge: Cambridge University Press, 2006.

Moore, R.I. *The War on Heresy: Faith and Power in Medieval Europe*. London: Profile Books, 2014.

Noonan, Jr., John T. *Contraception: A History of Its Treatment by the Catholic Theologians and Canonists*. Boston, MA: Harvard University Press, 1986.

Obolensky, Dmitri. *The Bogomils: A Study in Balkan Neo-Manichaeism*. Cambridge, UK: Cambridge University Press, 1948.

Outram, Dorinda. *The Enlightenment*. Cambridge: Cambridge University Press, 2013.

Pascal, Blaise. *The Pensées*. Translated by W.F. Trotter. https://sourcebooks. fordham.edu/mod/1660pascal-pensees.asp.

Pieper, Josef. "On St. Thomas Aquinas." *The Silence of St. Thomas*. South Bend, St. Augustine's Press, 1957.

——. "The Negative Element in the Philosophy of St. Thomas Aquinas." *The Silence of St. Thomas*. South Bend, St. Augustine's Press, 1957.

Pius XI, Pope. *Deus Scientiarum Dominus*. 1931.

Puech, H.C. *Le Manicheisme: son fondateur-sa doctrine*. Paris, 1949.

——. "The Concept of Redemption in Manichaeism." *The Mystic Vision*, 247–314. Princeton, NJ: Princeton University Press, 1968.

Ratzinger, Joseph. *Christianity and the Crisis of Cultures*. San Francisco: Ignatius Press, 2006.

Rozemond, Marlene. *Descartes's Dualism*. Cambridge, MA: Harvard University Press, 1998.

Runciman, Steven. *The Medieval Manichee: A Study of the Christian Dualist Heresy*. Cambridge, UK: Cambridge University Press, 1947.

Rutherford, Donald. "Descartes' Ethics." *The Stanford Encyclopedia of Philosophy*. Spring 2013 Edition. Edited by Edward N. Zalta, http://plato. stanford.edu/archives/spr2013/entries/descartes-ethics/.

Savage, Deborah. "The Centrality of Lived Experience in Wojtyła's account of the Person." *Roczniki Filozoficze*. LXI, 4, 2013.

——. "Metaphysical Realism as the Foundation of Environmental Stewardship and Economic Development." *Nova et Vetera*. Vol. 10, No. 1, 2012.

Schall, James V. *The Regensburg Lecture*. South Bend: St. Augustine's Press, 2007.

Schmitz, Kenneth L. *At the Center of the Human Drama: The Philosophical Anthropology of Karol Wojtyła/Pope John Paul II*. Washington, D.C.: Catholic University of America Press, 1993.

——. *The Recovery of Wonder: The New Freedom and the Asceticism of Power*. Montreal: McGill-Queens University Press. 2005.

Schouls, Peter. *Descartes and the Enlightenment*. Montreal: McGill-Queen's University Press, 1989.

Shorto, Russell. *Descartes' Bones: A Skeletal History of the Conflict between Faith and Reason*. New York, NY: Vintage Books, 2008.

Sokolowski, Robert. *Introduction to Phenomenology.* Cambridge: Cambridge University Press, 2000.

Sorell, Thomas. *Descartes' Reinvented.* Cambridge: Cambridge University Press, 2005.

———. "Morals and Modernity in Descartes." *The Rise of Modern Philosophy: The Tension between the New and Traditional Philosophies from Machiavelli to Leibniz.* Edited by Thomas Sorell. Oxford: Clarendon Press, 1993.

Sperring, Paul. "Descartes, God and the Eternal Truths." *Richmond Journal of Philosophy* 10. Summer 2005.

Stoyanov, Yuri. *The Other God: Dualist Religions from Antiquity to the Cathar Heresy.* New Haven, CT: Yale University Press, 2000.

Swieżawski, Stefan. *St. Thomas Revisited.* New York: Peter Lang, 1995.

Tardieu, Michel. *Manichaeism.* Chicago, IL: University of Illinois Press, 2008.

Taylor, Charles. *Sources of the Self: The Making of the Modern Identity.* Cambridge: Harvard University Press, 1989.

Vatican II. *Dogmatic Constitution on the Church* [Lumen Gentium]. 1964.

———. *Dogmatic Constitution on Divine Revelation* [Dei Verbum]. 1965.

———. *Pastoral Constitution on the Church in the Modern World* [Gaudium et Spes]. 1965.

Voss, Steven. "Descartes: The End of Anthropology." In *Reason, Will, and Sensation: Studies in Descartes' Metaphysics.* Edited by John Cottingham. New York: Oxford University Press, 1994.

Weigel, George. *Witness to Hope: The Biography of Pope John Paul II.* New York: Harper Collins Publishers, 2001.

West, Christopher. *Theology of the Body Explained: A Commentary on John Paul II's Man and Woman He Created Them.* Boston: Pauline Books and Media, 2007.

Williams, Bernard. Introductory Essay to René Descartes, *Meditations on First Philosophy: With Selections from the Objections and Replies.* Translated by John Cottingham. Cambridge: Cambridge University Press, 1996.

———. *Descartes: The Project of Pure Enquiry.* New York: Pelican Books, 1978.

Williams, George Huntston. *The Mind of John Paul II: Origins of His Thought and Action.* New York: The Seabury Press, 1981.

Williams, Thomas D. *Who is My Neighbor?: Personalism and the Foundations of Human Rights.* Washington, D.C.: Catholic University of America Press, 2005.

———. "What is Thomistic Personalism?" *Alpha Omega* VII, n. 2 (2004): 163.

Wippel, John. *The Metaphysical Thought of Thomas Aquinas.* Washington, D.C.: Catholic University of America Press, 2000.

Wojtyła, Karol. *The Acting Person.* Boston: D. Reidel Pub. Co., 1979.

———. "The Anthropological Vision of *Humanae Vitae.*" Translated by William May. http://www.christendom-awake.org/pages/may/anthrop-visionjpII.htm.

——. *Love and Responsibility*. New York: Farrar, Straus, & Giroux, 1981.

——. "The Person: Subject and Community." *Person and Community: Catholic Thought from Lublin, Selected Essays*, 219–261. New York: Peter Lang, 1993.

——. "The Problem of Experience in Ethics." *Person and Community: Catholic Thought from Lublin, Selected Essays*, 107–127. New York: Peter Lang, 1993.

——. "Subjectivity and the Irreducible in the Human Being." *Person and Community: Catholic Thought from Lublin, Selected Essays*, 209–217. New York: Peter Lang, 1993.

——. "Thomistic Personalism." *Person and Community: Catholic Thought from Lublin, Selected Essays*, 165–175. New York: Peter Lang, 1993.

Woolhouse, R.S. *Descartes, Spinoza, and Leibniz: The Concept of Substance in Seventeenth Century Metaphysics*. New York: Routledge, 1993.

ABOUT THE AUTHOR

David C. Hajduk, Ph.D., has over thirty years of experience in religious education and pastoral ministry, including youth, family life, and pro-life ministries. Since 1998, he has been a member of the Theology Department at Delbarton School in Morristown, New Jersey, where he also served as the Director of Mission and Ministry. He has been an Adjunct Professor of Moral Theology at Immaculate Conception Seminary School of Theology at Seton Hall University since 2008, and is the Director of Theology for Array of Hope, an apostolate that shares the beauty and truth of the Catholic Faith through high quality media and events. Dr. Hajduk is widely respected as a dynamic speaker and teacher, and is an award-winning author. He did his doctoral work in Theology at Maryvale Institute in Birmingham, England. He and his wife have 11 children and homeschool.

www.ingramcontent.com/pod-product-compliance
Lightning Source LLC
Chambersburg PA
CBHW021624120626
46545CB00002B/392